Beth,
Thanks for all your help &
support these last weeks & months.

Love,
Dell

# Out of Kentucky Kitchens

# OUT OF
# KENTUCKY
# KITCHENS

Marion W. Flexner

THE UNIVERSITY PRESS OF KENTUCKY

Copyright © 1949 by Marion Flexner

Originally published by Franklin Watts, Inc.

Copyright © 1989 by The University Press of Kentucky
Scholarly publisher for the Commonwealth,
serving Bellarmine College, Berea College, Centre
College of Kentucky, Eastern Kentucky University,
The Filson Club, Georgetown College, Kentucky
Historical Society, Kentucky State University,
Morehead State University, Murray State University,
Northern Kentucky University, Transylvania University,
University of Kentucky, University of Louisville,
and Western Kentucky University.

*Editorial and Sales Offices:* Lexington, Kentucky 40506-0336


**Library of Congress Cataloging-in-Publication Data**

Flexner, Marion, 1900-
    Out of Kentucky kitchens.

    Reprint, with new pref. Originally published: New
York: Watts, 1949.
    1. Cookery, American—Southern style.   2. Cookery—
Kentucky.   3. Kentucky—Social life and customs.
I. Title.
[TX715.2.S68F54   1989]        651.59769        89-16651
ISBN 0-8131-1712-7 (alk. paper)


This book is printed on acid-free paper meeting
the requirements of the American National Standard
for Permanence of Paper for Printed Library Materials.
∞

FOR
HELEN LEOPOLD

*who is in a large measure responsible for this book.*

*With much love,*

M. W. F.

# Contents

✠✠✠✠✠✠✠✠✠✠✠✠✠✠✠✠✠✠✠✠✠✠✠✠✠✠✠✠✠✠✠✠✠✠✠✠✠✠✠✠✠✠✠✠✠✠✠✠✠✠✠✠

# *Author's Preface to the Kentucky Edition*

✻✻✻✻✻✻✻✻✻✻✻✻✻✻✻✻✻✻✻✻✻✻✻✻✻✻✻✻✻✻✻✻✻✻✻✻✻✻✻✻✻✻✻✻✻✻✻✻✻✻✻✻✻✻✻✻

I was delighted indeed when the University Press of Kentucky asked my permission to add *Out of Kentucky Kitchens* to its list of Kentucky classics, and am happy now to give this latest edition my blessing.

Although I've sometimes said that this is not the best of my books, it has nonetheless become a favorite child: first, because of the lovely and generous people—friends, strangers, and friends of friends—who contributed their treasured recipes to this collection; and second, because of the new friends it has made for me in the forty years of its existence. *Out of Kentucky Kitchens* quickly became a kind of letter of introduction for me. Today I still receive letters and calls from people who want to know where they can find a copy (now I can tell them!) and from those who just want to tell me how much they and their families enjoy it. A letter from Wichita a few weeks ago said: "I couldn't tell you how many times I've prepared my two favorite dishes from your cookbook, Country Captain and Oscar Heims' Meat Loaf. I have served 'Oscar' to family, friends, and company in three states. . . . Last night as we were enjoying 'Oscar' again, I thought of you and wanted you to know."

In these times many young people, both women and men, probably learn their way around the kitchen earlier than I did. When I was married in 1922, I could make excellent fudge and a good herb mayonnaise, but little else. But I knew what good food tasted like and I set out to learn cooking as I would have studied anything else. If you can read, you can cook. So to a new generation of readers I say, welcome and enjoy!

*Marion W. Flexner*

Louisville, Kentucky
June 1, 1989

# *Acknowledgments*

✳✳✳✳✳✳✳✳✳✳✳✳✳✳✳✳✳✳✳✳✳✳✳✳✳✳✳✳✳✳✳✳✳✳✳✳✳✳✳✳✳✳✳✳✳✳✳✳✳✳

THE FOLLOWING PEOPLE have kindly allowed me to use their treasured recipes in this book: Judy Alexander, Barbara Anderson, Virginia Barker, Anne Clay Beaumont, Lorraine Bell, Irene Bohmer, Judith Bonnie, Charles Bronger, Sarah Buckner, Minnie Buechel, Alene Burger, Mary Helen Byck, Belle Christy, Dorothy Park Clark, Mary Clegg, Mina Cole, Elizabeth Colgan, Josephine Cox, William Crawford, Emily Davenport, Hattie Cochran Dick (The Little Colonel), Leila Dowe, Hortense Dreyfus, Helen Everhardt, Marguerite T. Finnegan, Morris Flexner, Rose Frankel, Peggy Gaines, Arnold Griswold, Camille Glenn, Alice Gray, Marion Green, Cissy Gregg, Katherine Harman, Corrie M. Hill, Julia Duke Henning Senior, Julia Duke Henning Junior, Corrie Hill Hurt, Lellie Ishmael, Lewis Kaye, Eleanor Mercein Kelly, Helen Leopold, Mary Shreve Long, Nick Marlowe, Marley Martin, Alexandra Matheson, Jane McFerran, Louise McKeithen, Isabel McMeekin, Mary Louise McNair, David Minifield, G. W. Munz, Mildred Neff, Mildred Nolan, Emma Ouerbacker, Sarah Parrant, Alice Pickett, Elizabeth Pleus, Josephine Randolph, Garnet Richards, Alice Roberts, Fred Rudolphi, Emily Rush, Noel Rush, Jean Russell, Jennie Selligman, June Smith, Louis Smith, Priscilla Stevenson, Dolly Sullivan, Lena Tachau, Carrie Todd, Allan Trout, Lillian South Tye, Sonia Uri, Mollie Walsh, Mary Lee Warren, Adele K. Weil, Edward West, Queenie Williams, Pauline Park Wilson, Nell Wolfe.

I wish also to express my deep appreciation to Stella Newhouse for her inestimable help in getting this manuscript together.

I wish to thank the following magazines and newspapers for allowing me to reprint various articles and recipes of mine published by them: *American Cookery, House and Garden, Gourmet, McCall's, American Home, Vogue,* the Louisville *Courier-Journal* and the Louisville *Times.*

I am also grateful to the following clubs, restaurants and inns for contributing their specialties: Ashbourne Inn, La Grange, Kentucky; Blue Moon Inn, Montgomery, Alabama; The Brown Hotel, Louisville, Kentucky; Charleston House, Charlestown, Indiana; Churchill Downs, Louisville, Kentucky; Old House, Louisville, Kentucky; Old Stone Inn, Simpsonville, Kentucky; Pendennis Club, Louisville, Kentucky; Pickwick Café, Montgomery, Alabama; Query Club, Louisville, Kentucky.

M. W. F.

# Introduction

✦✦✦✦✦✦✦✦✦✦✦✦✦✦✦✦✦✦✦✦✦✦✦✦✦✦✦✦✦✦✦✦✦✦✦✦✦✦✦✦✦✦✦✦✦✦✦✦✦✦✦✦

IT WAS SAID in the old days that if you had examined the contents of a Kentuckian's pocket you would have found: a bowie knife, the précis of a lawsuit to defraud his neighbor, and a copy of "Paradise Lost." There would also probably have been a sheaf of invitations—to a ball, a New Year's Day "Open House," a formal hunt dinner, a Derby breakfast or, in summer, a burgoo or barbecue party. For Kentuckians have always loved to entertain and have always been overly fond of good "vittals."

Back in 1874 when the good ladies of the Southern Presbyterian Church of Paris, Kentucky, compiled the now-classic cook book, "Housekeeping in the Blue Grass," they could boast in their introduction that "the Blue Grass region of Kentucky . . . is celebrated for the fertility of its soil, its flocks and blooded stocks, and last, but far from least, for the hospitality of the people, and their table luxuries."

But today the Blue Grass, comprising such cities as Danville, Harrodsburg, Georgetown, Lexington, Paris, Versailles, Winchester, etc., is not the only region in the state where a distinctive cuisine is to be found. From Shelbyville through Louisville (Derby Town) on the Ohio, to Irvin S. Cobb's Paducah in the "Purchase" strip; from Bowling Green, home of the well-known gourmet, Duncan Hines, in the "Pennyrile" (Pennyroyal) district; taking in Corbin, Williamsburg, Pineville, Middlesboro, Pikeville and on to the Blue Ridge and the Big Sandy—in fact, all over Kentucky, whether in prosperous river valleys or mountain districts, are to be found many noteworthy dishes.

A few of these were probably the brain children of unknown culinary artists, others were brought by the early settlers, English and Scotch, French émigrés, Austrian and German refugees, African slaves, who came to "Kentucke" (Land of Tomorrow) to make their homes. Other recipes crept in with the Yankee traders, steamboat passengers, Southern planters, foreign dignitaries, who passed through the state or made protracted visits. But no matter what the origin, all these sources have combined to enlarge and enrich our culinary knowledge, so that today Kentucky cooking is a unique blend of many old-world cultures seasoned with native ingenuity, a cross section of American cookery at its best.

13

They tell a story here about a certain Louisville host who gave his annual Derby breakfast, a celebrated affair where business and professional men, dowagers and debutantes rubbed elbows with horse trainers, politicians and farmers. At this gathering, after plying his guests with that particular "sippage" which has made Kentucky immortal (Mint Juleps to the uninitiated), the host finally led them into the dining room, where, as they say in Victorian novels, "a truly sumptuous repast had been spread."

The antique Hepplewhite table, decked out in its fabulous cloth of point de Venise, probably groaned as loudly as it ever did in its heyday in 18th-century England. Indeed, it is doubtful whether, a hundred and fifty years ago, it would have been possible to assemble at one season of the year such an infinite variety of hors d'oeuvres, canapés, pickles, condiments, aspics, green salads, entrées and sauces, smoked turkeys, country hams, ices, sherbets, cakes, pastries, fruits and cheeses as that Kentucky gentleman displayed.

The guests began to cram themselves with the tempting morsels—that is, all but one. Alone in a corner, the host spied a local farmer holding an empty plate. Asked if he were ill or if anything were wrong, the old man shook his head. "You know I got to admit all these here vittals," pointing to the table, "look mighty pretty. But now that I done seen these fancibles, I'm a-wondering whar's the fillables?"

A representative collection of Kentucky recipes should contain an equal number of fancibles and fillables, and I have tried to do justice to both. Some of them have never before been written down but were passed from one generation to another by word of mouth. Others were discovered in old ledgers and copy books and have had to be adapted for present-day use. Still others are recipes I have published from time to time in various magazines, or brought back with me from my travels and incorporated into our family menus. With few exceptions I have tested and retested these dishes in my own kitchen. All are contributed by competent cooks of recognized ability. To them and to all the friends, neighbors and interested Kentuckians who shared with me their heirloom recipes I extend my gratitude. I wish also to express my appreciation for the kind words of approval from Duncan Hines, whose own cook book, *Adventures in Good Cooking*, offers further exciting adventures in good eating.

MARION W. FLEXNER

Louisville, Kentucky

# Notes Concerning the Recipes
# in This Book

✠✠✠✠✠✠✠✠✠✠✠✠✠✠✠✠✠✠✠✠✠✠✠✠✠✠✠✠✠✠✠✠✠✠✠✠✠✠✠✠✠✠✠✠✠✠✠✠✠

C *equals* Cup
t *equals* teaspoon
T *equals* Tablespoon
F.G. *equals* few grains

Wherever possible, the number of servings has been given with each recipe. If a recipe serves 4 and you want only 2 portions, cut it in half. If you want 8, double it, and so on. Where the number of servings is not given, such as in the soup recipes, this means the recipe should be made up and kept in the icebox and served until it has been used up. It is not practical to cook small amounts of certain soups or cuts of meat (such as pot roast).

If a recipe in this book calls for an herb or spice you do not have, substitute another for it or leave it out entirely. There will be a subtle difference in flavor, but the basic recipe will not suffer materially.

The recipes that can be quickly prepared are marked (*Quickie!*).

# Table of Measurements

## SIZE AND CONTENT OF CANNED FRUITS AND VEGETABLES

No. 1 can *equals* 1⅓ cups
No. 2 can *equals* 2⅕ cups
No. 3 can *equals* 4 cups

15

## STANDARD WEIGHTS AND MEASURES

**F.G.** *equals* less than ⅛ teaspoon
2 teaspoons *equal* 1 dessert spoon
3 teaspoons *equal* 1 tablespoon
4 tablespoons *equal* ¼ cup
5 tablespoons *equal* ⅓ cup
16 tablespoons *equal* 1 cup
2 cups *equal* 1 pint
2 pints *equal* 1 quart
4 quarts *equal* 1 gallon
8 quarts *equal* 1 peck
1 pound liquid *equals* 2 cups
1 pound white sugar *equals* 2 cups
1 pound brown sugar *equals* 2 cups (firmly packed)
1 pound powdered sugar *equals* 2⅔ cups
1 pound cocoa *equals* 4 cups
1 pound wheat flour *equals* about 4 cups
1 pound cake flour *equals* 5 cups
1 pound corn meal *equals* 3 cups
1 pound nuts (chopped) *equals* 2 cups
1 pound butter or margarine *equals* 2 cups or 16 ounces
1 pound uncooked rice *equals* 2⅓ cups (rice triples its bulk when cooked)
1 pound raisins or currants *equals* 3 cups
1 cup liquid *equals* 8 ounces
1 ounce *equals* 2 tablespoons
1 ounce or 1 square of Baker's bitter chocolate taken from a half pound package *equals* 3 grated tablespoons of chocolate
1 ounce flour *equals* 4 tablespoons
Juice of an average-sized lemon *equals* 3 to 4 tablespoons
1 pound ground meat *equals* 2 cups (firmly packed)
1 average-sized egg, beaten lightly with a fork, *equals* 3 tablespoons of liquid
9 average-sized eggs usually weigh a pound
1 egg yolk usually *equals* 1 tablespoon
8 to 10 average egg whites will fill 1 cup
A 2½-pound lobster will produce about 1 pound of meat

*Unless otherwise noted, all measurements are level.*

# About Gourmet Powder

## (VE-TSON), MSG
### ("The Element of Deliciousness")

✦✦✦✦✦✦✦✦✦✦✦✦✦✦✦✦✦✦✦✦✦✦✦✦✦✦✦✦✦✦✦✦✦✦✦✦✦✦✦✦✦✦✦✦✦✦✦✦✦✦✦✦✦✦✦✦

MANY YEARS AGO a friend of mine introduced me to Gourmet Powder. "Put the tiniest pinch in sauces and gravies," she told me, "and it will give them a subtle, intangible flavor." I accordingly bought a whole carton of small flat bottles of Gourmet Powder, each accompanied by a tiny silver scoop to measure out the precious powder, termed by the Chinese, who originated it, "the element of deliciousness." Now this powder has been put on the American market under various trade names, called MSG by American chemists, "short for monosodium glutamate," a salt of "an amino acid made from high-protein by-products of wheat, corn, soy beans and sugar beet processing."

In an article about this "magic powder" in the *Reader's Digest* recently, it was stated that "salt and pepper may become a threesome" when American housewives learn the usefulness of MSG.

MSG looks like powdered sugar and has a slightly acid, salty taste. It so intensifies flavors that it has been claimed that if a drop of lemon juice is put in a glass of water, no one can detect it. But if a pinch of MSG is added to the glass, the lemon flavor will be slightly discernible.

Gourmet Powder or MSG has many uses other than those I've mentioned. It is said that if a small amount is added to vegetables which have been steamed or cooked too long, the fresh taste will be restored. Some use it in coffee, others in biscuits and hotbreads. If the tiny dispenser or scoop doesn't come with your bottle or can, an eighth of a teaspoon is about the right amount of MSG for a pint of gravy. You will have to experiment to see how much you will need to sprinkle on steaks or roasts, but I should imagine one-fourth of a teaspoon would be sufficient. You can use MSG either before cooking or afterwards, and it is said that freezing, baking, etc., will not affect its wonderful properties.

# For That Real Kentucky Flavor

❖❖❖❖❖❖❖❖❖❖❖❖❖❖❖❖❖❖❖❖❖❖❖❖❖❖❖❖❖❖❖❖❖❖❖❖❖❖❖❖❖❖❖❖❖❖❖❖❖❖❖

## GRUB, VITTALS, AND REPASTS
### (Suggested Menus for Everyday and Special Occasions, Using Recipes in This Book)

KENTUCKY FOOD is said to be divided into three classes: GRUB, or common fare such as hog jowl and greens, corn pone and 'lasses or native sorghum, washed down with sassafras (spicewood) tea. VITTALS are a cut higher— for example, fried country ham and gravy, biscuits, greasy beans (beans and bacon cooked until beans are almost transparent and coated with the bacon grease), fried apple pies or sweet 'tater puddin', coffee, etc. RE-PASTS constitute the top-drawer menus served for all formal occasions, from the feasts at the Governor's inaugural ball to receptions for visiting dignitaries, weddings, etc. Here follow a selection of menus for all three types of Kentucky meals.

## KENTUCKY DERBY BREAKFASTS

Derby Day in Kentucky! To the uninitiated this phrase has little meaning, but lovers of horse racing all over the country thrill at the mention of the word. For the Derby is the most important race of the year. Thousands of visitors pour into Louisville just for this event, the first Saturday of May—the date when the Derby is usually held. Excitement is in the air, a spirit of carnival prevails, all roads into the city are crowded as the vast mob slowly wends its way in the direction of Churchill Downs.

The first race will not be run until about noon. What matters that? At ten the crowd has annexed most of the free seats in the grandstand and clubhouse. Many have left home at seven in order to be sure of a place from which to watch the show, carrying the traditional shoe box filled with hard-boiled eggs, sandwiches, and pickles. Surely no better place could be found for a picnic than beautiful Churchill Downs! But if the visitor has any friends in Louisville he is almost certain to be invited to a Derby breakfast.

"Breakfast?" he will ask his host, "and at what time?"

"Ten-thirty."

"Thank you, I accept with pleasure, but surely I misunderstood. Is breakfast always served in Kentucky at this hour?" The host will shake his head, not knowing exactly how to explain this custom. He only knows that on Derby Day one always invites one's guests to "breakfast," even though the party is a very formal one, the service Georgian, the china Spode, and the menu perhaps like one of these:

## 1.

Mint Juleps or Whiskey Sours

Canapés of Caviar, Anchovy Paste and Chutney

| Chicken Croquettes with Mushroom Sauce | Sliced Old Kentucky Ham in Beaten Biscuits |
|---|---|
| Vegetable Aspic and Hearts of Bibb Lettuce with Tarragon Dressing | Shoestring Potatoes Black Raspberry Jelly Homemade Relish |

Fresh Strawberry Ice Cream in Individual Meringue Shells

Mints            Coffee            Salted Nuts

## 2.

Seafood Aspic in a Fish Mold
on a bed of Watercress

Herbed Mayonnaise                    Toasted Crackers

Whole Country Ham, Parboiled and Baked

Grape Jelly                Crystallized Cucumber Chips

Buttered Hot Rolls

Vegetable platter consisting of the following hot vegetables on a round tray:

Boiled Whole Cauliflower in the center with Cheese Sauce
and Gratings of Yellow Cheese, surrounded by
Broiled Tomato Halves
topped with Buttered Bread Crumbs
Radiating from this, Asparagus Vinaigrette

General Robert E. Lee Cake                Union Cake

Coffee

## 3.

Old Fashioneds or Kentucky Whiskey Toddies

Avocado Cocktail with Foam Dressing

Italian Bread Sticks

Tennessee Spice Round, Fall Fruit Conserve

Scalloped Potatoes                Lettuce Steamed Peas

Buttermilk Biscuits                        Butter

Woodford Pudding and Brandy Sauce

Coffee

## DERBY BREAKFASTS, COUNTRY STYLE

Besides the many charming old Colonial mansions in Kentucky, there are quite a few glorified log cabins, furnished in pioneer style (with just enough modern equipment to insure comfort). There is a real treat for any visitor fortunate enough to receive an invitation to dine with the owner of such a home. The rough-hewn logs, stone fireplaces, quartered-oak floors, lend a picturesque background for a Derby breakfast, country style, and as is to be expected, the menu will be in keeping with the surroundings. The food will probably be served on an old cherry drop-leaf table, the cloth red-checkered damask, the plates pewter or Sandwich glass, the menu:

**1.**

Tomato Juice Cocktail
Country Fried Chicken with Cream Gravy
Apple Rings
Corn Cakes with Sorghum or Preserves
Coffee in large cups

**2.**

Jellied Tomato Bouillon
Hot Brown Sandwich
Bibb Lettuce with Liberty Hall Maple Syrup Salad Dressing
and Fresh Green Asparagus
Iced Tea and Lemon
Transparent Pie
Coffee

**3.**

Fried Country Ham Steaks and Red Gravy
Batter Pudding        Green Apple Sauce
Green Beans and Jowl
Beaten Biscuits or Graham Gems with Butter
President Tyler's Puddin' Pies (Individuals)
Coffee

**4.**

Eggs Derby (Mary Shreve Long's recipe)
Tossed Green Salad with tart French Dressing
Garlic Bread
Fruit Cup with fresh Pineapple Water Ice
Butter Cookies or slice of Plain Cake
Coffee

## JUDITH BONNIE'S MENU FOR
## THE DERBY BREAKFAST

**Corn Meal Waffles topped with Turkey Hash**
**Sausage Patties                              Fried Apples**
**Endive, Artichoke Bottoms, Tomatoes, Cucumbers**
**with French Dressing**
**(Maple Syrup on Waffles for Dessert)**
**Hot Coffee**

## THE MOST FAMOUS OF ALL
## KENTUCKY BREAKFASTS

**A steak                              A man**
**1 quart bourbon whiskey          A dog**
**(bottled in bond)**
**The man throws the steak to the dog and drinks**
**the whiskey.**

(*Yes, it's corny, but in case anyone hadn't heard it, I thought I'd better include it—just for the record.*)

## KENTUCKY EGGNOG, MULLED WINE
## AND WASSAIL PARTIES
### (*For Christmas or New Year "At Homes" or Receptions*)

In Louisville, on both Christmas and New Year's Day, many people have "open house" in the afternoon and evening. Eggnog is usually given the place of honor on the refreshment table. Salted almonds, pecans and mixed nuts are stationed beside it and a large platter of "Raggedy Britches" or Christmas crullers. Rosettes—those wafer-thin wheels made of fritter batter and fried in deep, hot fat, then sprinkled with sugar—are constantly being cooked and brought to the table, for they do not last long once the guests have sampled their crisp and delicate goodness. Snowflakes might alternate for the rosettes if no wheel form is handy. These, too, are a fried light pastry—thin as gauze, golden-brown, only slightly sweet, well dusted with sugar. For by this time you have guessed that with eggnog, which is apt to be rich, a sweet cake is not in order, although there are some die-hards who insist that no other escort is fit for such a royal beverage as eggnog except a member of the fruit cake family. Some Kentucky hostesses will display slices of Jam Cake with Butterscotch Icing as superior to old-fashioned Fruit Cake, or perhaps they will offer you Kentucky Pecan-Bourbon Cake, a rich relative of the fruit cake clan, its sides a solid mosaic of pecan halves, seeded raisins and rich brown spiced cake batter, tipsy with bourbon whiskey. Many also offer hot Wassail as a contrast to the cold eggnog, and Wassail is at home with any of the cakes and pastries named. Sandwiches, cheese dips, etc. are not usually served at these parties, although country ham and hot homemade biscuits might make a belated appearance for those who do not have a sweet tooth. Kentucky Tom and Jerry and Champagne Punch often understudy the Wassail or Mulled Wine.

### 1.

Salted Almonds          Marion Green's Eggnog (cold)
Crullers or Raggedy Britches
Hickory Nut Cake          Wassail (hot)
Kentucky Black Cake
Country Ham in tiny hot homemade Southern Biscuits
Coffee

### 2.

Not-So-Rich Eggnog (cold)
Mulled Wine (hot)
Rosettes or Snowflakes          Kentucky Pecan-Bourbon Cake
Hot Sliced Capon in tiny buttered Whole Wheat Rolls

### 3.

Kentucky Tom and Jerry (hot)
Mixed Green          Ground Chicken and Almond Spread in
and Ripe Olives          Graham Gems or Rye Bread Rolls
Jam Cake with Butterscotch Frosting
Coffee

### 4.

Pendennis Club Champagne Punch or Cold Wassail
(Baltimore Fish House Punch)
Whole Sliced Country Ham          Hot Homemade Rolls, buttered
Hot Beaten Biscuits, buttered          Whole Baked Turkey
White and Dark Sliced Fruit Cakes          Salted Nuts
Coffee

## A LAVISH KENTUCKY COLLATION

In 1848 when Joseph A. Humphreys was making the "grand tour" he purchased in Prague, for the then "outrageous" sum of a thousand dollars, an etched, ruby-glass dinner service, made originally for Napoleon Bonaparte. This he presented to his bride when he returned home to Kentucky. The set created quite a sensation and on the 29th of July, 1856, the young Humphreys used all five hundred pieces of their prized glassware. The occasion was their entertainment for their good friend and neighbor, John J. Crittenden, ex-Governor of Kentucky and its newly elected Senator. Twenty-four selected guests sat down to a lavish collation—in the vernacular of the period. Each guest was given a printed menu; one of them is now the property of Sarah Buckner of Lexington, a descendant of the Joseph Humphreys. Here is the menu of the collation served at SUMNER'S FOREST, July 29, 1856:

SOUPS—Gumbo, Boulli Soup

BOILED MEATS—Ham, Champagne Sauce
            Brisket, White Sauce
            Leg of Mutton, Caper Sauce
            Pig's Head, Mint Sauce

BAKED MEATS—Beef á la Mode                Roast Beef
            Ham                     *         Calf's Head
            Ducks garnished with Olives   Brain Sauce

ROASTS—Saddle of Mutton          Shoat

ENTREES—Chickens, dressed with Mushrooms   Oyster Pies
        Croquettes                        Sweetbreads
        Kidneys Broiled

VEGETABLES—Corn Pudding  Boiled Corn  Tomatoes,        Okra
           Cucumbers     Potatoes        cooked and raw  Peas
           Beans         Onions       Squash           Radishes
           Cauliflower   Rice         Cabbage

PASTRY—English Plum Pudding       Apple Pie
       Soufflé                    Cocoanut Pies

DESSERT—Iced Pudding              Strawberry Ice
        Meringues                 Cake
        Sherbets                  Chocolate Ice Cream
        Jelly

NUTS AND FRUITS—Almonds        Brazil Nuts     Pecans      Figs
               Peanuts        Filberts                    Apples

WINES—Claret    Sherry    Champagne    Sauterne    Madeira
COFFEE

Most of these dishes are still served on Kentucky tables, although not at the same meal. Many foods were raised on the Humphreys' plantation, I am sure, all except the figs, and those must have come up by packet from New Orleans, Mrs. Humphreys' former home.

## MODERN KENTUCKY MENUS WITH
## TRADITIONAL DISHES

I have worked out some modern Kentucky menus based on the above
Gargantuan repast, and using the same dishes.

1.

Chicken Gumbo Soup with Rice
Crisp Corn Pones      Dressed Cucumbers
Sweet Butter      Spiced Ice Tea
Apple or Cocoanut Pie

2.

Ham Baked in Champagne or Ginger Ale
Corn Pudding      Green Beans in Brown Sauce
Buttered Hot Rolls      Bread and Butter Pickle
(June Smith's)      Nell Wolfe's
Tomato and Lettuce Salad
Piquant Dressing
Peach Ice Cream or Raspberry Water Ice
Iced Pudding (Plombière) and Marble Cake

3.

Leg of Mutton with Caper Sauce, Pickled Pears or Peaches
Cauliflower with Browned Buttered Crumbs      Hot Biscuits
Okra, Corn and Tomato Mélange      Sweet Butter
Strawberry Ice
The 100-Dollar Chocolate Cake

4.

Chicken, Veal, or Oyster Croquettes
with
Mushrooms in Double Cream Sauce
Lettuce-steamed Peas (Green Peas)
Boiled Potatoes with Chives or Parsley Butter
Buttered Wedges of Kentucky Sally Lunn, Honey
Orange-lemon Wine Jelly
Sour Cream Spice Muffins with Cinnamon Icing

5.

Ducks Garnished with Olives or Ducks in Orange Sauce
Candied Sweet Potatoes      Purée of Squash or Cymlings
Graham Gems      Damson Preserves      Green Tomato Pickles
Chocolate Soufflé with Sweetened Whipped Cream
Flavored with Vanilla
Cup Cake

**6.**

Roast Beef with Brown Gravy and Horseradish Sauce
Batter Pudding        Creamed Onions        Browned Potatoes
Dill Pickles        Fried Green Tomatoes with Homemade Chili Sauce
Hot Biscuits and Butter
English Plum Pudding with Hard Sauce
Coffee

# Out of Kentucky Kitchens

# Canapés, Hors D'oeuvres and Sandwich Spreads

✜✜✜✜✜✜✜✜✜✜✜✜✜✜✜✜✜✜✜✜✜✜✜✜✜✜✜✜✜✜✜✜✜✜✜✜✜✜✜✜✜✜✜✜✜✜✜✜✜✜✜✜✜✜✜✜✜

THE OPENING bid for a good party is often an attractive hors d'oeuvres tray or platter of dainty canapés or sandwiches. Here follows a list we serve in Kentucky for cocktail parties, wedding receptions, formal dinners or, in fact, any affair where such a course would be indicated.

## ALABAMA CHEESE BALLS (French Fried)
### (For Cocktail Parties or with Salads)

1½ C grated aged Cheddar
  cheese (do not use processed
  cheese)
1 T flour
3 egg whites, well beaten

¼ t salt
⅛ t dry mustard
⅛ t cayenne pepper
⅛ t paprika

To the cheese add the flour, salt, mustard, cayenne pepper, and paprika. Fold into the well-beaten whites of eggs. Shape into tiny balls, the size of a butterball. Roll heavily in cracker crumbs and fry in basket in deep hot lard, vegetable shortening or salad oil. If you have a kitchen thermometer, 375° is right. As soon as balls are golden-brown, they are done. Lower heat if balls begin to get too dark-brown. Remove from fire and drain on absorbent paper. Serve at once while piping hot. Some people stick a toothpick in each cheese ball.

## ANCHOVY CHEESE CANAPÉ    (Quickie!)
## OR SANDWICH SPREAD

2 cream cheeses (6 oz.)
3 drops tabasco sauce
1 T French dressing

2 drops garlic (or rub mixing
  bowl with split pod of fresh
  garlic)
½ tube anchovy paste, (1 oz.)

Blend cheese with anchovy. Add other ingredients. Spread on toasted bread cut into fancy shapes, or plain bread fried brown in butter. This sandwich can also be rolled and toasted in oven.

Variation: A small can of domestic caviar mixed with the above spread makes a welcome addition. This is also a delicious stuffing for tomatoes, served with French dressing.

This filling is often stuffed into minute cream puffs and served heated, at Louisville cocktail parties or receptions. It is a favorite hot addition to the hors d'oeuvres tray, too.

## BEER CHEESE                    (*Quickie!*)

In the days when free lunches were served in Kentucky saloons with every 5-cent glass of beer, we were told of a wonderful Beer Cheese that decked every bar. Finally we found someone who had eaten it and who told us vaguely how to prepare it. So Dorothy Clark and I experimented until we had what proved to be a very tangy sandwich spread. It will keep for weeks in a covered jar in the icebox and is a boon to the busy housekeeper. It makes wonderful sautéed sandwiches, or it can be dumped into a double boiler and allowed to melt, when it makes a perfect understudy for Welsh Rabbit. But we usually put the jar of cheese on a tray, surround it with toasted crackers and let each guest eat his fill. We may not have unearthed the bartenders' secret recipe, but ours is a concoction of which we're rather proud.

| | |
|---|---|
| 1 lb. aged Cheddar cheese (sharp) | 3 T Worcestershire sauce |
| | 1 t salt, or more to taste |
| 1 lb. American or "rat" cheese (bland) | 1 t powdered mustard |
| | Dash tabasco sauce or cayenne |
| 2 or 3 garlic pods (to taste) | pepper |
| ¾ of a 12-oz. bottle of beer (about 1 C more or less) | |

Grind the cheese (do not use processed cheese) with the garlic pods. Mix with this: Worcestershire sauce, salt, mustard and tabasco or cayenne. Put in a bowl in an electric mixer and add slowly enough beer to make a paste smooth enough to spread. Store in covered jars and keep in the icebox until needed.

## BENEDICTINE SANDWICH SPREAD
### (*Quickie!*)

This delicious spread was the brain-child of Miss Jennie Benedict, a beloved Louisville cateress of a generation ago. It is still a favorite at local cocktail parties and weddings.

| 2 cream cheeses (6 oz.) | 1 saltspoon salt, or more to taste |
| Grated pulp of 1 medium-sized cucumber | Mayonnaise |
| 1 grated onion | 2 or 3 drops green coloring |
| | Dash of tabasco |

Mash the cheeses with a fork. Work into them the grated pulp from a peeled, medium-sized cucumber, first extracting the juice by placing the pulp in a napkin and squeezing it fairly dry. Add the onion juice (more if a stronger onion flavor is liked), tabasco and salt and enough mayonnaise to make a smooth filling, easily spread. (Miss Jennie used mayonnaise made of lemon juice, real olive oil and egg yolks.) Last of all, add the green coloring—just enough to give a faint green tinge, for too much will look unappetizing.

## BROWN HOTEL SANDWICH SPECIALS
### *(Quickie!)*

These two sandwiches are specialties of Louisville's Brown Hotel.

## BROWN SANDWICH (cold)
### *(1 serving)*

| 1 thin slice rye bread, crust removed | 1 slice ripe tomato, peeled (large) |
| Thin slices baked chicken or turkey | 1 egg, hard-boiled and sliced in rings |
| Bibb or leaf lettuce to cover bread | Thousand Island dressing to top sandwich |

This is an open-face sandwich. To make it, place the bread on the salad plate. Butter it lightly if you wish. Cover with the lettuce, then the meat, then the tomato (cut ½ inch thick). Frame the tomato with the egg circles. Surround with more Bibb lettuce leaves or shredded leaf lettuce. Pass Thousand Island dressing to douse all over sandwich. This is, of course, a meal in itself—an excellent luncheon or supper or after-theater dish. In summer we serve this with iced tea in which a scoop of lime or lemon sherbet has been placed.

## BROWN SANDWICH (hot)
### *(4 servings)*

For some reason, this sandwich seems to be more popular than the cold Brown Sandwich and visitors to the Brown Hotel will often order this without consulting the menu. I like it in winter or on a cold day, but I am still partial to the cold Brown Sandwich when the weather is hot.

| | |
|---|---|
| 4 slices of toast | ¼ C American cheese, grated |
| 4 slices baked chicken or turkey | 8 strips bacon, fried crisp |
| (cut from the breast) about | 4 T grated Parmesan cheese |
| ¼ inch thick | 1 C cream sauce |

Blend yellow cheese with cream sauce until cheese has melted. Place a piece of chicken on each piece of toast, and cover with ¼ cup of sauce. Place 2 strips of bacon (previously cooked) on each sandwich, and sprinkle with 1 tablespoon of grated Parmesan cheese. Place sandwiches in a pan under the flame until the cheese melts and becomes a golden-brown. Serve at once. This recipe makes 4 portions. If you have individual shallow baking dishes, either pottery or copper, use them. This sandwich should really be served in the dish in which it was browned.


### CHILI SPECIAL          *(Quickie!)*

An excellent sandwich filling is this lovely, dusty-pink one:

| | |
|---|---|
| 1 cream cheese (3 oz.) | Chili sauce to make a smooth |
| 1½ t grated onion pulp and | paste |
| juice | Salt and cayenne pepper to |
| | taste |

Cream the cheese with onion, salt, pepper, and enough chili sauce to make a smooth paste. Spread thickly on rounds of bread. Top with second rounds of bread and fry until delicately brown, in a skillet where a small amount of butter has been melted. (Enough filling for 4 sandwiches.)

This is often made into open sandwiches, cut into any desired shape with your cookie cutters. Another popular way of serving the Chili Special is to pile it into a small bowl, place on a tray, and surround with potato chips.


### FILLED CHEESE BISCUITS (Chester Cakes)
#### *(A Canapé or Salad Accompaniment, or for Afternoon Tea)*

| | |
|---|---|
| ¼ lb. aged Cheddar or Old | ⅛ t nutmeg |
| English (sharp) cheese | ¼ t paprika |
| (grated) | ¼ t salt |
| ¼ lb. butter or margarine | 1 small can deviled ham |
| 2 C flour | 2 to 4 T cream |

or margarine. Sift flour, nutmeg, paprika, and
ese mixture to the flour mixture and crumble
is well blended, and mixture resembles corn
cher the better—and blend until the dough re-
not get it too moist. Roll a little bit at a time,
). A floured board and rolling pin are required.
r round biscuit or cookie cutter. Spread one
ith deviled ham. Top with another round and
ork to hold rounds together. Bake in hot oven
es are golden-brown. Takes 15 to 17 minutes.
d, single rounds of dough can be spread with
ricked to form a turnover.

## IN CHEESE JACKETS
### *n of Filled Cheese Biscuits)*

Cheese Biscuits very thin. Cut out with a
ded date on each round and fold the dough
g edges and seams together. Place, seamside
kie tin in a hot oven (450°) and cook until
his takes about 15 minutes. Serve hot as an
s, or for afternoon tea.

## AN'S GARLIC CHEESE ROLL
### *(For Cocktails)*

| Ched- | 1 T Worcestershire sauce |
| te | 1 T homemade mayonnaise or French dressing with olive oil |
| a paste | ¼ t dry mustard |
| | ½ box chili powder and ½ box paprika for rolling |

ldar cheese with cream cheese. Add all other
d chili powder, and work with fingers until
ivide into 2 portions. Mix paprika and chili
powder and spread thin on wax paper placed on table. Shape the cheese
into 2 rolls, one at a time, making them about the diameter of a silver
dollar or small round cracker, rolling them in the chili-paprika mixture,
and completely coating the outsides with the mixture. Flatten the ends
of the rolls in the mixture, also. Roll in clean wax paper and slip onto a
flat pan—we use a cookie tin. Put in the icebox for 24 hours to ripen.

To serve, remove paper, place the roll on a platter, and surround with round crackers the same size as the roll. A thin slice of the cheese is put on each cracker.

## GROUND CHICKEN—ALMOND OR PECAN SPREAD

1 C ground cooked chicken (baked chicken preferred)
1 C ground almonds or pecans
1 T finely chopped parsley

Mayonnaise to make a smooth paste not too runny
Salt and lots of black pepper to taste (freshly ground if possible)

Mix in order given. Serve in tiny hot baking powder or cream biscuits, or spread on rounds of bread sautéed on one side only, or put on a round of bread cut out with a doughnut cutter, minus the center. Top with a ring of bread from which the center has been removed. Put a sprig of parsley in the open ring and use discarded bread rounds to spread with another filling.

## HAM AN' BISCUITS      *(Quickie!)*

A Kentucky cocktail specialty is minute slivers of old ham, bedded in tiny, hot, buttered beaten or homemade biscuits.

## SONIA URI'S ICEBOX COCKTAIL PÂTÉ

Sonia spent so much time in France, her table is more French than American—sophisticated food at its very best. We had this pâté at her house not long ago and since then I have determined to keep some in the icebox at all times for emergencies. It is simply delicious and Sonia says it is even better if a slice of genuine truffle is placed in the bottom of the mold or container before the mixture is chilled.

½ lb. smoked liverwurst (I use Milwaukee Braunschweiger)
A 3-oz. package cream cheese
¼ lb. softened but not melted butter

1 t Worcestershire sauce, or more to taste
Dash tabasco or cayenne
1 slice truffle (optional)

Mash all ingredients with a potato ricer and beat with a fork until thoroughly blended (I use my hands). Place in a jelly glass or small mold lightly greased with olive oil and set in the icebox until needed. Serve with cocktails, highballs or sherry before dinner with salty crackers, or put on the hors d'oeuvres table.

## PICKLED MUSHROOMS FOR HORS D'OEUVRES, SALADS, OR COCKTAILS

Substitute 2 pounds of hothouse mushrooms, washed and boiled five minutes in salted water, then drained, for the two pounds of cooked shrimp in Alice Gray's Pickled Shrimp recipe which follows. Drained canned mushrooms can be substituted for the fresh ones if desired. These mushrooms are delicious in a chef or tossed salad or to serve as an hors d'oeuvre. They can also pinch-hit for pickles in sauces, stews, etc.

## ALICE GRAY'S PICKLED SHRIMP

Alice Gray introduced this pickled shrimp from Maryland and it has been a favorite at cocktail parties in Louisville ever since. It is also wonderful for the hors d'oeuvres tray. It should be made and served in an old-fashioned candy jar—the sort with a pressed glass stopper and mouth large enough to admit the hand. If you do not have one of these antiques, substitute a 2-quart Mason jar and dump the shrimp, onions, etc. into a cut-glass or pottery bowl before serving. Surround with toasted crackers and let each guest help himself and make his own canapés.

| | |
|---|---|
| 2 lbs. peeled boiled shrimp | A blade of mace |
| 1 large Bermuda onion or 2 medium ones, sliced | 1 small piece of ginger root |
| 1 medium-sized lemon, sliced in thin rounds | 4 medium-sized bay leaves |
| | 1½ C salad oil (use ½ C olive oil in this if possible) |
| ½ C mixed pickling spices | 1 pt. apple cider vinegar |
| ½ t black peppercorns | 1 t salt, or more to taste |
| 1 t sugar (optional) | ¼ t dry mustard |

Slice the onion, also slice the lemon in thin rounds. Place in jar first a layer of lemon, then of onion, then of shrimp. Add bay leaves. Pour over this the salad oil. Set aside. Meanwhile, boil the vinegar and if it is strong, use 1½ cups vinegar and ½ cup water. If not, use full strength. Add to this the pickling spices, peppercorns, mace and ginger root. Let boil hard. Add salt and dry mustard. Let cool. Strain the vinegar mixture over the shrimp and shake hard. Put in the icebox. Let remain at least 24 hours before using. Be sure to shake the bottle every 5 or 6 hours. This will keep 2 weeks in the icebox. If the vinegar mixture is very acid, add a teaspoon of sugar, but the original recipe did not call for it.

The pickled shrimp are also delicious in salads. Serve plain on a bed of shredded lettuce or watercress and pass plain or garlic mayonnaise to top them.

# "Sippages"

✠✠✠✠✠✠✠✠✠✠✠✠✠✠✠✠✠✠✠✠✠✠✠✠✠✠✠✠✠✠✠✠✠✠✠✠✠✠✠✠✠✠✠✠✠✠✠✠✠✠✠✠✠✠✠✠

"Kentucky, Oh Kentucky—
'Mid the blossoms newly born;—
Where the corn is full of kernels
And the Colonels full of corn."

Mr. Solger, Louisville's fabulous Gay 'Nineties caterer and coiner of apt phrases, dubbed alcoholic drinks "sippages." So we have borrowed this phrase to apply to the traditional as well as the modern punches, cocktails, and other alcoholic beverages served in Kentucky today.

## APPLE TODDY (Kentucky Style)

| | |
|---|---|
| 6 apples, peeled and cored | 2 C boiling water |
| 1 C sugar | Sugar to taste |
| 1 C water | Nutmeg, freshly grated |
| Cinnamon, powdered | 1 pint bourbon whiskey |

Pare and core the apples. Place them in a baking dish and pour over them a syrup made of sugar and water. Dust the apples with cinnamon and bake until done, basting frequently. This takes about 1 hour. Remove apples and juice from stove and mash in bottom of a silver or china punch bowl. Pour over apples boiling water, sugar to taste, and whiskey. Grate nutmeg over this and ladle into cups. Serve at once with crullers or rosettes.

## ELEANOR MERCEIN KELLY'S
## BALTIMORE FISH HOUSE PUNCH
### (Family Cold Wassail Bowl, 1732 recipe)

Eleanor Mercein Kelly is the dean of Louisville fiction writers. Famous throughout the country as the author of *Basquerie* and other short

36

stories, she is equally well known among her friends as one of the South's most gracious hostesses. Her food is always exciting, different. This punch recipe is a family one dating from 1732. They refer to it also as their Wassail Bowl, for of course a wassail, which was a holiday punch often ladled out to Christmas carolers or mummers in the old days in "Merrie England," may be either a cold or a hot drink. She says this is potent but perfectly delicious, and I am delighted to be able to present it to you. To make it you will need:

| | |
|---|---|
| 2 qts. Jamaica rum or Bacardi | 2 qts. water |
| 1 qt. (cognac) brandy | 1 qt. freshly squeezed lemon or |
| ¾ lb. sugar (loaf sugar origi- | lime juice |
| nally) | 1 wineglass peach brandy |
| 1 large single block of ice | |

Put sugar in punch bowl, add water and stir until dissolved. "Then contribute the various spirits and liquids," the old recipe runs. "Center as great a lump of ice in the punch bowl as may be, permitting the brew to stand unmolested for a couple of hours." In conclusion it states, "you may use a quart of Bacardi instead of the Jamaica rum if the ladies prefer." Before serving, ladle the punch over the ice to be sure it is well blended. Fruit cake, pound cake or any of the jam cakes or pecan cakes are the traditional companions for this robust punch.

## PENDENNIS CLUB CHAMPAGNE PUNCH

### *(35 to 40 punch cups)*

Another favorite Louisville Christmas beverage is the Champagne Punch served at the Pendennis Club. Mr. William Crawford, the manager, has kindly given his permission to reprint it here.

| | |
|---|---|
| Juice of 1 doz. lemons | 2 C strong tea (optional) |
| 1 qt. carbonated water | ½ pt. curaçao |
| ½ pt. maraschino liqueur | 2 qts. champagne |
| 1 pt. brandy | Fruits for decorating |
| Powdered sugar to taste | |

Mix lemon juice with carbonated water. Sweeten to taste with powdered sugar. The strong tea may be added if desired, but it is optional. Place a large block of ice in a punch bowl. Pour the mixture over it and add the maraschino liqueur, curacao, brandy and champagne. Mix well and decorate with fruits in season. Ladle into punch cups.

## CHURCHILL DOWNS MINT JULEP
### (Quickie!)

*(The julep you would be served at the famous
Louisville race track)*

### (1 serving)

1 or 2 ounces Kentucky bourbon whiskey

1 T chopped mint leaves

1 T water

1 t sugar, or more to taste

Shaved or crushed ice to fill each
cup

1 small bunch fresh mint

2 straws, cut short

Place sugar and chopped mint in a small crockery bowl. Bruise the leaves
well with a muddler or the back of a wooden spoon, until mixture forms
a paste. Add water and continue stirring. There should be a thick green
syrup by this time. Now you are ready for the whiskey. Fill a julep cup
half full of crushed or shaved ice. Add the mint syrup and the whiskey.
Fill the cup or glass with crushed ice. Slip the bunch of mint into the
ice, and beside it the straws. They should be no taller than the mint.
Lift the cups onto a tray, being careful not to touch the sides with the
fingers, and put them into the icebox to frost. This will take from one-
half to one hour. Serve at once. This appears to be a most innocuous
concoction, but it has a potent kick, as anyone who has tasted it for the
first time can testify. It should be sipped slowly and not tossed off at a
gulp!

NOTE: A silver julep cup is preferable for making this famous old
drink, although it is by no means essential. If you are lucky enough to own
such heirlooms, chill the cups thoroughly before mixing the juleps. Glass
tumblers may be substituted for silver cups if necessary—they will not
frost, however!

## MARION GREEN'S EGGNOG SUPERB
### (20 servings)

Marion Green is the society editor of the Louisville *Times*, and one of
Louisville's most delightful hostesses. Her kitchen is presided over by
genial David Minifield, and between them they make delicious concoc-
tions. Here's their recipe for eggnog, described by all who are lucky
enough to sample it as "the best and richest eggnog in the world."

Yolks of 12 eggs

2½ C sugar

1 qt. aged bottled-in-bond Kentucky bourbon whiskey

1 qt. double cream

Beat the egg yolks very, very light with the sugar—an electric mixer helps. They should be spongy and lemon-colored. Add whiskey very, very slowly, beating between each addition—Marion's directions say "a drop at a time," but I add about a tablespoon or two. Beat the cream stiff, but watch carefully that it does not get buttery. It is better on the runny than the too-thick side. Fold this cream into the batter mixture and pour into a crystal or silver bowl. The bowl should be placed in a larger one and chipped ice put around it to keep it thoroughly chilled. Grate nutmeg over the top, or put a little over each serving.

Marion says this will serve twenty, but if you want to make it go farther, take the 12 egg whites you did not use, beat them to a stiff froth and fold into the mixed eggnog. This also makes a brew a little less rich.

## NOT-SO-RICH EGGNOG   *(Quickie!)*
### *(16 punch cups)*

Our family prefers this recipe for eggnog because it is not too rich.

| | |
|---|---|
| 3 eggs, separated | 1 pt. cream (single) |
| ¼ C sugar | ½ pt. whiskey (aged bourbon) |
| F. G. salt | 2 T Jamaica rum |
| Grated nutmeg | 2 T sugar |

Separate the eggs. To the yolks add ¼ cup sugar. Continue beating until light and lemon-colored—an electric mixer is wonderful for this. Add the single cream and pour the whiskey and Jamaica rum into it, stirring well. Beat the egg whites with salt. When stiff, add 2 tablespoons sugar. Fold gently into the other mixture and pour into the eggnog bowl. Dust the surface with freshly grated nutmeg or grate a little nutmeg over each serving. Chill, if necessary, by putting the bowl filled with the eggnog into a large bowl, and packing crushed ice around the smaller bowl to fill the cavity between the two bowls.

## HOT SPICED WASSAIL
### *(32 punch cups)*

No winter beverage warms the cockles of the heart more effectively than Hot Spiced Wassail. I gave a party for some debutantes several years ago and served Wassail along with the eggnog. To my surprise, many preferred it, and since then I have had any number of requests for it. In fact, I was quite pleased when it was served at one of the large debut balls last year. Here's how to make it:

| 1 gal. apple cider | ¼ t powdered ginger |
|---|---|
| 1 T whole cloves | ¼ t grated nutmeg |
| 1 T allspice | ¼ t salt |
| 2 sticks cinnamon bark | 2 lemons cut in slices |
| ½ lb. dark brown sugar | (seeds removed) |
| 1 pt. Holland gin or grain | 3 oranges cut in slices |
| alcohol | (seeds removed) |
| 2 blades of mace | |

Mix the cider with salt and sugar. Drop into it a bag containing spices. Let this come to a hard boil, and simmer 15 minutes in a covered pot or kettle. Remove from fire and taste to see whether or not mixture is sweet enough. If not, add more white sugar to taste—a tablespoonful at a time. Set aside until ready to serve. Then boil cider once more and remove spice bag. Pour into the wassail bowl, which has been prepared as follows:

Use a large punch bowl made of heavy china or silver. Place it over a kettle of boiling water to heat. Add lemons and oranges cut in thin slices. When fruit and bowl are warm, add the Holland gin or grain alcohol. When this becomes warm, pour the boiling cider over it. Ladle into cups or mugs and serve at once. Do not try to boil the gin—this will cause the alcohol to evaporate. You merely want the liquor to be hot enough not to chill the cider mixture.

Another way to serve this is in a deep crockery pot kept over an alcohol burner—the kind used to serve a large quantity of soup. This was the method used at one of the Louisville clubs and it was very successful.

## KENTUCKY TOM AND JERRY
### *(12 servings)*

This is a wonderful drink for a cold wintry night; not as rich as eggnog but just as satisfying.

| 6 eggs, whites and yolks beaten | ½ t ground cloves |
|---|---|
| separately | 1 t ground cinnamon |
| 12 T sifted powdered sugar | Whiskey |
| ½ t ground allspice | Jamaica rum |

Fold the yolks and whites together after beating, adding the sifted powdered sugar and spices. Put 2 tablespoons of this mixture in the bottom of a Tom and Jerry mug or a regular coffee cup. Add a jigger of whiskey, warmed in the bottle but not heated. Then stir well to make an emulsion. This keeps the mixture from curdling. Add ½ teaspoon warmed Jamaica rum along with each jigger of whiskey, if the flavor is liked. Fill up the mugs or cups with boiling water, stirring as the water is poured. Serve at once, as the spices have a tendency to settle at the bottom of the mug.

## KENTUCKY WHISKEY TODDY    *(Quickie!)*

½ t sugar (or 1 t if you have a    A spilling jigger of bourbon
   sweet tooth)                          whiskey
1 T tap water, or more if you       (2 to 2½ T)
   like a mild drink

Mix sugar and water. Add the whiskey. Pour into an Old-Fashioned glass
and fill with crushed ice, or add 2 ice cubes. Stir until chilled. Serve. This
is our favorite whiskey drink.

## MULLED WINE
### *(For New Year's Eve)*

In some old books Mulled Wine made with claret was called "The Arch-
bishop"; when made with port it was dubbed "The Bishop." This drink
is especially delicious with "Raggedy Britches" (crullers) or jelly cookies.
Here's the Louisville recipe:

1 C sugar                           2 T whole allspice
1 C water                           1 T whole cloves
3 qts. claret                      ½ t grated nutmeg
2 qts. water                     1 T coriander or cardamon
6 sticks cinnamon bark          seeds
2 or 3 pieces dry ginger root    ¼ bottle arrack, if you can find
2 blades mace                   it. If not, you can substitute
¼ bottle Jamaica rum         a mild rum.
Juice of 3 lemons              Cinnamon sticks
Lemon rinds

Boil sugar and water for 5 minutes. Cover and set aside. To the claret
add 2 quarts of water, lemon juice and the empty rinds. Taste and
sweeten to your fancy with the sugar syrup. Add a spice bag containing
the spices. Let the mixture boil hard, then turn off heat, cover, and let
the spices steep. Heat again if necessary, and add the Jamaica rum and
arrack. If no arrack can be found, substitute any one of the mild rums—
Bacardi, Ronrico, etc. Be sure the bottles of rum and arrack have been
warmed before pouring into the heated wine. Remove spice bag. Serve
a cinnamon stick with this, to use as a straw.

## OLD-FASHIONEDS    *(Quickie!)*

According to Irvin S. Cobb, Kentucky's gifted writer and raconteur, these
cocktails originated at the Pendennis Club in Louisville, Kentucky.

To the Kentucky Whiskey Toddy add a dash of Angostura bitters, a
slice of lemon, half a slice of orange and a maraschino cherry.

### "SHOW ME A LAND" TODDY    *(Quickie!)*

When Dorothy Clark and Isabel McMeekin collaborated for the first time under the name "Clark McMeekin," they wrote the popular historical novel about Kentucky called *Show Me A Land*. To commemorate this occasion, the chef at the Brown Hotel (where many delectable dishes originate) introduced two *Show Me A Land* items on the hotel menu—a toddy and a sandwich. Here is the toddy:

| | |
|---|---|
| 1 ounce water (⅛ cup) | A sprig of mint |
| 2 small cubes sugar | 1½ ounces bourbon whiskey |
| A mint cherry (green) | |

For the winter version of this toddy, the sugar is mixed with boiling water and muddled. When it has dissolved, pour it into an Old-Fashioned glass with the whiskey and mint cherry. Have the glass hot and the liquor warm but not boiling. It should be warmed in the bottle before being added to the toddy.

To make the summer version of this drink, cold water is used and the ingredients are poured into an Old-Fashioned glass filled with crushed ice. The mint cherry is added as before and a small sprig of mint slipped into the corner.

This is guaranteed to transport you to another era—to the lush days before the Civil War, when the "Colonel Suh" sat on his wide verandah and, holding just such a beverage in his fine aristocratic hand, rocked back and forth whiling away the midday hours.

# Soups

✛✛✛✛✛✛✛✛✛✛✛✛✛✛✛✛✛✛✛✛✛✛✛✛✛✛✛✛✛✛✛✛✛✛✛✛✛✛✛✛✛✛✛✛✛✛✛✛✛✛✛✛

## ALABAMA CHICKEN GUMBO
### (12 servings)

I like this recipe because it calls for ingredients that can be bought anywhere. It differs somewhat from the traditional Creole version, but is deserving of praise in its own right.

| | |
|---|---|
| A 5- or 6-pound hen | 1 pt. fresh green butterbeans |
| 1 qt. fresh or canned tomatoes | 2 large onions, chopped |
| 1 qt. okra, cut in rings | 1 green pepper, chopped |
| 2 T chopped parsley | 1 T salt, or more to taste |
| ½ t black pepper | 2 small pods garlic |
| ¼ t thyme | 3 bay leaves |
| 1 T filé powder (optional) | Corn cut from 5 ears |
| 1 gal. water | 2 T flour |
| ¼ lb. lean raw ham, diced | 1 tiny hot red pepper (optional) |

Disjoint fowl. Salt and pepper and roll in flour. Fry in deep fat until golden-brown, but not done. Remove chicken to soup kettle and set aside. Now pour off all but 2 tablespoons of fat from the pot in which the chicken was fried. Brown the diced raw ham. Put the ham with the chicken, and braise the onion, green pepper and garlic in the same fat. Add to soup kettle. Add the flour to the remaining fat, and brown, but be careful not to burn. Add a cup of the water to make a thick gravy and when thick add this to the chicken and ham. Now put the rest of the water and all other ingredients, except the corn, in the soup kettle. Cover, set on the stove and simmer gently until chicken is thoroughly done (4 or 5 hours). Remove chicken from the soup, discard the bones and add the meat to the rest of the soup. Add the corn and cook 20 to 30 minutes longer, or until it is thoroughly done. Care must be taken that the soup does not scorch or burn. Rice is always passed with this soup, a tablespoon or more being added to each plate at the table. The filé powder adds a great deal to the flavor, but the soup is very good without it. The excess fat should be removed before pouring the soup into the tureen. Correct

43

the seasoning and serve at once. This is a meal in itself. Serve with beaten biscuits or hot Southern biscuits and lots of butter. A piece of pie makes a fine dessert. President Tyler's Puddin' Pie can't be beat. Lots of coffee to follow, too.

## BOUBA                                                    (Quickie!)
### (6 hearty servings)

Bouba is the name of a delectable fish chowder our French-Canadian guide once prepared for us on the shores of a beautiful emerald lake not large enough to be placed on the regional map, and hence a fisherman's paradise. Neither the guide nor we could trace the origin of the name, but here's the recipe for Bouba:

12 small potatoes, peeled, or 6 medium ones cut in half
6 medium-sized onions, sliced ¼ inch thick
Freshly ground pepper (black)
4 T butter (no substitutes)

Enough water to cover (about 6 C)
6 bass filets (about 2 lbs.)
Parsley and paprika for garnishing

Cover the bottom of the pot with the onions, add salt, black pepper and butter. Add enough water to cover. Cover the pot and let come to a hard boil, then reduce the heat and cook 15 minutes. Add the bass filets and when this begins to boil once more, simmer for ½ hour. Serve the broth in soup cups and garnish with parsley and paprika. The fish and vegetables are eaten in a soup plate, and make a very satisfying meal. In case you have 12 bass heads, substitute them for the filets. Strain the soup and serve with chopped parsley.

## BOUILLABAISSE

1 lb. red snapper, halibut, or whitefish
1 qt. tomatoes
⅛ t paprika
1 bay leaf
1 slice orange peel
⅛ t saffron
½ lemon, juice and rind
Salt, black pepper to taste

1 lb. mixed shellfish—shrimp, crab, oysters, scallops, lobster, etc.
½ C olive oil
2 garlic cloves
2 onions
2 T chopped parsley
½ t mixed herbs—basil, thyme, marjoram

Rub fish with part of olive oil, herbs, lemon juice, and 1 pod garlic (crushed). Salt and pepper and let stand 1 hour. Fry onions, parsley, and remaining garlic in rest of oil. Add fish cut in 2-inch pieces. Cook

10 minutes (a Dutch oven is excellent for this). Add water, tomatoes, shellfish and remaining ingredients, and cook 10 minutes longer or until all fish are done. Serve in soup tureen. Pass croutons with this.

## TANDY ELLIS'S BURGOO
### *(8 to 20 servings)*

For many years Tandy Ellis, the Kentucky wit and raconteur, ran a daily column in the Louisville *Courier-Journal*. It was considered quite an honor to be invited to his sanctum (Rambeau Flats) at his home in Ghent, Kentucky. Once, when I published a recipe for burgoo which called for cabbage, he took exception and sent me his own version of this distinctive Kentucky dish. He wrote:

"I have been asked many times for my recipe for burgoo, especially for home use. I learned to make burgoo from Gus Jaubert of Lexington, and from several of the other old-time makers of Kentucky burgoo. I trailed with Gus Jaubert on one occasion when he went to Ohio and served 10,000 people. He had one kettle that held 600 gallons. I have made burgoo for several meetings. My recipe to serve at the home for about 8 people* follows":

| | |
|---|---|
| 2 lbs. beef cut from the shank (soup bone included) | 2 C diced onions |
| ½ lb. lamb (baby lamb, not mutton) | 2 C fresh butterbeans or 1 pkg. frozen butterbeans |
| 1 medium-sized chicken | 3 carrots, diced |
| 2 C diced potatoes | 1 C minced parsley |
| Red pepper to taste (1 small pod, or more to taste) | 2 green peppers, diced, seeds removed |
| 3 C corn cut from the cob (young field corn is best) | 2 C okra, diced or cut in rings |
| Salt and black pepper to taste | 4 qts. water, or more if soup cooks too thick |
| 1 "toe" of garlic | 12 tomatoes or 1 qt. can |

Put the beef, lamb, and dismembered chicken in a soup kettle with water, salt, black and red pepper. An old-fashioned iron kettle was specified by Mr. Ellis, but any heavy aluminum or metal kettle with a tight-fitting lid will do. Let this come to a hard boil, reduce the heat, and simmer about 2 hours with the lid on. Add potatoes, onions, and at intervals of 10 minutes, the butterbeans, carrots, green peppers. Then add corn and simmer for 2 hours or until mixture seems very thick. Watch carefully so that it does not stick. Add more water from time to time if

* I disagree with Mr. Ellis's figures. I have served 20 people with this recipe. But if it is kept in the refrigerator it can be used for several days.

necessary, but use as little as possible. Add okra and tomatoes and the garlic and let simmer another 1½ hours, or until these vegetables too are done and blended with the others. Mr. Ellis insisted that the stew should cook for 7 hours, but 4 to 5 hours should be quite sufficient. As soon as soup is taken from stove, stir the parsley into it. This soup improves by standing and can be kept for a long time in the refrigerator. It is delicious when reheated. Serve with corn pones and follow it with a piece of pie— a most satisfactory repast, Kentucky style.

## CARCASS SOUP

Use only *baked* fowl to make this soup—capon, chicken, turkey, duck, or goose. Boiled fowl has not sufficient flavor.

| | |
|---|---|
| 1 carcass of turkey or chicken, etc. | Scraps of dressing, meat, skin, gravy |
| 1 bunch celery leaves, or 3 stalks celery with leaves | 3 sprigs parsley |
| | Salt, pepper to taste |
| 1 onion | Leftover giblets |
| 1 pod garlic (optional) | Water to cover fowl (about 2 qts.) |

Put all ingredients in soup kettle and boil 2 to 3 hours, until all seasoning has gone into soup. Strain and add ¾ to 1 cup of cooked barley, rice or noodles, and fresh chopped parsley.

NOTE: This soup also makes an excellent base for meat gravies. If put in the icebox and sealed in a sterile jar, it will keep for several weeks.

## CREAM OF MUSHROOM SOUP SUPERB
### *(6 servings)*                    *(Quickie!)*

This is our favorite recipe for Mushroom Soup and one we serve for many occasions. The flavor is improved if it stands an hour or so before serving. It keeps well in the icebox for a few days, in a covered container. Heat before serving. We usually make it with fresh hothouse mushrooms, although wild ones would probably do. Do not make it with canned mushrooms, however.

| | |
|---|---|
| ½ lb. fresh hothouse mushrooms | 1 bay leaf |
| 2 T olive oil | 1 t salt, or more to taste |
| 2 T butter or margarine | 1 T Worcestershire sauce |
| 1 "toe" of garlic | 1 t mushroom catsup (optional) |
| 1 T flour (rounded) | 1 qt. milk |

Grind mushrooms. Heat olive oil and butter in the bottom of a Dutch oven or large skillet with a tight-fitting lid. Add mushrooms, garlic, bay leaf, salt, and black pepper. Cover and simmer 5 minutes. Stir occasionally. Add flour and mix until smooth with mushrooms. Gradually add milk, stirring to make a smooth paste. Add all other ingredients, seasoning to taste with more salt and pepper, if necessary. Stir to keep from lumping. Let come to a boil, and turn off the heat. Set aside for an hour or so and reheat before serving. Remove bay leaf and garlic, if you can find it. This soup is vastly improved in flavor if allowed to stand and mellow before being served. Dust each portion with paprika, or top with a teaspoon of one of the following:

### Paprika Cream Topping

½ C double cream                    Dash of cayenne pepper
F. G. salt                          1 t bright red paprika

Beat the double cream with the salt and cayenne pepper. When stiff add the paprika. Serves 6.

### Pimento Cream Topping

Follow above recipe, substituting 1 canned pimento, put through a ricer or food mill, for the teaspoon of paprika.

## BARBARA ANDERSON'S CUCUMBER CRÊME
### (Quickie!)

Barbara Tunnell Anderson, one of Louisville's most gifted writers, author of the charming novel, The Days Grow Cold and the more recent South Bound, gave me this delicious and unusual recipe.

4 cucumbers, peeled and diced       1 C celery, diced
½ C leeks or shallots or onions,    1 qt. chicken broth
  diced                             1 C heavy cream
Chopped chives or parsley, and      Salt and freshly ground black
  paprika, for garnishing             pepper to taste

Put cucumbers, celery, leeks or shallots (if neither leeks nor shallots are to be had, use chopped onion) in a Dutch oven with a lid. Add chicken broth and cook 25 to 30 minutes, or until vegetables are tender. Strain soup and mash vegetables through a fine sieve, or use a food mill if you own one. Add cream and serve soup hot or cold. Garnish each portion of cold soup with a few chopped chives or a little chopped parsley. Pass croutons with the hot soup.

## DIXIE OKRA SOUP

| | |
|---|---|
| 1 qt. okra | 2 sprigs parsley |
| 3 qts. water | 1 T salt |
| A 2-lb. beef bone with meat | ½ t black pepper |
| 1 lb. lean beef | 2 onions |
| 1 slice hot red pepper or a dash | Bunch of celery leaves |
|    of cayenne | 1 pt. tomatoes, peeled and quar- |
| 1 green pepper, diced |    tered (fresh or canned) |

Cook soupbone, meat, water, celery, 1 onion, salt and pepper in a covered soup kettle until meat is tender. Strain. Add meat to the stock plus another diced onion, okra cut in slices, green pepper, diced, and fresh or canned tomatoes. Simmer ½ hour or until vegetables are done. Add more salt and pepper if necessary.

Delicious with Skillet Corn Pones and Pecan or Chess Pie. This makes a meal in itself.

## HAM-BONE SOUP

You will want to know about this hearty soup, which dates from Colonial times in old Virginia. Serve it to your family after they have had an outing in the woods on a cold winter's afternoon.

| | |
|---|---|
| 1 qt. fresh or canned tomatoes | 1 ham hock with meat, or ham |
| ¼ t black pepper |    bone plus 1 lb. ham scraps |
| 4 medium potatoes, cut in cubes | 3 qts. water |
| 1 small head cabbage, shredded | 3 onions, chopped |
|    (remove hard parts) | Dash cayenne |
| | Salt to taste |

Boil ham in water with pepper and onions. If ham has been previously cooked, 2 hours will be sufficient; if not, 3 hours. Do not add salt until later, as the ham is so salty more may not be necessary. Add potatoes and cabbage and tomatoes and simmer 1 hour longer. Skim off excess fat before serving. This is an excellent way to use the leftover ham bones and scraps of ham. Ham-bone Soup is usually served with Skillet Corn Bread.

## HAYMARKET FRESH GREEN PEA SOUP
### *(With meat stock base)*     *(Quickie!)*

The Haymarket is the picturesque open market on Jefferson Street where the farmers of Louisville display and sell their produce. The wholesale market opens at 4 or 5 A.M., the retail at 8, and continues until after dark. All through the summer months are to be found, in this colorful spot, stalls of garden jewels—herbs, onions, garlic and everything else needed to make the summer soup a dish to remember.

| | |
|---|---|
| 1 onion | 2 T chopped parsley |
| 1 qt. shelled peas (fresh peas) | ½ C cream |
| 1 bunch celery tops | Salt, pepper to taste |
| 1 T flour | 2 T butter or chicken fat |
| 1 qt. chicken broth or sweet-bread stock | |

Boil peas in chicken broth with celery, onion, salt and pepper, until peas are thoroughly done. Strain and mash through a sieve. Melt butter in a skillet. Add flour and brown. Then add cream to make a thick sauce. Add this to the soup and then season well. Sprinkle with parsley and serve at once.

## KENTUCKY BLACK BEAN SOUP

### *(A recipe from pre-Civil War days—another Kentucky culinary masterpiece)*

| | |
|---|---|
| 1 lb. black beans, soaked over night in water | 1 veal knucklebone with meat |
| | 4 cloves stuck in lemon pieces |
| 1 lb. lean veal | ¼ t allspice |
| 1 lemon cut in eighths | ¼ t black pepper |
| ½ t nutmeg | 1 C sherry |
| 3 T salt, or more to taste | 2 T butter |
| 2 T Worcestershire sauce | Lemons |
| 3 onions, chopped | Hard-boiled eggs for garnishing |
| 3 qts. water | |

Cover beans with water and soak overnight. Drain. Next morning put 3 qts. of water in a soup kettle. Add meat, knucklebone, lemon, beans, salt, pepper, Worcestershire sauce and spices and boil slowly until beans are mushy (3 to 4 hours). Remove meat and set aside. Remove lemon and cloves and discard. Press beans through a strainer or food mill. As this is hard to do, it may be necessary to add a bit more water to dissolve the remaining pulp or to thin the soup. Shred meat into strained soup. Fry onions until brown in butter and add to the soup. Add sherry and more salt and pepper if necessary. Heat to the boiling point. Serve 1 slice of lemon and 1 slice of hard-boiled egg in each plate or cup.

## EMILY RUSH'S TARRAGON SHALLOT CRÊME
### *(6 servings)*

This is a wonderful rich soup of the Vichysoisse type. It is simple to make, and is delicious hot or cold.

| | |
|---|---|
| 1 qt. chicken or sweetbread stock | Celery leaves (about ½ C) or a few stalks celery with leaves |
| 8 shallots, tops and all (if small, use 12) cut in rings | Salt and black pepper |
| | 1 pt. heavy cream |
| 2 sprigs fresh tarragon (24 leaves) or ¼ t dried herb | Chives |
| 6 egg yolks | Dash of paprika |

Add the shallots to chicken or sweetbread stock. (For the latter see recipe for Boiled Sweetbreads on page 134.) Add the tarragon (fresh or dried), celery leaves or stalks with leaves. Simmer soup 20 minutes after it comes to a hard boil. Add salt and black pepper to taste. Set aside. Beat egg yolks with cream. Add to cool soup and strain. Return to stove and cook soup in a double boiler, stirring constantly until it coats the spoon like a custard. Do not boil. Pour into a covered dish and set in icebox. Garnish with chives and a dash of paprika.

## CHARLES BRONGER'S LOUISVILLE TURTLE SOUP
### *(16 servings)*

This version of turtle soup is typical of Louisville and is blood brother to Burgoo, being a conglomeration of meat stock, tomatoes, vegetables, including corn, celery, green beans, etc., plus the turtle meat, of course. This is the recipe of Mr. Charles Bronger. He gave it to Cissy Gregg, who published it in the *Courier-Journal* and gave me permission to use it here. She writes: "Before Prohibition there were camps near the edge of town where stag parties would gather on week-ends, around kegs of beer and 40-gallon kettles of turtle soup, which was cooked all Saturday night. At the Oak Park Outing Camp on Bickel's Lane the elder Bronger (now aged 78) used this recipe. The turtles are at their soup peak in late summer or fall when they are fat, before they hibernate for the winter."

Even Mr. Bronger's cut-down recipe that Cissy used made 7 gallons of soup, so I have done another operation on it to trim it to home-kitchen size. This should make about 2 gallons of soup—enough for 16 hearty eaters.

2 lbs. or 4 C turtle meat (if you don't have that much, fill out the amount with fresh beef tongue, says Mr. Bronger)

2 carrots

½ C fresh green beans

3 stalks celery with leaves (¼ whole large bunch)

3 large onions

2 medium-sized potatoes

2 oz. tomato purée

1 T whole allspice

½ C green peas, fresh, frozen, or canned

1 No. 1-size can tomatoes

¼ bottle catsup (about ½ C)

¼ pod hot red pepper (⅛ t)

¼ C browned flour* (see note at bottom of page)

¼ bottle claret (about ¾ C)

1 gal. water (4 qts.)

2 hard-boiled eggs

1 whole lemon

Extra salt and black pepper to taste

1 t sugar if wine is dry

½ C corn, cut from cob, or canned, Niblet type

⅛ medium-sized head of cabbage, core removed

Put turtle meat and (if you are using it) fresh beef tongue in a large soup kettle with the cold water. I add salt and black pepper but the original recipe did not call for it. Cover and let come to a hard boil, then turn down the flame and simmer gently until the meat is falling apart. If you own a pressure cooker, cook 45 minutes to an hour at 15 pounds pressure, cutting the water down to 6 cups. But if you want to make it the traditional way, Mr. Bronger and Cissy say the meat must simmer 2½ to 3 hours in a soup pot or kettle with a tight-fitting lid. While meat is cooking, get vegetables ready, and put the allspice and pepper pod into a muslin bag—allow room for the spices to expand. Then when the meat is tender, strain the broth, and mix it with the flour, a little at a time to form a smooth paste. Set it aside. If you have used tongue, trim it, removing bones and skinning it. The meat must be put through a meat grinder along with all the vegetables, even the tomatoes, unless you want to strain them. One whole hard-boiled egg is also ground and half a lemon, peel and all (seeds removed). Save the juices that drip from the meat and vegetables you have ground, and put back in the soup kettle with the meat, vegetables and the thickened soup stock. Now add to this more salt and pepper if necessary, the spice bag, catsup, sugar and claret, tomatoes and tomato purée. Simmer for 1 to 1½ hours longer— Cissy said 4 but I have cut her recipe in quarters, so I believe the time specified will be sufficient. In a pressure cooker, 8 minutes at 15 pounds will be sufficient. Continue to cook until well blended. Watch carefully so that it does not burn—"it will scorch as easily as jam, when it is thick," Mr. B. said. Serve in a tureen, floating a sliced hard-boiled egg and

* To brown the flour see recipe under General Hints at the beginning of the chapter on Cakes (page 231).

thin lemon slices also, or serve one slice of each in every plate. Add more
claret to each plate if you like a strong wine flavor. If more water has
to be added in the cooking, use boiling water.

# You'll Want These with Your Soup

## CEREAL BITS FOR SOUP OR SALAD

Toasted Cheerios, Rice Krispies, Puffed Wheat or Rice can be served
with soup, salad or cocktails in an emergency. They can also be sprinkled
with grated cheese and heated in the oven before serving.

## CROUTONS (Fried)

Take stale baker's bread, remove crusts, and dice into inch squares. Melt
1 tablespoon butter in a skillet and keep stirring the croutons until each
side is brown. Fry the cubes from only one slice of bread at a time.

## DUMPLINGS FOR SOUP OR STEWS

| | |
|---|---|
| 1 C flour | ¼ C milk, or enough to make |
| 2 t baking powder | dough stiff enough to roll |
| ¼ t salt | 2 T butter or substitute |

Sift dry ingredients. Add fat and mix well. Add milk slowly. Roll on
floured board to about ¼ inch thickness. Cut with a small biscuit cutter
or thimble and drop into boiling soup or stew. Cook 10 to 15 minutes
or until dumplings are thoroughly done. Serve 3 to 6 per plate, according to size. Two tablespoons of chopped parsley mixed with the sifted
dry ingredients are a nice addition when the dumplings are used for
soup.

## EGG FOR SOUP

To each quart of highly seasoned clear broth, allow 1 well-beaten egg.
Drop by teaspoonfuls into the boiling clear chicken soup or meat broth.
Serve hot.

## MARROW BALLS

1 C cracker or bread crumbs
3 T marrow or butter (melted)
½ t baking powder
1 t grated onion
2 T chopped parsley
1 egg, beaten

4 to 6 T soup stock or milk
  (enough to make a stiff
  paste)
F. G. black pepper
Salt to taste

Mix crumbs, baking powder, and onion. Add well-beaten egg, and marrow or butter. Add soup stock or milk, gradually, stirring all the while. The mixture must be stiff enough to hold together. Add parsley, salt and pepper to taste. Roll into tiny balls the size of marbles. Keep in refrigerator until ready to use. Just before serving add the balls to the boiling soup and cook until thoroughly done. This takes 10 to 20 minutes. Serve 4 small balls in each cup of soup.

## RICE BALLS FOR SOUP

⅔ C cooked rice
2½ T flour
1 t grated onion and juice

1 T chopped parsley
1 egg
Salt, pepper to taste

Mash rice. Add all other ingredients. Mix well. Drop from the end of a teaspoon into clear boiling soup. Continue boiling 5 minutes. Serve 3 balls to each plate.

# Breads

❖❖❖❖❖❖❖❖❖❖❖❖❖❖❖❖❖❖❖❖❖❖❖❖❖❖❖❖❖❖❖❖❖❖❖❖❖❖❖❖❖❖❖❖❖❖❖❖❖❖❖❖❖❖❖❖❖❖❖❖❖❖❖❖❖

## Baking Powder and Soda Breads

### ON MIXING AND COOKING BAKING POWDER AND SODA BREADS

All measurements are level unless otherwise stated. Standard measuring spoons and cups are used exclusively.

*     *     *

All-purpose flour has been used in all recipes in this book unless otherwise stated. It should be sifted once before measuring.

*     *     *

For all recipes in this book calling for sweet milk, I have used baking powder having a cream of tartar base, such as Royal brand; for recipes calling for buttermilk, cultured milk, sour milk, or sour cream, I have used Double Acting baking powder or Calumet brand.

*     *     *

Use salad oil, lard or vegetable shortening for greasing pans. Margarine and butter are apt to cause the bread to stick because of the salt they contain.

*     *     *

The oven should be preheated for five or six minutes (depending on your stove heat regulator) before the breads are put in.

*     *     *

Recipes calling for sugar require white sugar. Brown, maple or powdered sugars will be indicated where needed.

*     *     *

To test biscuits or muffins after cooking them the specified time given in each recipe, break one open. If the centers are done, remove from the stove. Avoid overcooking, as it dries out the bread. Undercooking is apt to produce gummy or heavy breads or biscuits.

To cream shortening, soften it to room temperature. Do not melt before measuring unless specifically instructed to do so. "2 T shortening" means to measure it before melting, "2 T shortening *melted*," means to measure, then melt, while "2 T *melted* shortening" means that the shortening should be melted before being measured.

\* \* \*

Do not grease pans unless instructed to do so in a particular recipe. Roll dough on a floured board, or marble slab if you are lucky enough to own one. Flour the rolling pin also.

\* \* \*

There is often an argument among housewives, especially in the South, about the best method of blending the fat with the flour in making hot breads. Having been taught by "Mammy cooks" in Alabama, I use my fingers, crumbling the shortening and flour together until the mixture resembles coarse corn meal. I find this quicker and easier than trying to cut the fat into the flour with two knives or even using a modern pastry blender. Frankly, I don't think it makes any difference which method is used.

## CORRIE HILL'S BANANA BREAD
### (2 small loaves)

Corrie M. Hill is the wife of the well-known and beloved Judge Will Hill of Montgomery, Alabama. Mrs. Hill's great-great-grandfather was the brother of George Washington's mother. Corrie Hill is known throughout the South for her excellent table. Banana Bread is one of her specialties. Serve it for dessert where a not-too-sweet cake is liked, or with coffee or chocolate for Sunday brunch.

| | |
|---|---|
| ½ C butter or margarine | 1 t soda |
| 3 large ripe bananas (1 C banana purée) | ½ t salt (if sweet butter is used. If salty butter or margarine is used, omit salt entirely.) |
| 1 C sugar | |
| 2 C flour | 2 whole eggs |
| | 1 C chopped pecans |

Cream butter and sugar well. Beat eggs and add to butter and sugar. Mash bananas through strainer or food mill, and add them to butter, sugar, and egg mixture. Mix salt and soda with sifted flour, stir into batter, add nuts. Mix well. Pour into 2 medium-sized greased loaf pans. Bake one hour in moderate oven (15 minutes at 375°, 45 minutes at 350°). Test with straw. When done, turn out on platter and sprinkle top with powdered sugar. Delicious hot or cold. I often omit nuts.

## AUNT ROSE'S TEA BISCUITS     *(Quickie!)*
### *(A Southern biscuit roll)*

| | |
|---|---|
| 2 C flour | ½ t salt |
| 2 t baking powder | 2 T lard |
| 2 t sugar | 1 egg yolk |
| ½ C milk (about) | 1 T butter |

Sift dry ingredients. Add lard and butter and mix with the fingers, or use a pastry blender if you prefer. Add beaten egg yolk and enough milk to make the dough the proper consistency to roll. Roll on a floured board to ¼ inch thickness, and cut out with a biscuit cutter. Brush with butter, lap over. Place on a greased biscuit pan, brush with butter again, and bake in a hot oven (450°) 15 to 20 minutes or until biscuits are done inside and golden-brown outside.

## HARDIN COUNTY CHICKEN BISCUITS
### *(To accompany fried chicken)*     *(Quickie!)*

These are delicious hot breads closely akin to puff paste. I'm told that the recipe originated in Hardin County, where these biscuits always appear on the platter with fried chicken and cream gravy.

To make the biscuits, follow the recipe for Dumplings on page 52. Roll the dough ½ inch thick and cut in small squares with the pastry wheel, or use an ordinary small biscuit cutter. Fry the biscuits in the deep hot fat in which you have just fried your chicken. The fat should be smoking hot—375°—when the biscuits are put into it; lower the flame, and let the biscuits cook until golden-brown all over. If the biscuits are not covered by the fat, cook 2 minutes on one side, then turn over, and cook 1½ to 2 minutes on the other side until the biscuits are brown outside and done throughout. (Break one open to see if the centers are done.) Place on the platter with the fried chicken and douse with cream gravy.

## MY OWN BISCUITS (with Buttermilk or Cultured Milk)
### *(10 to 12 biscuits)*     *(Quickie!)*

When I was a child our cook used to make a delectable hot biscuit unlike most of the other Southern biscuits. It was so flaky on the outside it almost resembled puff paste, and the inside was the consistency of a homemade roll. Finally, after years of trial and error, I worked out this formula, which is pretty foolproof, as far as I am concerned.

| | |
|---|---|
| 1 C flour (measured before sifting) | ¼ t salt |
| | ½ t sugar |
| 1 t baking powder | ⅓ C buttermilk or cultured milk |
| ¼ t soda | |
| 4 T bland lard or vegetable shortening | Extra flour to roll biscuits (¼ to ⅓ C) |

Sift the cup of flour with the dry ingredients. Add the lard and mix with the fingers as for any other biscuits, blending until it resembles corn meal, or use a pastry blender. Add all the buttermilk or cultured milk and mix well. It will be a light spongy dough, a little on the soft side. Dump the rest of the flour on a board or marble slab. Place the dough on top of this and roll it around, letting it take up just enough flour so that you can handle it and so that it will not stick to the rolling pin. You do not want to work any more flour into it than necessary, but the dough should be smooth like marble and rather soft, just stiff enough to roll. Flour the rolling pin and roll dough ⅓ to ½ inch thick, depending on whether or not you like your biscuits thin or thick—we like the thin ones. Bake 15 to 20 minutes in a moderate oven (375°). When biscuits are golden-brown on the outside, break one open to see whether it is done throughout. If so, serve them at once. Butter at the table. These biscuits are equally good next day if split and buttered and browned on the buttered side only under the oven's flame or grill. We also serve them hot for breakfast with maple syrup, instead of pancakes. These biscuits can be made up in the morning, rolled out and covered with a cloth, and kept in the icebox to be baked in the evening, if desired. This recipe makes 10 to 12 biscuits, depending on size of biscuit cutter.

## MY OWN BISCUITS (with Sweet Milk)
### *(Quickie!)*

Follow the recipe for My Own Biscuits with Buttermilk or Cultured Milk, substituting sweet milk, and using 2 level teaspoons of cream of tartar baking powder instead of the soda and double-acting baking powder.

## JOSEPHINE RANDOLPH'S WHOLE WHEAT HONEY BREAD

| | |
|---|---|
| 1 C milk | 1 C graham flour or whole wheat flour, sifted before measuring |
| ½ t salt | |
| 2 t baking powder | |
| ½ C honey | 1 C white flour, sifted before measuring |

Mix milk and honey. Sift white flour, salt, and baking powder into graham or whole wheat flour. Mix honey and milk with dry ingredients. Beat hard until smooth. Pour into greased loaf pan and bake 1 hour in a moderately hot oven (400°). Turn out on a wire cake rack to cool. When cold, slice and spread with softened butter for sandwiches, or serve with honey for tea. It's a wonderful sweet bread, a Kentucky taste treat.

# *Batter Breads*

## DOLLY SULLIVAN'S BREAD-CRUMB PANCAKES

Dolly Sullivan cut quite a figure in the Louisville newspaper world a decade ago, and ran a syndicated column under the name of Cynthia Gray. When radio station WHAS started here, she was one of the early continuity writers and had an excellent daily radio program for women. On the air she was known as Dolly Dean. Here is her recipe for Bread-crumb Pancakes, an old Kentucky dish very popular to this day, and an excellent way to use up leftover bread from sandwiches, etc.

| | |
|---|---|
| 1½ C fine dry bread crumbs | 1 egg |
| 1½ C milk | ½ C flour |
| 2 T white corn syrup or honey | 1 T butter, melted |
| 2 t baking powder | ½ t salt |

Heat milk and pour over crumbs; let stand 15 minutes. Meanwhile sift flour, baking powder and salt. Add to crumb mixture with well-beaten egg, syrup or honey, and melted butter. Beat once more until thoroughly blended and free from lumps. Drop by tablespoons onto a well-oiled griddle, letting one side brown before turning to brown on the other side. (Turn only once!) Serve hot with melted butter and brown sugar or maple syrup.

## FEATHER PANCAKES
### *(6 servings)*

These are the original old-fashioned Southern breakfast pancakes.

| | |
|---|---|
| 2 C flour | 2 eggs, well beaten |
| 1 T baking powder | 1½ C milk |
| 6 T melted lard, butter or margarine (butter preferred) | ½ t salt |

Sift dry ingredients. Add milk well beaten with eggs, beating all the while to make a smooth batter. If it lumps, use electric beater or Dover egg beater, but do not beat too long—1 minute is quite sufficient. Add melted fat. Drop by tablespoons onto a well-greased griddle or skillet and brown first on one side and then on the other. NEVER TURN PANCAKES MORE THAN ONCE. Be sure they are thoroughly brown before turning—lift up the edge of a pancake and peek—when golden-brown, turn. If batter is too thick, thin with a little extra milk. Serve piping hot as a brunch, breakfast or supper dish. Crisp bacon or sausage cakes, coffee and orange juice are a happy combination. Another variation is to fill each cake with 1 tablespoon of chicken or turkey hash and put them in a baking dish. Spoon more hash over them, cover with a thin blanket of grated Parmesan or grated American cheese and run under the flame to brown. This makes a most wonderfully filling and appetizing brunch—I've even had it for an appetizer at a formal dinner.

For still another variation add ½ cup of washed, thoroughly dried fresh blueberries or huckleberries to the batter just before frying the cakes.

## KENTUCKY SALLY LUNN
### *(A marvelous company hot bread)*
### *(6 servings)*

| | |
|---|---|
| 2 C flour | ½ C milk |
| 2 eggs, separated | ½ yeast cake |
| ½ C butter | ½ t salt |
| ¼ C sugar | |

Cream butter and sugar. Add well-beaten yolks, salt, and flour, alternating with pasteurized milk that has been heated until lukewarm, and mixed with yeast. Fold in well-beaten egg whites. Put in a greased pie pan, either treated glass or pottery, and let stand until it doubles its bulk (2½ to 3 hours). Bake 25 to 30 minutes in an oven set at 375°.

When the bread is golden-brown and tests done, remove from the oven, cut into pie-shaped wedges and butter while hot.

Leftover Sally Lunn can be buttered, and toasted under the flame in stove. Brown on buttered side only.

## ROSETTES

Many of us remember the wheel-like, wafer-thin rosettes our grandmothers used to serve for tea. They are equally good with hot Christmas drinks. Here is a grand family recipe. You can't make it without the proper irons, but if you are lucky enough to own some, here's how:

| 1 egg | 1 T olive oil or salad oil or |
| ½ C milk | melted butter |
| 1 t sugar | 1 lb. lard, salad or peanut oil |
| ⅔ C sifted flour | for frying rosettes |
| ¼ t salt | Powdered sugar |

Beat the egg and milk until well mixed, but do not beat too long or the batter will blister when cooked. Add sugar, salt, and 1 tablespoon of oil or melted butter. Pour this mixture into the flour, beating vigorously all the while. If this is lumpy, it must be strained, as it should be a smooth thin batter the consistency of thick cream.

Heat the lard or oil in a deep skillet or chicken fryer. When fat is hot (about 375°), dip the iron into it. When the iron too is fairly hot, dip it into the batter. Do not submerge more than ¾ of the iron, however, and let the batter set on the iron a moment before putting it back into the hot fat. The rosette should cook until golden-brown (about 40 seconds). Remove from the iron at once with a dull knife, but be careful not to break, as rosettes are very brittle. Drain on absorbent paper, dust at once with powdered sugar, and pile on a plate.

These rosettes are tricky to make, and you must expect a few cripples the first few times. For instance, if the iron is too hot, the batter won't stick to it. You'll have to regulate your heat each time. If the wafers brown too quickly, lower the heat. If the cooked rosette is soft or gummy, or falls off the iron before it is done, the fat is either too hot or you have fried the rosette too quickly. Don't let all this scare you, for once you get going the rest is easy, and the delicately crunchy rosettes beside your bowl of punch will well be worth the trouble and effort you have taken to prepare them.

# *Waffles*

## GINGERBREAD WAFFLES

| ¼ C sugar | 1¼ C sifted flour |
| 2 T butter | ½ C molasses |
| 2 T lard | ¾ t soda |
| ½ t ginger | ½ t cinnamon |
| ¼ t cloves | ⅛ t salt |
| ½ C hot water | |

Cream butter, lard and sugar. Add well-beaten egg and molasses. Sift dry ingredients. Add to butter mixture. Last of all add hot water. Beat hard to make a smooth batter. Cook in waffle irons and serve one section to each person. A tablespoon of Mock Devonshire Cream or whipped cream sweetened and flavored with vanilla usually accompanies this dessert. Some like a Butterscotch, a Brandy or an Old-fashioned Brown Sugar Sauce with it.

## PERFECTION WAFFLES

These are really the best waffles I ever ate—crisp on the outside, yet they have body. As one colored cook used to say when she made them, "They don't get 'sobby' (soggy) like other waffles when you pour syrup on them." We use them as a basic waffle, varying them to suit the occasion.

| | |
|---|---|
| **2 C flour, measured after sifting** | **1½ C milk** |
| **½ t salt** | **¾ C melted fat (half bland lard** |
| **2 T sugar** | **or vegetable shortening, half** |
| **3 rounded t baking powder** | **butter or margarine)** |
| **2 eggs, separated** | |

Sift flour with salt, sugar, and baking powder. Beat the yolks with the milk and pour slowly into the dry ingredients, stirring to prevent lumping. Add melted fat (yes, ¾ cup is the right amount) and beat until batter is smooth, then fold in the two well-beaten whites. If salted butter or margarine has been used, no extra salt will be needed; otherwise, add a little to taste.

To bake these waffles, have the iron smoking hot. If you use an electric iron, brush it lightly with grease the first time (I use a little melted lard), but this will not be necessary thereafter. I use 4 tablespoons of batter for each waffle. Close the iron and cook 4 minutes by the clock. Serve at once with hot butter, hot syrup, honey or anything you like. If you use an old-fashioned waffle iron, it must be well greased each time a waffle is made. Cook the waffle 2 minutes on one side, turn and cook 2 minutes on the other.

Where this waffle is used for hash, creamed oysters, chicken à la king, etc., in place of toast, omit 1 tablespoon of sugar from the batter. If waffles are used for shortcake, a teaspoonful of vanilla may be added before they are cooked.

*Leftover batter can be kept in the refrigerator in a covered bowl and cooked the following day. Add ½ to 1 teaspoon of baking powder dissolved in 1 or 2 tablespoons of water to every cup of leftover batter, and mix well before cooking the waffle. If this batter is too thick, thin with an extra tablespoon or two of milk. This batter also makes good pan-*

cakes, although it should be just a little thinner than the waffle batter. Add a tablespoon or two of milk before dropping from a tablespoon onto a hot, lightly-greased griddle. Cook until one side is brown, then turn and cook on the other side. See recipe for baking Feather Pancakes (page 58).

## About Corn Breads

Always bake corn meal muffins, breads, etc., in heavy metal (we use iron) utensils, heating them well before the batter is put into them and being sure they are well greased and that the grease is hot. Explicit directions are given with each recipe, but, on the whole, tin pans or lightweight metal pans are not as satisfactory as heavy ones, as in the light ones corn bread is apt to brown too much on the outside before the inside is done. Pyrex or pottery baking dishes or custard cups are better than tin ones. They must be well greased and very hot, as a rule, before the batter is added. Leave in a hot stove 5 minutes before filling.

\* \* \*

Southern corn bread made with white corn meal is crisp and crunchy on the outside, moist inside. It is not "raw" or "doughy" but is not as dry and fluffy as the Northern yellow corn bread.

\* \* \*

Water-ground corn meal is the favorite Southern type. It is much coarser than "Pearl" meal, or finely ground meal, and is not sifted, but dumped into the bowl and mixed with the other ingredients. Directions are given with each recipe.

\* \* \*

Keep corn meal in dry, clean glass jars with ground-glass, tight-fitting tops, or in tin containers. Never leave them open. Buy small amounts at a time, as the meal sometimes gets weevils in it or becomes moldy.

\* \* \*

I prefer buttermilk or cultured milk to sweet milk for mixing corn meal breads, but I have given recipes for both as it is a personal matter, and you must make your own choice.

\* \* \*

Do not try to cook corn meal pancakes on a griddle—they need the extra fat and are only good when fried in the proper amount of grease or lard in a skillet.

Corn bread must be served hot to be good, although it can be buttered and toasted under the flame if any is left over next day. It's good that way with syrup or honey.

## JOSEPHINE COX'S BATTER BREAD

This recipe was given me by my good friend, Josephine Cox, who got it over forty years ago from her friend, Mrs. Carrie Pace Hite, a distinguished Louisville gourmet. Mrs. Hite is said to have brought the recipe with her from her native Virginia. It resembles our Kentucky Spoon Bread and is equally delicious. It was served for breakfast in the old days, with spare ribs or bacon or sausage. It makes a wonderful brunch dish too, or can pinch-hit for a starchy vegetable at dinner.

2 eggs, well beaten
1 C rich buttermilk or cultured
   milk
½ t soda
½ t salt

1 T butter (no substitutes)
1¼ C boiling water
1 C white corn meal (water-
   ground if possible)

Pour meal in a bowl without sifting. Scald meal by pouring the boiling water over it and stirring to prevent lumps forming. Add water slowly, beating all the while. If lumpy, the mixture must be strained. Add salt and butter and let butter melt. Mix well and set aside to cool slightly. Then add eggs beaten with buttermilk and soda. Beat well. Pour into a greased baking dish or casserole—the batter bread is served in the same dish in which it is baked. Set in a hot oven (450°) and leave from ½ hour to 40 minutes or until mixture just sets and no longer shakes in the middle. Do not overcook. If properly baked, this is light and airy, just like a soufflé. Serve at once.

## CORN MEAL MERINGUES
### *(6 or 8 servings)*

These delicious, though not so familiar, members of the Southern Hot Bread Brigade must be served piping hot, and cannot be heated over or used again. This recipe will serve 6 or 8; if the crowd is small, cut ingredients in half.

5 T white corn meal
1½ C boiling water
¼ t salt

4 egg whites, beaten with more
   salt

Mix the corn meal with the boiling water, stirring to prevent lumping and beating until smooth. Put in a saucepan and allow to boil 3 minutes, stirring constantly. Add salt and set aside to cool slightly. Beat the egg whites with more salt. When stiff enough to stand alone (we turn bowl upside down and shake, and the eggs should be so stiff they will not fall out), fold into the cool mush. Mix well. Drop from end of a tablespoon onto a cookie tin lined with greased heavy brown or wax paper. Bake ½ hour in a slow oven (300°) or until outside becomes a golden-brown and center is cooked through. If the meringues are not brown enough, increase the heat to 350° and leave in stove 5 minutes longer. Remove meringues from paper with a spatula or pancake turner. Serve hot with soups or salads.

## CREAM CORN PONES
### *(6 small pones)*

| | |
|---|---|
| 1 C unsifted white corn meal | ½ C boiling water |
| ½ t salt | 1 T melted lard or butter |
| ¼ C thick sweet cream | 1 t baking powder |
| 1 T melted lard for skillet | |

Put corn meal into a bowl. Get the water-ground meal if you would have your pones taste the way ours do in Kentucky. Don't try to make this recipe with yellow meal. Add salt to meal and stir in the boiling water. The mixture will resemble dry crumbs. Cover the bowl and set in the refrigerator an hour or so to chill. Just before you are ready to make your pones, bring your corn meal mixture into the kitchen. Be sure that your oven is hot by this time—450° is about right. Add to meal mixture the 1 tablespoon of melted lard or butter, and baking powder mixed with the sweet cream. Stir well. Now the mixture should be a paste, firm enough to handle. Take heaping tablespoons of this paste and form them into croquette-like shapes, placing them in a preheated iron skillet in which there is another tablespoon of melted lard or butter. Then pat the tops with your fingers to flatten them slightly. Put pones in the oven and leave them there for half an hour. By this time they should be brown, and cooked on the inside. If not, turn them over and let them stay in the stove an extra 5 minutes. Serve them piping hot with beans or greens or soup or salad, and allow at least two to each person. As with biscuits, you always "butter 'em while they're hot."

These pones are equally good made with thick sour cream. Use same amount as you would of sweet cream, but substitute ¼ teaspoon of soda for the baking powder.

## OKEFENOKEE HUSH PUPPIES
### *(4 servings)*

Dorothy Clark brought this recipe back from Georgia where she went fishing in the Okefenokee Swamp. It is light and spongy and goes well with any fried fish. I had always thought that Hush Puppies were made famous by Marjorie Rawlings in her *Cross Creek Cookery,* but I'm told on very good authority that they originated in Georgia or Alabama and that when the fishermen sat around the campfire frying their fish, the hound dogs whined so loudly they threw them some meal cakes to stop the noise, saying "Hush, puppies." Whatever the origin, these onion-flavored corn pones have become very popular in Louisville in recent years. Dorothy's are by all odds the best I've ever tasted. Don't be alarmed at the amount of baking powder—it's not a misprint but the secret of the puffball lightness of this unusual hot bread.

1 C white corn meal (water-ground if possible)
1 pod garlic, crushed
1 T finely chopped onion
½ t salt
2 T baking powder

2 T (very heaping) flour (about ¼ C)
2 eggs
¾ to 1 C buttermilk or sweet milk

Rub the bowl with garlic as for salad. Discard the garlic. Dump the unsifted corn meal into the garlic-rubbed bowl. Sift the flour, salt and baking powder into this. Beat the eggs and then add just enough milk to make a stiff batter. Add the onion and beat again. Cover bowl and let set an hour or so in the icebox until the batter becomes spongy.

To fry the Hush Puppies, have a deep kettle of lard or vegetable shortening very hot (375°). Drop batter into fat from a tablespoon. Do not cook too many at a time—4 to 6 are enough. Fry golden-brown on one side and, if necessary, turn and fry on the other; or if the fat is deep enough to cover, they should cook without turning. If Hush Puppies brown too quickly, lower the heat. Be sure they are done inside before removing from the fire. (Remove one and break it open, to see.) When done, remove the Hush Puppies, drain on absorbent paper and serve piping hot. Butter and eat. A must with fried fish.

## OLD-TIMEY CRISP CORN MEAL WAFFLES
### *(3 to 4 waffles)*

I've tried dozens of recipes for corn meal waffles and none of them satisfied me, because I wanted a waffle that would be light and airy, crisp and crunchy, and yet at the same time would retain its corn meal flavor and consistency. Finally I came across one in an old Virginia cook book and adapted the present concoction from it. The first time I baked these waffles they were perfect, and I will never try another corn meal waffle recipe. Some Southerners will question the sugar, but it is needed to make the waffle brown.

| | |
|---|---|
| ¾ C white corn meal (water-ground if possible) | ¼ t soda |
| 2 T flour | ½ t baking powder |
| ⅓ t salt | 1 t sugar |
| 1 C buttermilk or cultured milk | ¼ C melted lard or butter |

Dump the corn meal into a bowl without sifting. Add the flour sifted with the dry ingredients. Add the egg and beat, then add the milk gradually, beating to prevent lumping. Add the melted fat. Have the waffle iron smoking hot and, if you are using an electric iron, grease very lightly for the first waffle only. My waffle iron is unusually large and therefore I use 5 tablespoons of the batter to make each waffle. The new models seem to be smaller, and 4 tablespoons should be sufficient. Place them in each section near the center—they will spread to the edges. Cook 4 minutes. Serve with hot melted butter and your favorite syrup or honey. If an old-fashioned waffle iron is used, grease heavily each time. Cook the waffle 2 minutes on each side, or until it is golden-brown.

## SKILLET CORN PONES        *(Quickie!)*
### *(4 servings)*

This is a quick, light, crunchy corn pone like Mammy used to make.

| | |
|---|---|
| ¼ C flour | ¼ t soda |
| ¾ C white corn meal (water-ground if possible) | 1 t sugar |
| 1½ t baking powder | ½ C buttermilk |
| ¼ t salt | Lard for frying |

Mix sifted flour with all dry ingredients except corn meal, and sift again. Add meal and gradually beat the buttermilk into this. It makes a stiff batter.

Put a rounded tablespoon of lard or vegetable shortening in a 10- or 12-inch skillet and let it melt. When it is smoking hot, drop the corn mixture into this—a tablespoonful at a time, cooking 4 pones at a time. Brown pones on one side, then with the pancake turner turn and brown on the other. Split one pone to see whether or not it is done in the center—as soon as it has cooked through, it is ready to serve. Cook 2½ to 3 minutes on each side. Have fire very hot at first, then lower the flame. If pones cook too quickly, they will be too brown outside and raw inside. Serve very hot—pass the 4 that have been cooked, then start over again.

These pones are wonderful with soup or salad or a regular meal, especially with pork.

# Southern Sauces and Syrups for Pancakes and Waffles

## HOT SPICED MAPLE-HONEY SYRUP

A Colonial recipe to be used on pancakes, waffles, puddings or what you will. It is deliciously different.

| | |
|---|---|
| 1 C maple syrup | ½ t cinnamon (powdered) |
| ½ C strained honey | ¼ t caraway seeds |

In a saucepan, mix the maple syrup with the honey. Add cinnamon and caraway seeds. Set over a flame and allow to come to a hard boil. Remove from stove and pour into a sauceboat or pottery pitcher or syrup jug and carry to the table. When this is to be used with pancakes or waffles, serve it with a pitcher of hot melted butter. Use the butter first and then top with the Spiced Maple-Honey.

## OLD-FASHIONED BROWN SUGAR SAUCE
### (For waffles, pancakes or puddings)

| | |
|---|---|
| 1 C dark brown sugar, firmly packed | 4 T water |
| | 1 T butter |

Mix ingredients in a saucepan and put over flame or burner on top of stove. Let boil until sugar melts and is the consistency of maple syrup, stirring occasionally to keep from sticking. This does not take long— 2 to 3 minutes. Have the flame high at first, then reduce it to low. Do not cook too long or the mixture will sugar. Many old-time, dyed-in-the-wool Kentuckians prefer this sauce to any other for their waffles and pancakes.

# Bread Doughs and Rolls

## ICEBOX AND REFRIGERATOR BREADS

Any of the recipes for refrigerator rolls given in this book will make very good bread if the loaf is properly shaped, and allowed to rise a long enough time before being properly baked. The Icebox or Refrigerator Buttermilk or Cultured Milk Dough recipe given in this book, as well as the Sweet Refrigerator Roll Dough, will produce excellent loaves.

## SHAPING, RAISING AND BAKING ICEBOX OR REFRIGERATOR BREAD

You will need 2 full cups of dough to make an average-sized loaf. Remove from the icebox and knead on a floured board, working more flour into it if necessary. Make into a ball, roll lengthwise until dough is 3 times as long as the pan. Fold one side into the middle, fold the other to the middle, then lap the two. Pinch ends together and fold under. Roll the dough gently to round the edges, then put in pan, seam side down. Press to fit pan and even dough. The pan should be well greased with melted butter or margarine before adding the dough. Brush top and sides with more melted butter or margarine. Cover pan. Set dough in a moderately warm room and let rise until double its bulk—2 to 3 hours. Bake the loaf 25 minutes in a hot oven (400°), then reduce heat to 375° and cook 25 minutes longer. Brush the loaf once more with melted butter or margarine, then cook 10 minutes longer at 350°. Remove bread from oven and turn upside down on a wire rack to cool, or set on a cloth-covered board. Cool before slicing.

This bread makes very good toast, especially when cut in ½-inch-thick slices and browned on one side in the oven. The untoasted side is generously buttered and put under the flame once more to bubble and brown. Serve at once.

## RAISING AND BAKING ICEBOX OR REFRIGERATOR ROLLS

Dough takes longer to rise in winter than in summer. In winter, if I am having dinner at six-thirty, I take the dough out of the icebox at three to make my rolls. Then I let them rise until six o'clock or six-ten—about three hours, in a moderately warm room—about 70°. More or less time does not seem to matter. In summer, 1½ to 2 hours is usually enough.

If you find the rolls are not rising quickly enough or if you should forget to take them out in time, light the oven and set the rolls on top—not directly over the heat but where they will get quite warm. Then they will rise quickly. This method is not recommended for general use, because the quickly risen rolls are not as fine-textured as the slowly risen ones. Therefore, use this method only in an emergency.

The usual refrigerator roll takes from 18 to 20 minutes to bake in a hot oven (450°). Should your stove register "very hot," 15 minutes might do them. They should be brown on the outside, but not burned, and light and cottony inside.

Any of the dessert roll variations given under Sweet Refrigerator Roll Dough may be used with the other All-Purpose Icebox Buttermilk Dough. The only difference will be that the Sweet Refrigerator Roll Dough makes a lighter and richer roll.

Note on scalded versus lukewarm milk: Old-fashioned bread dough recipes often required the milk to be scalded or boiled and then cooled to lukewarm before being used in rolls. I believe this was because raw milk was probably used, and the dough soured without this treatment. Pasteurized milk only needs to be heated to lukewarm, I have found.

# *Icebox or Refrigerator All-Purpose Dough for Bread or Rolls*

## BUTTERMILK OR CULTURED MILK REFRIGERATOR DOUGH

This is a quick roll or bread dough for immediate use or to be kept in the refrigerator until needed. It's the easiest of all my icebox roll dough recipes and the one I use more often than any other.

| | |
|---|---|
| 2 C buttermilk or cultured milk | 6 C flour |
| 1 cake yeast | 1½ t salt |
| ½ t soda | ½ C lukewarm water |
| 1½ t baking powder | ½ C bland lard or vegetable |
| 4 T sugar | shortening |

Dissolve yeast in warm water. Set aside. Sift dry ingredients. Add shortening and crumble with the fingers or use a pastry blender as for biscuits. When ingredients are well mixed, add yeast and warm water, and buttermilk or cultured milk. Knead well with the hands. Place in a bowl and cover. Set in the icebox until ready to use. The rolls can be made at once but are better if left in the icebox for at least 12 hours. To make these rolls, shape according to the following directions: For Parker House Rolls, see the recipe for June Smith's Southern Potato Rolls (page 78); for Bread Sticks, see Buttermilk Refrigerator Rye Salt Sticks (page 71); for Twin Rolls, see Twin Dinner Rolls following recipe for Icebox Refrigerator Sweet Roll Dough (page 73). After making dough into shapes, set aside to rise from 1½ to 2 hours in a warm room. When rolls are light, bake 15 to 20 minutes in a hot oven (450°) or until golden-brown. Serve hot. Return the unused dough to the icebox in a covered bowl. This dough will keep for several weeks if kept chilled. Here is a quick roll shape you will find handy if you are in a hurry:

## BUTTER ROLLS

I'm proud of this one, for I thought it up myself. Roll out the Icebox Roll Dough ¼ to ⅓ inch thick. Brush with butter or margarine, then roll up like a jelly roll, pinching ends together to keep in the butter or fat. Cut in inch slices and place side by side in a greased pan, or put in a greased muffin tin. Brush the surface with melted butter or margarine. Let rise and bake according to directions given above, for Buttermilk Refrigerator Dough.

To form this icebox dough into loaves, consult note at beginning of this chapter, on Shaping, Raising and Baking Icebox Bread. For a richer, more cake-like loaf, substitute 1 cup of sour cream for 1 cup of the buttermilk or cultured milk in the Buttermilk or Cultured Milk Refrigerator Dough, and add an extra ¼ cup of sugar. It makes a firm-textured, old-timey homemade bread.

## BUTTERMILK REFRIGERATOR RYE ROLLS

Follow recipe for Buttermilk or Cultured Milk Refrigerator Dough (page 69) adding 1 tablespoon of caraway seeds and using half rye flour and half white flour instead of all white flour. Two tablespoons of strained honey and 2 tablespoons of sugar are also used, instead of 4 tablespoons of sugar as required in Buttermilk or Cultured Milk Refrigerator Dough. To make bread of this rye dough, consult the note at the beginning of this chapter.

## BUTTERMILK REFRIGERATOR RYE SALT STICKS

Make the rye bread recipe above. Take a tablespoon of this risen dough at a time and roll into ropes or pencils the size of your corn bread stick pans. If the ropes do not fit, clip off the ends to the proper length, using your kitchen scissors. It may be necessary to add a little flour to keep dough from sticking to your palms when rolling. Brush surface with beaten egg and ice water—1 tablespoon water to 1 egg—the yolk or white can also be used instead of the whole egg. Sprinkle surface with coarsely crushed freezing salt, using this sparingly. Then sprinkle once more with a few caraway seeds. Let rise 2 to 3 hours and bake according to directions given for Raising and Baking Refrigerator Rolls (page 68).

## BUTTERMILK REFRIGERATOR
## WHOLE WHEAT ROLLS

Follow recipe for Buttermilk or Cultured Milk Refrigerator Dough, using half whole wheat flour and half white flour instead of all white flour, and substituting 2 tablespoons of sugar and 2 tablespoons of honey or white corn syrup for the 4 tablespoons of sugar. Consult the note at the beginning of this chapter, for raising and baking.

## FROZEN BUTTERMILK ROLL DOUGH

The Icebox Buttermilk or Cultured Milk Dough given in this chapter makes excellent frozen rolls. Let dough remain in the refrigerator overnight, make into shapes and place in pans. Cover the pans with freezing-paper and tie securely over the pan. Freeze. These rolls are delicious when thawed properly, then allowed to rise before being baked. This takes several hours, depending on the temperature of the room. They will, of course, take a longer time to rise than if they had been kept in the icebox. Do not store in the deepfreeze too long, but they are good for 6 to 8 weeks. Rye and whole wheat rolls made from the Buttermilk Roll recipe freeze equally well. Once frozen, the rolls can be wrapped separately in wax paper and stacked in bags or boxes.

## ICEBOX OR REFRIGERATOR SWEET ROLL DOUGH
### (Basic recipe for sweet dinner rolls,
### dessert rolls or coffee cakes)

There used to be a restaurant in Louisville so famous for its rolls that people came from all over Kentucky just to taste them. They were twin rolls, with that true homemade flavor, the outside flaky and brown, the inside light and fluffy, almost the consistency of angel food cake. They came to the table in a wicker basket, buried in a snowy white napkin, and were served piping hot. We buttered them immediately, and I still remember how they almost dissolved without chewing when we popped them into our mouths. Of course we tried to get the recipe—everyone did—but no amount of cajolery, or even bribery, would induce the manager to part with it.

One day, I went to a luncheon at Peggy Gaines's house and by a lucky chance was served a roll that in every respect resembled those wonderful ones we had raved about all those years. Peggy was sure it was made from the old formula. She had gotten it via the kitchen grapevine, from a maid, who had a friend who had worked in the old restaurant. Good recipes, like good deeds, have a way of getting around, and my friend was generous enough to share her secret with me.

When I made up the dough I noticed that it was sweeter and richer than most refrigerator rolls and I began to experiment with it, using it for Raised Doughnuts, Jelly Doughnuts, etc. I found that with this basic dough I could make any number of sweet breads that could pinch-hit for dessert. Here's the recipe, and I hope you too will be inspired to try it in various ways.

6 C flour (sifted once before measuring)
1 t salt
1 cake yeast
½ C sugar
2 C pasteurized milk
1 well-beaten egg

10 T melted butter, and more to use when making out rolls. (Vegetable shortening may be substituted for butter, but the rolls will not be as rich.)

After the flour has been sifted, measure 6 cupfuls. Take 3 of those cupfuls and put into the sifter again with the sugar and salt. Sift into a bowl and set aside.

Warm 2 cupfuls of pasteurized milk—if raw milk is used, it must be boiled and cooled to tepid before using. With ½ cup of lukewarm milk, mix a yeast cake. With the other 1½ cups mix the well-beaten egg, and melted butter or vegetable shortening. Pour liquid ingredients into the flour mixture, stirring to make a smooth batter. It will resemble a thick soup, but don't worry. Cover the bowl with a clean towel and set aside in a warm place until it rises to 2 times its bulk. This takes from 1½ hours in summer to 2 in winter. Then stir into the sponge the remaining 3 cups of sifted flour. The dough will be soft—too soft to handle at first. Place it in the refrigerator in a covered container for 24 hours before using. In an emergency, the dough can be made up early in the morning and rolled out at 4 o'clock that same afternoon. But the rolls are better if left undisturbed until the next day.

## TWIN DINNER ROLLS

The original twin dinner rolls made from this sweet roll dough and served at our famous Louisville restaurant, were shaped as follows:

Roll a small piece of dough ½ inch thick on a floured board. Cut out with an average-sized biscuit cutter. Submerge these biscuits in melted butter or margarine, then fold in half, pinching the edges together in the center. Put 2 of these folded biscuits side by side, smooth side up, in a greased muffin tin. Let rise until very light. This will take 2 hours in summer, 2½ to 3 in winter. Bake the rolls in a hot oven (450°) until they are golden-brown. This takes from 15 to 20 minutes. Serve very hot.

# *Variation of Icebox or Refrigerator Sweet Roll Dough*

## ALMOND-COFFEE CREAM FILLING FOR ROLLS OR FRENCH PANCAKES

½ lb. grated or ground almonds
2 T honey
2 T strong coffee

2 T thick cream
1 heaping T sugar, or more to taste

Make a paste of the above ingredients. Spread on ⅓ of the Refrigerator Sweet raw dough, which has been rolled thin. Roll up like a jelly roll, pressing ends together. Slice into 1½-inch pieces and press into well-greased muffin tins (allowing ½ teaspoon of melted butter or margarine and 2 blanched almonds for each piece). Let rise 2 hours and bake in a moderate oven (375°) for 25 to 30 minutes, or until rolls brown and seem done. Turn out upside down and dust with powdered sugar. Frost with Vanilla Glaze if desired—see recipe following Rum Rolls (page 76).

Sometimes I add 4 drops of almond extract and 4 drops of rose-water to the above paste and it tastes rather like almond paste. It can be substituted for almond paste in many recipes.

## FILLED HORNS OR CRESCENTS

Take individual pieces of the Sweet Refrigerator Dough (1 tablespoon) and pat or roll ¼ inch thick on a floured board. Brush with butter and put 1 tablespoonful of the filling given below on the dough. Spread evenly. Roll diagonally, pinch ends together, and place on a greased pan. Turn ends of roll in to form a crescent or horn. Brush with melted butter and set aside to rise, 2 or 3 hours. Bake according to directions for baking rolls.

### Filling for Butter Horns or Crescents

This is enough for the full roll recipe. Cut in half or fourths for smaller amounts.

| | |
|---|---|
| 1 C raisins | 2 t cinnamon |
| 1 C citron, chopped | ½ t mace or nutmeg, or ¼ t |
| 1 C brown sugar | of each |
| Grated rind of 1 lemon | 1 C chopped almonds or pecans |
| 1 C currants | |

Mix all ingredients and use as directed above (Filled Horns or Crescents)

## GLAZED ORANGE ROLLS
### (6 servings)

The filling for these dessert rolls must be made the day before it is to be used. Squeeze juice and pulp from a large orange. Remove the seeds but do not strain. Then put the orange skin (white part as well as yellow) through the finest blade of meat grinder.

In a saucepan mix the orange juice, pulp and rind with 1 cup of sugar and ½ cup of butter or margarine. Place on the stove over a low flame, stirring until butter and sugar are dissolved. Simmer until thick—about 8 minutes by the clock. Then pour into a bowl, cool, cover, and put in the refrigerator until ready to use.

Roll out ⅓ of the Sweet Refrigerator Dough. Spread the thick orange filling over the dough. Roll up like a jelly roll, pinching the ends to keep the filling from escaping.

Into the bottom of a 9-inch-square pan put 4 tablespoonfuls of melted butter or margarine and spread evenly. Sprinkle lightly with a tablespoonful of white sugar. Cut the orange roll into inch slices and place side by side in the pan. When the pan is full, mash the rolls flat with the palm of the hand, distributing the dough evenly over the surface. Set in a warm place to rise—2 to 3 hours.

Bake rolls 30 minutes in a moderate oven (375°), or until the tops are brown. Turn out immediately onto a plate (bottom side up) and scrape all the orange syrup out of the pan over the surface of the rolls. If the under side is not sufficiently caramelized, slip the rolls back into the pan in which they were cooked, leaving the bottom side exposed. Return to the oven for 5 to 10 minutes, or until the rolls become glazed and golden-brown, but watch carefully to see that they do not burn. Serve warm.

## JELLY DOUGHNUT BALLS
### *(From Refrigerator Sweet Roll Dough)*
### *(6 servings)*

At the same time we make the Raised Doughnuts (see next recipe), we prepare Jelly Doughnut Balls from the center rounds left from cutting out the doughnuts. Or, if all the dough is made into Jelly Doughnut Balls, use a small biscuit cutter. Prepare the balls according to directions given for Raised Doughnuts. When they have been cooked, allow to cool slightly. Then split and place ½ teaspoonful of firm jelly in the center of each—we used currant and raspberry, but grape, blackberry or apple would do. Dust with powdered sugar before sending to the table.

## RAISED DOUGHNUTS
### *(6 servings)*

Mix ⅓ of the Sweet Icebox or Refrigerator Roll Dough with ½ teaspoonful of freshly grated nutmeg. Then roll ½ inch thick on a floured board. Cut out with a floured doughnut cutter, saving the small balls from the center to use later; see Jelly Doughnut Balls (preceding recipe). Place on an ungreased cookie tin, letting rise 1 hour on one side, then turning and letting rise 1 hour on the other.

To cook, have a skillet or pan of hot salad oil, or melted lard or vegetable shortening (365°). Place 2 or 3 doughnuts at a time into the hot grease. When one side is brown, turn and brown on the other, being careful not to puncture the doughnuts when handling. Drain on brown or absorbent paper. Dust with powdered sugar, or a mixture of ½ teaspoonful of cinnamon and a heaping tablespoonful of powdered sugar, or ice while still warm, with Vanilla Glaze (page 76).

## RUM ROLLS
### (6 servings)

In many old Washington restaurants, such as the Occidental, in days gone by, Rum Rolls were the specialty of the house. Sometimes they were plain, or sometimes filled with raisins or currants. But all of them were iced with a delicious rum frosting. They are nice to serve at home with a pot of tea on a cold winter afternoon, or for a light dessert after a heavy meal.

Work 1 tablespoonful of Jamaica rum into ⅓ of the Icebox or Refrigerator Sweet Roll Dough. Roll thin on a floured board. Brush with melted butter, sprinkle with ¼ cup of currants and ¼ cup of sugar. Dust with freshly ground nutmeg—about ¼ teaspoonful. Roll up like a jelly roll, pinching the ends together. Cut this roll into slices about 1 inch thick, and place side by side in a 9-inch-square cake pan, well greased with 2 tablespoons of melted butter. Then, with the palm of the hand, mash them very flat, spreading the dough to cover the whole surface of the bottom of the pan. Let rise in a warm place 2 to 3 hours, or until light, then bake in a hot oven (450°) for 20 minutes, or until rolls seem done. Turn onto a plate and frost immediately with rum icing made by mixing ½ cup powdered sugar with 1 teaspoon melted butter and 1 tablespoon Jamaica rum, or enough to make the icing the proper consistency to spread. Smooth over the surface of the rolls while they are still hot and let harden slightly before serving. Or, if desired, substitute this:

### Vanilla Glaze for Rolls

½ C powdered sugar
1 t melted butter or margarine
⅛ t vanilla

1 T cream, or more to make a
paste the proper consistency
to spread

Mix all ingredients together. If too thick, add more cream; if too thin, more sugar. Spread over rolls, doughnuts or pastry while they are still hot and the icing will glaze them.

# About Salt-Rising Bread

Frankly, I have never been able to make a successful loaf of salt-rising bread. I have tried dozens of recipes, and all of them have failed. I even talked to a baker here who had long been famous for his so-called salt-rising bread, and he told me that the product he puts out now is made with yeast. His explanation of present-day failures is that most of our commercial corn meal has been bolted and will not ferment as easily as the unbolted variety. For, of course, the "rising yeast" used in the genuine article is made only of salt water and sugar and corn meal.

Cissy Gregg, the able food consultant and editor on the Louisville *Courier-Journal*, once published a really workable recipe, but Cissy cheated, too, for she used soda as well as raw potatoes, and she knows, as I do, that a pioneer Kentucky housewife would have held up her hands in horror at the thought.

## MOCK SALT-RISING BREAD OR ROLLS
### (Corn Meal Bread)

I have admitted defeat when it comes to making salt-rising bread. However, this old Southern recipe for Mock Salt-Rising Bread or Corn Meal Rolls or Bread is a very good substitute, with a flavor very similar to salt-rising bread, and it is ten times easier to make.

2½ T white corn meal (water-ground if possible)
¼ C white corn syrup, honey or sugar
1⅓ C lukewarm milk
2 T warm water

2 C flour, measured after sifting
4 T melted butter, margarine or lard
½ t salt
1 well-beaten egg
1 yeast cake

Mix the corn meal with the corn syrup, honey or sugar. Add ⅔ cups of the warm milk, mixed with the melted butter, margarine or lard. Add salt. Put in a saucepan, place over a flame and let come to a boil, stirring constantly to prevent lumping. Have the flame high at first until the mixture begins to boil and then reduce it as low as possible. Let cook until mixture becomes a mush (3 or 4 minutes, continuously stirring). Set aside to cool until lukewarm. To the cooled mush add the beaten egg, the remainder of the warm milk, the flour, and the yeast cake dissolved in the warm water. Cover and let set in a warm room about an hour. Then toss dough on a floured board and roll smooth, working as little extra flour into the dough as possible. The dough is soft like biscuit dough, but it can be handled.

*To make rolls from this dough*, roll ½ inch thick on a floured board. Cut out with a small biscuit cutter and put on a well-greased pan, brushing each biscuit roll with margarine or butter. Or, if you prefer, make pocketbook rolls by doubling the biscuit rolls in half after first submerging them in melted butter or margarine, then pressing them together on the center edge. Let these rolls rise another half hour or until they seem light. They will never be as light as the rolls made without corn meal, but it is their very texture that makes them distinctive. Put the pan of rolls in a preheated oven (450°) and bake until a golden-brown—20 minutes should be sufficient. Serve hot with honey or jam or pats of sweet butter.

*To make this dough into 2 small loaves,* divide the dough in half. Roll each half as nearly as possible the length and width of the loaf pan. Press dough into loaf pan well greased with melted margarine or butter. Flatten the dough with the palm of the hand, making it cover the pan; then brush with melted fat. Let loaves rise 1 to 2 hours longer or until dough is light. Bake 25 minutes in a hot oven (400°), then reduce heat to 375° and cook 25 minutes longer. Brush with melted margarine or butter but do not take from the oven for another 10 minutes. As soon as bread is taken from oven turn out on a wire rack. Cool before serving, though dyed-in-the-wool Southerners relish this bread while it is still warm. To toast next day, slice this bread ½ inch thick and toast under the flame on the buttered side only. Delicious! Recipe makes two 9″ x 9″ pans of rolls or 2 small loaves of bread, or one pan of 9 rolls and 1 small loaf.

## JUNE SMITH'S SOUTHERN POTATO ROLLS

I've never tasted a better example of the light, fluffy, old-fashioned Southern hot roll than this one of Isabel McMeekin's capable cook, June Smith.

| | |
|---|---|
| 1 C hot riced mashed potatoes | 8 C flour |
| (about 3 medium ones) | 2 C milk |
| ¾ C fat (lard, vegetable short- | 1 cake compressed yeast |
| ening, butter, or margarine) | 1 egg, well-beaten |
| 2 t salt | ½ C sugar |

To the hot potatoes add the fat, sugar and salt. Mix well. Add the well-beaten egg. Scald milk and cool slightly. Add the warm (but never hot) milk to the potatoes, alternating with 2 cups of the flour. Beat hard. Dissolve the yeast cake in ¼ cupful of this batter and add to rest of batter. Cover with a kitchen towel and let batter rise ½ hour in a warm place. Now add 6 cups of flour (measured after sifting). Knead the mixture well for 5 minutes. Return dough to bowl, cover again and let rise until it has doubled its bulk (from 1½ to 2 hours). Roll dough out to ½ inch thickness. Cut into rounds with a large biscuit cutter. With a dull knife press through the center of each round of dough (do not cut through) and fold in half. Pinch the edges of the rolls together and place close together in a greased pan. Brush tops with melted butter. If desired, the tops of the rolls may be brushed with egg (either yolk or white, slightly beaten with water) and sprinkled with poppy seeds. Let rolls rise again until they double their size (about 2 hours). Bake in a hot oven (450°) 20 to 30 minutes.

# Cheese and Eggs

✦✦✦✦✦✦✦✦✦✦✦✦✦✦✦✦✦✦✦✦✦✦✦✦✦✦✦✦✦✦✦✦✦✦✦✦✦✦✦✦✦✦✦✦✦✦

## EGG AND TOMATO SCRAMBLE  *(Quickie!)*
### *(4 servings)*

This is a favorite Kentucky and Alabama dish, served for breakfast, lunch or Sunday night supper, and although its preparation is simple, few people tasting it for the first time realize just what it is. My grandfather, being French, may have introduced it to us from his native land, for I have seen this recipe in French cookery books. It isn't good if made with canned tomatoes. They should be dead-ripe, garden-fresh, to make this dish reach its peak.

4 eggs
2 medium-sized, dead-ripe tomatoes
4 strips jowl or breakfast bacon
(optional)

2 T bacon fat, butter or margarine
Salt and freshly ground black
pepper

Fry bacon in a skillet until brown, and drain on absorbent paper. Set aside. If bacon is not to be used, measure 2 tablespoons of butter or margarine and melt. Peel the tomatoes and cut out all hard parts. Then slice in quarters or eighths and put in the fat in the skillet. Add salt and pepper and cover the skillet. Reduce the heat and let the tomatoes simmer until they become a thick paste, about the consistency of bought tomato purée; stir occasionally to prevent sticking. This takes 10 to 15 minutes. Add the well-beaten eggs and stir until mixture is fluffy and eggs are done. It is always soft, never gets hard as some scrambled eggs do. Serve at once on a platter, surrounded by the bacon. Garnish with parsley.

## A VARIATION OF EGG AND TOMATO SCRAMBLE

We dress up the Egg and Tomato Scramble according to taste and what our garden or our grocer offers. A small diced onion, a tablespoon of

minced green pepper, a few chives, a little parsley can be added to the
tomato while it is cooking. A teaspoon of Worcestershire and a dash of
tabasco and Maggi sauce or soy sauce are also good.

## JULIA HENNING JUNIOR'S EGGS CREOLE
### *(6 servings)*                              *(Quickie!)*

| | |
|---|---|
| 2 T butter | Few drops tabasco |
| 1 green pepper, chopped | 1 t Worcestershire sauce |
| 1 small onion, grated | 1 C grated American cheese |
| 2 T flour (heaping) | (Cheddar) |
| 1 can tomato soup, undiluted | 6 hard-boiled eggs, cut in half |
| 1 C consommé or 2 bouillon | ½ C buttered bread crumbs |
| cubes dissolved in 1 C water | Salt to taste |

Melt butter. Add pepper and onion. Cook 5 minutes. Add flour, and
brown. Add consommé, soup and seasoning. Cook 20 minutes. Add
cheese. Sauce must be the consistency of cream sauce. Into a dish put
the hard-boiled eggs, which have been cut in half. Pour the sauce over
them. Sprinkle buttered bread crumbs over this and brown under the
flame or grill, then serve very hot.

## MARY SHREVE LONG'S EGGS DERBY
### *(6 servings)*

Mrs. Long is one of Louisville's most charming citizens and her lovely
home on Fourth Street has been the Louisville address of many famous
movie stars and other visiting celebrities. She sent me this recipe with
the comment, "It is my favorite hot brunch Derby dish."

| | |
|---|---|
| 6 hard-boiled eggs | 2 T flour, mixed with |
| Salt, pepper, hot mustard to | 1 C sweetbread broth |
| taste | 4 T ground ham (country ham |
| Celery seed to taste | preferred) |
| 2 large sweetbreads, cut in | Cream, to mix with egg yolks to |
| thumb-sized pieces | make a firm paste |
| ½ C grated Parmesan and | 1 C cream |
| sharp New York cheese, | ½ lb. fresh mushrooms broiled |
| mixed | in |
| ½ C blanched, shredded | 4 T butter |
| almonds | 4 T sherry or more to taste |

Peel the hard-boiled eggs and cut in halves lengthwise. Mix the yolks
with the ham, mustard (use the powdered mustard), salt, pepper, and

celery seed. Add just enough cream to make the yolks the proper consistency to pile into egg whites and hold together—begin with a tablespoon and add a little more if necessary.

Boil sweetbreads (page 134). Drain, saving liquor, remove membranes, and cut sweetbreads into thumb-sized pieces. Add to the cream. Mix sweetbread liquor with flour, adding a little at a time to make a smooth paste. Add this gradually to the mushrooms sautéed in butter for 10 minutes or until done. Add sweetbreads, cream and sherry and season to taste.

Put the stuffed hard-boiled egg halves side by side in a flat baking dish with high sides. Pour the sweetbread-mushroom mixture over them. Top with the grated cheese and, last, the almonds. Set in moderate oven for 10 to 15 minutes or until cheese begins to bubble and brown. If not brown in 15 minutes run under the flame in the grill for a moment. Serve at once, piping hot.

## KENTUCKY CHEESE FONDUE
### *(A Lenten or luncheon dish)*
### *(4 servings)*

This is a delicious main dish and one I have never seen prepared in just this manner except in my adopted State. It should be accompanied by tart jelly (plum, grape or currant), or chutney, if you prefer it, and a green or fruit salad with a tangy French dressing.

| | |
|---|---|
| 4 t margarine or butter | 2 C milk |
| 4 pieces of bread | ¼ t paprika |
| 4 slices of yellow cheese (aged | ¼ t salt |
|    Cheddar) cut ¼ inch thick— | ¼ t dry mustard |
|    enough to cover 4 slices of | Dash of cayenne pepper |
|    bread | 2 t Worcestershire sauce |
| 3 eggs | |

Soften margarine or butter and spread the pieces of bread on one side only. Beat the eggs with the milk, Worcestershire sauce, paprika, salt, dry mustard and dash of cayenne. Set aside. Grease a rectangular baking dish with butter or margarine. Pour half the liquid mixture into this. Place two slices of the bread, buttered side up, in this mixture in the baking dish. Completely cover the buttered slices of bread with sliced cheese, to a thickness of ¼ inch. We use sharp Canadian or Wisconsin Cheddar, by preference. Now put the other two slices of bread over the cheese, buttered side next to the cheese, making two sandwiches. Pour the rest of the liquid mixture over these top slices, then top each slice with another slab of cheese. Place the baking dish in a hot oven (400°)

and cook until the cheese melts and bubbles and all liquor has been absorbed. The bread will swell and puff, and the cheese will give it a crunchy brown coating. It should be done in 35 or 40 minutes. Serve immediately.

## SWISS CHEESE TARTS
### (A luncheon dish especially for Lent)
### (4 servings)

These are so delicious we serve them for a first course at a luncheon, although they are often baked in miniature tins and passed with hot hors d'oeuvres at a cocktail party. But this recipe is intended for 4 average-sized individual pie pans.

1 C shredded Swiss cheese or Gruyère (American Swiss cheese is all right)
1 T butter
1 small onion, grated
3 well-beaten eggs
⅛ t salt

⅛ t grated nutmeg
1 C sweet or sour cream
Dash of tabasco or cayenne pepper
4 t butter (for dotting tops of cheese tarts)

Shred the cheese. Melt the tablespoon of butter and grate onion into it. Let get yellow and soft, but not brown. Fold in the shredded cheese. Set aside.

Line small individual pie pans with rich pie crust rolled very thin. Prick and cook about 8 minutes in a hot oven (450°). Divide cheese and onion among the 4 tarts. Then pour over them the following mixture:

Beat the eggs well—I use the electric mixer once more. Add to them the salt, nutmeg and cream. Add a dash of tabasco or cayenne. Dot each tart with 1 teaspoon of butter. Return to a moderate oven (375°) and bake until custard sets, 20 to 35 minutes. The tops should be golden-brown. Serve very, very hot. We accompany these with a green salad, hard water rolls, and hot coffee—a wonderful lunch or Sunday night supper menu, especially during Lent.

# *Fish*

✠✠✠✠✠✠✠✠✠✠✠✠✠✠✠✠✠✠✠✠✠✠✠✠✠✠✠✠✠✠✠✠✠✠✠✠✠✠✠✠✠✠✠✠

## BAKED BASS À LA REELFOOT LAKE
### *(8 to 10 servings)*

This recipe is from George, a guide we once had at Reelfoot Lake.

2 bass weighing 2½ lbs. each  
2 onions, sliced  
Salt and pepper  
1½ C tomato catsup  
½ C cider vinegar  
¼ t dried tarragon leaves  
  (optional)  
1 clove garlic

2 T chopped parsley  
2 T chopped chives or young  
  wild onion tops  
1 T Worcestershire sauce  
¼ C butter or margarine  
¼ t fresh thyme or dried leaves  
  (optional)

Clean the fish, scrape, and remove heads. Place in a roasting pan. Slice the onions in rings and place on top of the fish. Salt and pepper. Mix the tomato catsup with the cider vinegar and pour over the fish. Add the tarragon leaves, or a sprig of the fresh herb, and the thyme (this is my own addition). Add the garlic, parsley, chives or wild onion tops, and Worcestershire sauce. Dot with butter or margarine. Cover the pan and bake 1 hour in a moderate oven (375°). Remove fish to a platter, garnish with parsley or green celery leaves, and pass the sauce separately. This sauce lends itself to a large number of variations. For example:

1. Omit vinegar and substitute a whole lemon cut in ¼-inch slices. Place over the unbaked fish and proceed as above.
2. Add ½ pound of fresh mushrooms to the sauce before baking the fish.
3. Add ½ cup of sliced stuffed green olives and a diced green pepper to the sauce before cooking.
4. Add ½ teaspoon of powdered saffron to the original sauce before baking the fish. Or substitute 1 teaspoon of curry powder, if preferred.

## BAKED STUFFED LAKE TROUT, LANDLOCKED
## SALMON, BASS, DORÉ, PIKE, ETC.
### *(6 servings)*

A 2½ to 3-lb. fish                           Olive oil, or melted butter, or
Salt                                                     margarine
Freshly ground black pepper

Remove the head of the fish, if desired, and split fish down the back
so that it will lie open, but do not cut in half. Remove the central bone
with a sharp knife. Rub the fish inside and out with salt, pepper, and
olive oil or melted butter or margarine. Lay the dressing (see recipes
below for dressings) on the bottom half and smooth evenly. Cover with
the top side of the fish and secure the edges with toothpicks, or sew with
linen thread. Bake in a moderate oven (375°) for 40 minutes to an
hour, depending on the size of the fish.

No cover is put on the fish, so it should be basted from time to time
with melted butter or margarine, or the drippings in the pan. Some
people lay 3 or 4 strips of breakfast bacon over the surface of the fish,
but I have never cared for this flavor.

When the fish is done, transfer to a platter. Serve with Maitre d'Hotel
or Hollandaise Sauce. For stuffings, use any one of the three given
below.

## DRESSINGS FOR BAKED STUFFED LAKE TROUT,
## LANDLOCKED SALMON, BASS, DORÉ, PIKE, ETC.
### *(6 servings)*

1. HERB DRESSING: Soak 3 slices of baker's white bread cut ½ inch thick
in ½ cup of broth or milk. Crumble with the fingers. Add 1 tablespoon
parsley, ⅛ teaspoon thyme, salt, black pepper, a dash of ginger and
another of nutmeg. Melt 2 tablespoons margarine, butter or olive oil
in a skillet. Add a small chopped onion and a finely diced stalk of celery,
and braise until soft but not brown. Pour over the bread and mix well.
Add a whole egg and season to taste. Return the mixture to the skillet
and cook until stiff enough to hold together but not dry. Spoon onto the
bottom half of the fish. Smooth with a knife. Close the fish and secure
with a few toothpicks. Bake as above.

2. SPINACH DRESSING: To the basic dressing above add ½ cup of
spinach purée, made by boiling the spinach in salted water until tender,
draining it and putting it through the finest blade of the meat grinder.

3. MUSHROOM DRESSING: Add to the basic stuffing 1 cup of sliced mushrooms sautéed 5 minutes in 1 tablespoon of fat.

## COURT BOUILLON LOUISIANA
### *(12 servings)*

4 lbs. red snapper, cut in slices or fillets
2 bay leaves
1 C flour
¼ t marjoram, dried
2 T Worcestershire sauce
2 cloves garlic, chopped
½ red pepper pod, chopped
¼ t thyme, dried
2 C olive oil

5 green peppers, chopped
3 pts. tomatoes
Juice of ½ lemon
¼ t basil
6 small onions, chopped
2 T chives, chopped
1 bottle white wine (⅕ gal.)
¼ t nutmeg
Salt, pepper to taste

Wash fish well, season with salt and pepper, and soak for 30 minutes in oil to which lemon juice and herbs have been added. Remove fish and dip in flour. Place in a large soup kettle. Fry onions and garlic in oil in which fish was soaked. Add peppers and when vegetables are soft, add tomatoes and all other ingredients. Pour over fish. Cook slowly until fish is tender, watching carefully to keep from sticking and burning—15 or 20 minutes should be enough. Ladle into plates. Serve with French bread or hard water rolls. A meal in itself.

## JACK SALMON OR *(Quickie!)*
## CANADIAN WALLEYED PIKE PARISIENNE
### *(4 servings)*

This recipe was brought to Louisville from Paris by my husband's French grandmother in 1850.

2 lbs. doré or Canadian walleyed pike fillets or whole cleaned fish weighing not more than ½ lb. apiece
1 qt. water
½ lemon, sliced into rings
1 small bunch of green celery tops
3 sprigs of parsley
1 small onion, cut in rings
4 T finely minced parsley

¼ t ground ginger
½ t whole peppercorns or ¼ t grated black pepper
1 rounded t salt or more to taste
2 egg yolks
2 T flour
Lemon juice
4 T butter or margarine
2 C broth

For 2 pounds of fish make the following court bouillon: In a soup kettle with a tight-fitting lid or in a Dutch oven place the water, sliced lemon, green celery tops, parsley sprigs, onion, ground ginger, pepper and salt to taste; cover and cook 15 minutes. Then add the fish, and when the liquor comes to a boil let simmer 10 to 20 minutes depending upon the size and thickness of the fish. As soon as it is cooked through, it is ready to serve.

Pour off 2 cups of this broth and strain. Into a bowl place 2 egg yolks mixed to a paste with 2 tablespoons flour. Slowly add the fish broth, stirring to prevent lumping. Taste for seasoning, adding more salt, pepper, and lemon juice to taste.

Melt 4 tablespoons butter or margarine in the top of a double boiler. Add the egg-fish liquor and stir over a low flame until the mixture thickens. A wooden spoon is best for this. The sauce is really a mock Hollandaise and should be the consistency of thick cream. Just before serving add 4 tablespoons finely minced parsley.

Place the fish on a platter, garnish with parsley, and pass the sauce separately, dousing each portion with a generous serving.

## LOUISVILLE ROLLED OYSTERS
### (6 servings)

The rolled oyster is a distinctive Louisville culinary invention. It is a fist-sized, croquette-like affair composed of three or four juicy oysters encased in a smart jacket of cracker meal or white corn meal. Rolled oysters can be eaten with the fingers at alfresco backyard picnics, or given the place of honor at a Sunday night supper. Dip them into your favorite catsup or tartar sauce between each bite. If you have never eaten them before, you have a real taste treat in store for you.

The two old-time restaurateurs who battled (verbally) about how this particular concoction came into being are Al Kolb and Mr. Mazzoni. Al insists his mother brought the recipe to Louisville from New Orleans. Mazzoni's story is that back in the 1870's a Frenchman who ran a tavern on Third Street had a batch of oysters left over. Not knowing what to do with them, he had one of the cooks whip up a flour and water batter and mix the oysters in this. Then, because they were so small, three or four were rolled together in cracker meal to make one gigantic croquette.

Al Kolb's restaurant is no more, but Mazzoni's is going strong, and still prepares oyster rolls the old way. But I think I have made an improvement, in the recipe I'm giving you—my own rendition of the classic Louisville rolled oyster. This recipe will serve six, one oyster roll to a person. If your guests are hearty eaters, double the recipe.

18 medium-sized oysters, drained   1 t baking powder
½ C flour                          1 well-beaten egg
¼ C milk or more if needed         1 C white corn meal or cracker
¼ t salt                              meal or enough in which to
Lard or vegetable shortening for      roll batter-coated oysters
   frying oysters

Sift the flour, baking powder, and salt. Beat the egg and milk and add, to make a batter. It should be stiff, but if too stiff to coat the oysters, add a little more milk. Beat smooth. Put all the oysters in this and coat them well. Take up three batter-coated oysters at a time and form them in the hand into a croquette. Then quickly roll in the meal, covering them completely. The trick is to prevent the individual oysters from escaping the fist-sized mass and separating when fried. I find it best to coat them a second time, putting the rolled croquettes back once more into the batter, then giving them another dusting of corn meal or cracker meal. The six rolled oysters are now ready for frying and they do not suffer one whit if made up in the morning and fried in the evening.

When ready to fry, treat the oysters as you would doughnuts. Have a pan of deep lard on the stove. When it is smoking or reaches 375° by the kitchen thermometer, put the oysters in a basket and lower them into the fat. Do not cook too quickly, as you want them to cook through. I lower the heat as soon as they hit the fat. They should cook on both sides at once if enough fat is in the pan. If not, cook on one side, turn with a pancake turner and cook on the other. This will take about three to four minutes all together. Drain on absorbent paper. Cook only three of these oysters at a time and leave space around them so that they can brown evenly. Serve hot. My favorite dip-sauce is catsup in a small bowl with a teaspoon of very hot brown mustard to top it—*Mister* is the brand I prefer. Or, you can serve tartar sauce or anything you wish. A baked potato with butter and chives and sour cream (to make your own fixings at the table), a green salad, coffee, and a piece of coffee cake makes us leave the table smacking our lips.

## BOILED SHRIMP *(Quickie!)*

2 lbs. fresh raw shrimp in their shells  
1 qt. water

¼ t red pepper  
1 t salt (heaping) or more to taste

Boil water, salt, and pepper in a saucepan or kettle with a lid—we use a Dutch oven. Add shrimp. When water boils once more, cover and cook 5 minutes for medium-sized shrimp, 7½ to 10 for large or jumbo shrimp. Let shrimp cool in water in which they were boiled. Remove shells. Clean if desired, removing the black vein down the back. Two pounds of raw shrimp in their shells should yield approximately 1 pound of cooked, peeled shrimp. Use this recipe for all dishes in this book calling for cooked shrimp.

If desired, remove shells and black vein from shrimp before cooking. Prepare the salted water according to directions above. Add peeled, cleaned shrimp, cooking 3 to 4 minutes for medium shrimp, 5 to 7 minutes for jumbo or large shrimp. Let cool in water, drain, and use as directed.

## SHRIMP AND MUSHROOM CASSEROLE WITH ANGOSTURA SAUCE
### (6 servings)

This is one of the most delicious ways of preparing shrimp I know. The original recipe was baked in a casserole, but recently I have been serving it without recooking it—pouring the shrimp into a bowl and placing a twin bowl of rice beside it. Then each guest helps himself to as much as he wishes of both. However, here is the recipe as it was given to me and you can decide which method you prefer. Either way, it is an unusual, delightful dish.

2 T margarine or butter (for sauce)
½ lb. fresh mushrooms
1 small pod of garlic
½ t sugar
¼ t paprika
⅓ C heavy cream
3 T flour
1½ T Worcestershire sauce
2 T margarine or butter (for topping)
1½ T freshly chopped parsley

Salt and pepper
½ small onion, grated (about ½ t pulp)
2 C peeled fresh tomatoes (or canned ones)
Pinch of soda (⅛ t)
6 T good sherry
4 to 5 drops Angostura bitters
1½ pts. peeled cooked shrimp (3 C)
⅓ C freshly-made bread crumbs

To make the sauce, melt 2 tablespoons of margarine or butter in a large skillet or Dutch oven. Add the fresh mushrooms, caps and stems separated but not cut, and a small pod of garlic. Add salt and pepper. Cover and cook 5 minutes, stirring to keep mushrooms from sticking. Then add the grated small onion. Cover the pan and cook 5 minutes longer. Add the peeled fresh tomatoes or canned ones. Add a pinch of soda, sugar, paprika, and more salt and pepper. Simmer 15 minutes. Discard garlic pod. Mix the heavy cream with flour to make a smooth paste. Then add the sherry, Worcestershire sauce and drops of Angostura bitters. Pour the cream-sherry mixture into the tomato-mushroom mixture, stirring to make a smooth blend. Cook 3 minutes and add peeled cooked shrimp and parsley. Taste for seasoning, adding more salt and pepper if necessary. As soon as the shrimps are hot, pour the mixture into a serving bowl or a casserole dish. If you cook this as a casserole, sprinkle the freshly-made bread crumbs over surface and dot with the rest of the margarine.

Cook 10 minutes in a moderate oven (375°), then transfer to the broiler and let remain until crumbs brown and surface becomes bubbly. Serve at once. Mushrooms may be omitted from this recipe and the Shrimp with Angostura Sauce served in a dish, to be spooned over rice or toast squares.

## SHRIMPS DE JONGHE
### *(My version of this elusive recipe)*
### *(4 servings)*

There was once a restaurant in Chicago run by a Belgian couple named de Jonghe and one of their specialties was a shrimp-and-herbed-bread-crumb-and-butter dish which made a national reputation for itself. The nephew of this famous couple is now in business and again serves their specialty, although he refuses to divulge the secret family recipe. However, he does insist that his version has 12 herbs in it—a number greater than I can figure. However, here's the recipe I have worked out which is, to my taste anyway, an acceptable facsimile of the original Shrimps de Jonghe.

You will need 1 pound of cooked shrimp for 4 servings. Medium-sized shrimp are best. You can buy them already cooked and peeled if you are in a hurry, otherwise boil them according to directions given on page 87.

### Herbed Butter for Shrimps de Jonghe

| | |
|---|---|
| 1 C softened margarine or butter (butter is best) | 1 C bread crumbs |
| 1 t salt | ¼ t tabasco |
| 2 T lemon juice | 6 T strained court bouillon or consommé |
| 6 small shallots and green tops | 2 buttons of garlic (small) |
| 4 sprigs thyme, or ¼ t dried herb | 4 sprigs tarragon or ¼ t dried herb |
| 4 sprigs parsley, or ¼ t dried herb | Small bunch of chives (if in season) or 1 slice white onion |

Put shallots, garlic, parsley, chives or onion slice, thyme, and tarragon through the finest blade of the meat grinder. Add to softened butter or margarine. Add all other ingredients, folding in the bread crumbs last of all. This makes a rather stiff paste. It can be used at once or kept in a covered jar in the icebox.

To make the Shrimps de Jonghe, divide the shrimp into 4 piles. Spread a layer of herbed butter ¼ inch thick over the bottoms of 4 pottery baking dishes or individual casseroles. Place a covering layer of cooked, peeled, cleaned (if you wish) shrimp on top, pressing the shrimp into the herbed butter and arranging them spoon fashion in rows. They should be only one layer deep. Divide the remaining butter into 4 parts and coat the shrimp, blanketing them on top with the butter if enough remains. Place the pottery dishes in an oven set at 400° and preheated. Leave 10 minutes. Transfer to grill and let the tops brown. Serve at once. A green salad or fresh green peas or Chinese pea pods, new or baked old potatoes, tea and a light sponge pudding round out this very hearty meal.

## LOUISE McKEITHEN'S STUFFED CRABS
### *(3 to 4 servings)*                    *(Quickie!)*

| | |
|---|---|
| 2 T melted butter | ½ t prepared (yellow) mustard |
| 1 T flour | ¼ t salt or more to taste |
| ½ C top milk or cream | ½ t prepared horse-radish |
| 1 t lemon juice | Dash cayenne pepper or tabasco |
| 1 can crab meat (6½ to 7 oz.) | sauce |
| 1 hard-boiled egg, chopped | ¼ C bread crumbs or grated |
| Dabs of butter for tops of shells | Swiss cheese |
| 1 T chopped parsley | |

Melt the butter in a double boiler. Add flour and mix until it forms a smooth paste. Slowly add the top milk or cream, stirring until the mixture makes a smooth sauce. Add prepared mustard, salt, horse-radish, cayenne or tabasco, lemon juice and parsley. Stir well. Fold into this the crab meat and hard-boiled egg, chopped fine. Pile into shells and top with bread crumbs or grated Swiss cheese and dabs of butter. Put under the flame to brown or place in the oven for ten minutes (hot oven— 450°). Serve at once. Potato chips are nice with this, and a green or grapefruit salad.

Tuna fish (well drained) may be substituted for the crab meat, with equally good results.

# Game

✤✤✤✤✤✤✤✤✤✤✤✤✤✤✤✤✤✤✤✤✤✤✤✤✤✤✤✤✤✤✤✤✤✤✤✤✤✤✤✤✤✤✤✤✤✤✤

MANY HUNTERS hang their game for several days after it has been killed—in fact, one book suggests that this be done for ten days or two weeks. But by then the birds are "high," and to me have a spoiled flavor which I have never learned to appreciate. However, they can be plucked more easily when they are a few days old, as the feathers come out quicker. Pick game birds dry, as the skin is very tender and the flavor is impaired by scalding. I also wash my birds well in cold water after they are picked and cleaned, and if the gamy odor is too pronounced, I wash them in a soda solution and rinse in cold water before cooking. This, I know, is according to Flexner rather than Hoyle.

## LOUIS SMITH'S DOVES OR QUAIL IN WINE SAUCE
### (6 birds)

Louis Smith, our houseman, cooks doves and quail better than anyone I have ever known. He wisely uses the pressure cooker, for the birds are apt to be tough. For six doves or quail you will need:

| | |
|---|---|
| Salt and pepper | 1 T Worcestershire sauce |
| Flour in which to roll birds | ½ t Kitchen Bouquet |
| 2 t butter to each small bird | 1 C white wine |
| 1 pod garlic | ½ C water |

After the birds are picked and cleaned, they are salted and peppered and rolled in flour. The pressure cooker is heated and butter melted. When the butter has melted the birds are browned on each side and while they are cooking a pod of garlic is browned with them. We usually cook about 6 birds at a time. When the birds are brown, pour over them the wine and water and add more salt and pepper, the Worcestershire sauce and Kitchen Bouquet. Put the lid on the cooker. When it has steamed, screw down the petcock and allow the pressure to reach 15, then lower the heat and cook 20 minutes at that temperature. Release the steam, remove the garlic pod, if you can find it, and serve the birds with wild rice, dousing them with the gravy. You can thicken it if you wish, but we do not. These birds are as tender as butter, and the sauce, says my husband,

91

"good enough to eat on cotton." If you do not own a pressure cooker, cook the birds in a covered Dutch oven about 1 hour or until they are tender. More wine and water may have to be added if the liquid evaporates.

## POTTED DOVES OR QUAIL
### (4 servings)

Use a Dutch oven or chicken fryer for this. For 4 doves or quail you will need:

| | |
|---|---|
| 4 T butter | 2 T minced parsley |
| 4 tiny onions the size of walnuts | Salt and pepper to taste |
| (I use sets) | 1 C slivered sautéed mushrooms |
| 1 T flour | cooked in 1 T butter (op- |
| 1 C water | tional) |
| 1 pod garlic | |

Melt butter in Dutch oven or chicken fryer. Add garlic. Salt and pepper birds and cook until brown all over. Remove to a plate. Discard garlic and add flour. Cook until brown, stirring constantly. Add water to make a gravy. Return birds to gravy, cover and simmer until tender (45 minutes to 1 hour), adding more water if necessary. Fifteen minutes before taking birds from the stove, add the tiny onions and continue cooking. Just before serving, add the parsley. If desired, 1 cup of slivered mushrooms, sautéed 5 minutes in 1 tablespoon of butter, may be added to the gravy just before removing from the stove. Allow one dove to a person. Serve with wild rice and toast triangles if you like them, passing the gravy separately. I never put my birds on toast because I think the toast absorbs the juices. Quail and other small game are delicious prepared by this recipe. Domestic squabs are good, too, but will require longer cooking.

# Quail

In addition to the preceding recipes, here are a few of our favorite ways to cook quail:

## BAKED QUAIL WITH WILD RICE DRESSING
### (4 servings)

| | |
|---|---|
| 4 quail | 1 C stock or broth |
| 4 T butter | 4 T wild rice dressing (see page |
| Flour in which to roll quail | 112) |
| Salt and pepper | |

Salt and pepper birds and roll in flour. Stuff 1 tablespoon of dressing in each bird. Melt fat in a Dutch oven or chicken fryer. Brown birds. Add stock and seasoning to taste. Cover the pan. Set in moderate oven (375°) and cook 1 hour or until birds are tender. Serve with brandied fruit.

## BAKED QUAIL AND OYSTERS
### (4 servings)

4 quail
4 t butter or margarine
Flour in which to roll butter
Salt and pepper to taste
4 strips bacon (I use thin breakfast bacon)

4 to 8 oysters, depending on size
4 T consommé or meat stock made by dissolving 1 bouillon cube in ¼ C water

Wash and draw quail well. Be sure they have been well cleaned. Do not split. Salt and pepper the birds inside and out. Put a piece of bacon over the breast of each bird. Wrap around and tie securely with a piece of string—do not use a toothpick. Put an oyster or two in each bird, filling the cavity. Place the birds in a roasting pan, one beside another—a casserole dish or pyrex dish will also be adequate. The oven should be moderately hot—375°. Add the consommé or meat broth and do not put a lid on the cooking dish. Baste the birds with their own drippings every 15 minutes and cook until they are tender—40 minutes should be enough. Take the birds from the oven, remove bacon and discard it. Put the birds back in the pan. Drop into the pan 4 teaspoons of butter or margarine, each teaspoon of which has been rolled in flour until it will not hold any more. Cook 8 minutes longer or until butter melts and flour thickens gravy. Baste the breasts with the sauce. Serve with plain rice. Sprinkle the breasts with chopped parsley if you like the flavor. Serve toast triangles or hot biscuits with this and "dunk" them in the gravy.

## CASSEROLE OF QUAIL AND MUSHROOMS IN SOUR CREAM
### (4 servings)

4 quail
½ C butter
1 C water
Salt and black pepper to taste
Flour in which to roll quail
1 pod garlic
1 onion, ground

¼ lb. mushrooms, washed and ground
¼ t paprika
1 C sour cream
Extra flour for thickening gravy if necessary

Salt and pepper quail, and roll in flour. Melt butter in a skillet or Dutch oven and add the garlic. Put the quail in this and lower the heat. Brown quail on all sides but do not try to cook done. Transfer quail to a casserole with a lid. Add the ground onions and the ground mushrooms to the pan in which quail were browned and simmer 5 minutes. Add the water and let come to a boil. Pour the mixture over the quail after removing garlic. Put the top on the casserole and cook 1 hour in a moderate oven (375°), turning the quail after ½ hour. Just before serving add the sour cream, and extra salt and pepper if necessary. Thicken the gravy with a flour-and-water paste if necessary.

## VIRGINIA BARKER'S OVEN-BROILED QUAIL
### (2 servings)

Virginia Barker's husband is a great hunter and she tells me that, after trying numerous recipes, they find this their favorite way of preparing quail. It is simply delicious and we too have adopted it. You will need all the butter or margarine called for to cook the quail properly, but because some will be left over, Virginia uses it to pour over her wild rice, which she always serves with quail. Mushrooms and wild rice make an even better combination. With the remaining brown particles in the skillet, a gravy is concocted and poured over the game. Here are the directions:

2 quail, cleaned and split in     Salt and freshly ground black
    half                                 pepper
½ C butter or margarine,
    melted

Use a 6-inch skillet. The size of the skillet is important, for the butter or margarine must be ½ inch deep in the bottom of the pan and the birds should fit close together in it. Salt and pepper the birds and douse in the melted butter or margarine. Then put in the skillet, breast side down— this too is important. If you like your birds rare, cook only 6 minutes in an oven where the broiler flame is very hot. If you like well-done birds, cook 12 minutes. In either case turn the birds over and cook 3 minutes longer to allow the breasts to brown. The Barkers do not serve their quail on toast (nor do I), but you can if you wish. Pour off the excess butter to use on your rice or some other vegetable—it can be set aside and re-melted. Leave about 2 tablespoons of fat in the pan, and all the brown drippings. Add 2 or 3 tablespoons of water and set the skillet over a flame on top of the stove. Let cook until it makes a gravy, and pour at once over birds. Garnish the platter with parsley and serve. If you like lemon, put lemon wedges on the platter, too, and squeeze over your quail at the table.

## QUAIL IN HERBED WINE SAUCE
### (6 servings)

6 partridges or quail
6 T butter or olive oil
1 pod garlic, crushed
1 onion, chopped
½ lb. mushrooms (optional)
1 bay leaf
1 carrot, scraped and cut in rings

¼ t thyme
1 T chopped parsley
1 C white wine
1 C consommé or chicken broth
Salt and black pepper to taste
½ t sugar, if wine is dry
Flour in which to roll birds

Rub game with salt and pepper and crushed garlic pod. Roll in flour and brown in butter or olive oil. Add liquid slowly, then all other ingredients. We use a Dutch oven or chicken fryer with a heavy, close-fitting lid. Let the liquids come to a boil on top of stove. Then transfer the covered pot to a moderate (375°) oven, and cook the birds 1 hour or until they stick tender. Taste the gravy and add more salt and pepper and wine if necessary. Place the quail on a platter, garnish with extra chopped parsley and serve the sauce separately. If you like, you may surround them with toast squares.

## WILD DUCK (Teal or Mallard)

Draw 2 small wild ducks. Wash well in soda water and rinse in clear water. Drain. Rub well with salt, black pepper, and butter or olive oil. Stuff each with 1 onion and celery tops. Roast until brown in a slow oven (350°). This takes 1 to 2 hours, depending on size of ducks. Take out ducks and set aside, removing onions and celery tops. Skim off fat from bottom of pan. To drippings add 1 small glass (½ cup) of currant jelly and 1 tablespoon of flour mixed with ¼ cup of cold water. Let boil. Pour over ducks and serve with slices of stiff jelly or sliced oranges.

# *If You Can Find a "B'ar"*

## ALICE ROBERTS' ROAST BEAR

Alice Roberts got this recipe from her sister, Judie Alexander. Judie and her husband, Tom, run the fascinating dude ranch called Cataloochee, in the Great Smokies. I had heard that all who tasted this delicious bear roast begged to be invited again, so I asked Alice to send me the recipe, and she did, writing: "Here 'tis!! Assuming you have caught that b'ar." There was once a tree on the old Manslick Road outside of Louisville which bore the legend "D. Boone Kilt A B'ar 1803." The tree is gone but the bark with Boone's message can be seen in Louisville's Filson Club. I'll bet *his* "b'ar" didn't taste as good as Alice's. Alice says this is really a glorified pot roast and that the secret of this recipe lies in removing every trace of bear fat—which is apt to be strong, even in the tenderest "b'ar." The meat should also be marinated overnight and part of the next day with the mixture given below, turning the meat and basting occasionally. She also added this interesting bit of information: "As I said, this is Judie's recipe and since they have it more often than we, she has become quite an expert. You will be interested to know that they wanted her to fly to New York at Thanksgiving time to supervise the cooking of the bear Tom sent for the Tar Heel Society's annual meeting at the Hotel Lexington. She couldn't go but sent her recipe and the Governor of New York was loud in his praises in next day's Sun."

### Herb Mixture for Marinating Bear

| | |
|---|---|
| 1 C Wesson oil (or half Wesson and half olive oil) | 1 t dry mustard |
| | Dash of Worcestershire sauce |
| 1 large onion, chopped | ½ C catsup |
| 1 clove of garlic, crushed | Celery salt |
| 2 or 3 bay leaves | Stalk of chopped celery |
| Rosemary—a few needles | Salt and pepper |

Marinate meat as described above. Remove meat from herb mixture, scraping off all clinging ingredients. Rub with salt and pepper and sear well in a very little fat. Pour boiling water a quarter of the way of the roast. Add marinating mixture of oil and herbs and cover the pot. Simmer very gently, allowing 45 minutes cooking time to the pound. Be sure to keep the liquid up—always a quarter of the roast. Turning the meat keeps it moist. Before serving, remove roast from the liquid, thicken the gravy, and strain.

# *Poultry*

✿✿✿✿✿✿✿✿✿✿✿✿✿✿✿✿✿✿✿✿✿✿✿✿✿✿✿✿✿✿✿✿✿✿✿✿✿✿✿✿✿✿✿✿✿✿✿✿✿

## ABOUT PREPARING POULTRY

All fowl should have been killed at least 24 hours, and thoroughly chilled
before cooking. Place in a covered hydrator in icebox until ready to use.

\* \* \*

Be sure the birds are well cleaned, lungs, etc., removed and all blood
washed away before storing in icebox. Always see that the gall bag has
not broken as its contents, spilled on the fowl, will cause a bitter, un-
pleasant taste.

\* \* \*

To freshen birds, wash them in a strong soda solution and then rinse
thoroughly in cold water before cooking.

\* \* \*

Do not try to make soup from leftover boiled chicken, as most of the
flavor will have cooked out of it in the first boiling. I bake chickens to use
for croquettes, soufflé, salad, etc., so that I can recook the skin and what
meat is left on the bones and make delicious Carcass Soup (page 46).

\* \* \*

Even a few shreds of poultry meat can be turned into a delightful
luncheon dish—see recipes for Hot and Cold Brown Sandwiches (page
31).

\* \* \*

Use a small paint brush or basting brush to baste fowl. Keep it for that
purpose and remember to wash the fat out of it each time it is used to
keep it from developing a rancid odor.

\* \* \*

NOTE *on frozen poultry.* The method of thawing frozen poultry has
been often disputed. I have one friend who insists that thawing it in
water improves the bird. Others say that this will cause the meat to be
watery. I've tried both methods and can see no difference. If you are in
a hurry to use the frozen poultry, however, it can be thawed much more

quickly by placing it in a bowl of cold water and leaving it in a warm, but not hot, room. Frozen chickens are sold in parts or whole. After they have been thawed, they can be prepared by any of the recipes given in this book. Never refreeze them, but if you do not use a whole package, wrap the remainder well in wax paper or cellophane and store in a hydrator in the icebox until needed.

# Chicken

## BROILED SPRING CHICKENS
### (4 servings)

2 spring chickens (1½ lbs. to       ¼ lb. butter
   1¾ lbs. each)                      Salt, pepper to taste

Clean the fowl and split down the back but do not disjoint. Sprinkle with salt and pepper. Smear with some of the softened butter. Put chickens on a wire rack over a dripping pan and place under the flame in the grill. Brown first on one side and then on the other, turning the fowls constantly and basting with butter. The chickens require constant care to keep them from burning. They should be done in 45 minutes to 1 hour. A properly broiled chicken is among the South's most delectable culinary achievements. The fowl should be crisp and crunchy outside, the meat juicy and tender inside. Serve with baked potatoes and plenty of browned butter. Allow ½ chicken to each person.

Do not try to serve large chickens prepared this way—even a 2-pound chicken (weighed after being fully dressed) is too large. Cook large birds (2 to 3 lbs.) first by the above method, then transfer them to a roasting pan and add 1 cup of water, which has been poured into the pan where the chickens were broiled, and allowed to mingle and blend with the drippings. Cover the roaster and put it in a moderate oven (350°) and leave for an hour or so or until chickens stick very done. In the South we call this dish Smothered Chicken.

## HELEN AND KAK LEOPOLD'S CHICKEN AU VIN
### (3 servings)

A 2-lb. chicken                        2 T olive oil, salad oil, etc.
1 crushed garlic pod                   Salt to taste
Black pepper, freshly ground           ½ C white wine
½ C water                              Mushrooms (optional)

Rub the chicken with crushed garlic, pepper and oil. Brown in a Dutch oven until chicken is as brown as if broiled under the flame. This should take about ½ hour. Two more tablespoons of oil may be necessary to keep the chicken from sticking to the pan. Salt well when browned and add the water and wine. Cover and let simmer slowly another ½ hour, or until chicken is very tender and almost all the gravy has cooked away. Mushrooms may be added with the white wine if desired.

## ASHBOURNE INN CHICKEN CACCIATORE
### *(6 to 8 servings)*

Ashbourne Inn is the newest of the gourmet restaurants within an hour's driving-time from Louisville. Close to La Grange, Kentucky, amid lush farmlands, near the picturesque Ohio River, and on Route 42—the direct road from Cincinnati to Louisville—it is easily accessible. The original old farmhouse has been carefully remodeled and charmingly decorated. There is a terrace, too, where guests may dine out-of-doors when the weather permits. Ashbourne Inn has many specialties and this one has been generously shared with us.

A 4-lb. hen sprinkled with salt and pepper
Flour in which to dredge chicken
Butter in which to brown chicken (about ¼ C)

Disjoint chicken. Sprinkle generously with salt and pepper and dredge with flour. Melt butter or margarine in a Dutch oven and brown chicken. Cover with the following sauce and cook slowly until chicken is tender.

¼ C butter
1 T finely minced onion
1 slice carrot, cut in cubes
1 slice turnip, cut in cubes
¼ C flour
1 C white wine
1 t salt, or more to taste
⅛ t black pepper

F. G. cayenne pepper
2 C stewed strained tomatoes
1 C boiling water
1 clove garlic
1 C sliced mushrooms sautéed 5 minutes in 1 T butter (to be added 10 minutes before chicken is done)

Pour off fat from the pan in which the chicken was browned and add enough butter to make ¼ cup. Add flour, salt, pepper, and cayenne and stir in skillet until flour is browned. Add tomatoes gradually and cook 5 minutes, then strain over chicken. Add all other ingredients, except sautéed mushrooms. Put the top on the pan and simmer slowly until chicken seems very tender when stuck with a fork—1 to 2 hours. Ten minutes before removing from stove add the sautéed mushrooms. If mixture cooks too thick, add more water and wine mixed in equal proportions. Serve with Spanish or Yellow Rice (page 159).

## ALENE BURGER'S CHICKEN CHOW MEIN WITH FRIED NOODLES

Cook a 5-pound hen as for Stewed Chicken and Dumplings (page 106). Prepare the chicken the day before the chow mein is to be made and let the chicken stand in the broth overnight. This isn't obligatory, but it does improve the flavor. Then remove the chicken from the bones. Discard the skin. Strain the broth and reserve for the sauce. How to make the chow mein:

| | |
|---|---|
| 1 lb. mushrooms, cut in quarters | 1 can bean sprouts, drained |
| 4 T chicken fat or butter | 3 C diced celery |
| 1 T flour | 2 cans tomato sauce or tomato |
| 2 onions, chopped | soup |
| 1 green pepper, chopped | 2 C chicken broth |
| 1 pod garlic, minced | ¼ C soy sauce |
| 1 T Worcestershire sauce | Salt, pepper to taste |

Melt fat, add mushrooms and cook 5 minutes. Add pepper, celery, onions and garlic and cook 10 minutes longer. A large iron pot with a close-fitting lid, or a Dutch oven, is best for this. Add all other ingredients, except chicken. Thicken gravy with a flour-and-water paste and add seasoning to taste. Simmer 30 minutes. Add chicken and let cook a few minutes to heat. Pour into a dish and sprinkle with parsley. Serve with canned or homemade fried noodles prepared as follows:

### Fried Noodles

½ lb. finely-cut egg noodles          Lard or peanut oil

Place the egg noodles in a wire basket and cook in a deep pot in smoking fat (375°) until golden-brown. This will take only a few seconds. Drain on absorbent paper and place on a platter. Cover with the chicken mixture made for the chow mein. Garnish with shredded chicken, shredded green onion tops, and shredded toasted almonds.

VARIATION: In an emergency the dry cereal known as Corn Soya Shreds may be substituted for the fried noodles. Be sure that they are crisp before serving.

## SOLGER'S CHICKEN CROQUETTES
### (12 croquettes)

Toward the end of the past century and during the first decade of this one, there was a Louisville restaurateur by the name of Solger, a veritable Mrs. Malaprop, who delighted the palates of the local gourmets with his wonderful food and amused them by his "Solgerisms." Once, at a very fashionable party, he served a croquette, its casing brown and crunchy, its well-seasoned filling moist almost to the point of being runny. When asked for the recipe, he bridled and replied, "But I won't tell anyone— it's my own composure." However, he agreed to give his employer all the ingredients—except one. That one, though, was very important, for without it the croquettes would not have the proper consistency. The lady consented. "Then," said the old man, with his tongue in his cheek, "I tell you what I'll do. You guess the missing ingredient and if you get it the very first time, I'll tell you if you are right." She agreed, and being a superior cook herself, she did guess it—the answer was *calves' brains.*

Mr. Solger would make his croquettes only of chicken or veal, but I have been equally successful with turkey or capon. However, the meat must first have been baked. Do not attempt to make them with meat that has been boiled. It is too moist and hasn't enough flavor. For a dozen croquettes you will need:

| | |
|---|---|
| ½ lb. baked turkey, chicken, or veal, ground fine and weighed after grinding | Salt and black pepper to taste |
| | ⅛ t freshly grated nutmeg, or more to taste |
| ¼ lb. freshly ground bread crumbs weighed after grinding | 2 whole eggs, well beaten |
| | 2 t grated onion juice and pulp |
| 2 C strong broth or unthickened gravy from the chicken, or canned consommé | 1 T finely chopped parsley |
| | ¼ lb. calves' brains boiled in salt water, drained and mashed |
| ½ C butter (no substitutes) | ¼ C heavy cream |
| 1 t Worcestershire sauce | 2 egg whites, lightly beaten with 1 T water, in which to roll croquettes |
| Extra bread crumbs for rolling croquettes | |

Mix the meat and crumbs in a large bowl. Slowly add broth, gravy, or consommé. Melt butter in a large skillet. Add onion with juice, and brown. Add this to the meat-crumb mixture. Now add the well-beaten whole eggs and all the other ingredients except the lightly-beaten egg whites, and mix again. The filling will be a little soft, but no matter. Pour it into the skillet once more. Set on the stove over a low flame and *stir* and *stir* and *stir* until it gets stiff enough to leave the sides of the pan. But do not cook until it gets dry. Put into a covered bowl and set in the icebox for 2 hours or until the mixture can be handled easily. Leaving it in the icebox overnight will not harm its flavor. Remove the bowl from the icebox and form the croquettes into balls or oblongs, using a tablespoonful of the mixture for each one. Roll them first in bread crumbs (no cracker crumbs, please), then into the egg-white mixture, and back into the crumbs once more. By this time they should be nicely tailored with a thick coat of crumbs. Fry them in a wire basket in deep, hot, melted lard or vegetable shortening (385°). Cook only a few croquettes at a time, and if the fat gets too hot lower the flame, so that the croquettes will not burn. Two to 3 minutes should cook them, for as soon as they are hot through and a golden-brown color they are ready to serve. We always send ours to the table with mushroom sauce, made as follows:

## MUSHROOM SAUCE FOR CHICKEN CROQUETTES
### *(Quickie!)*

½ lb. mushrooms, cut in quarters
½ C milk
½ C cream
2 t flour
½ t Kitchen Bouquet
2 T butter
2 t Worcestershire sauce
Salt and pepper to taste

Separate mushroom caps from stems, cut in quarters, and simmer in butter until thoroughly tender—about 5 minutes. Add milk mixed to a paste with flour. Add cream, Worcestershire sauce, and Kitchen Bouquet. Then add salt and a dash of pepper, and cook until sauce is the consistency of thick cream, stirring constantly.

## EMMA OUERBACKER'S CHICKEN CURRY
### *(Quickie!)*
### *(A delicious dish concocted from leftover cooked chicken)*

4 or 5 onions, chopped
5 T salad oil or melted shortening
5 T flour
1 C cream
2 to 4 T curry powder
1 qt. chicken stock
1 C seedless raisins
1 C drained crushed pineapple
Juice of ½ lemon
Strip of lemon peel
2 C cut-up cooked chicken (or more)
Salt to taste

Simmer the onions in the salad oil or melted shortening until they are soft and golden. Stir in the flour and cook, stirring constantly, over low heat. Add chicken stock. Stir until smooth and slightly thickened. Add raisins and crushed pineapple. Now add the lemon juice and lemon peel. Simmer about 5 minutes. Add cream. Blend curry powder to a paste with a little water and stir into mixture. Better to start with 2 tablespoons and work up to the point where it is just right for your taste. Last of all, add chicken, and salt to taste. Simmer over low heat until it reduces to a good consistency. Serve with freshly cooked rice that is fluffy and dry. Serve with condiments in side dishes, to be sprinkled over the top. *Suggestions:* Chutney (a must), grated cocoanut, pickle relish, chopped bacon, chopped eggs, chopped salted peanuts or almonds, and French-fried onions.

## CHICKEN LIVERS IN WINE SAUCE
### *(4 servings)* *(Quickie!)*

1 lb. chicken livers
4 T butter
4 T wine (sherry or Madeira)
2 T flour
Salt, pepper to taste

¼ t sugar
1 pt. meat stock (chicken stock is best)
1 pod garlic
3 sprigs parsley

Melt butter in skillet. Salt and pepper livers. Roll them in flour and fry in butter until golden-brown. Care must be taken not to let livers get hard. A slow fire is best. Add stock, garlic, and parsley and simmer 20 minutes or until livers are tender. Remove garlic and parsley from sauce and thicken with flour dissolved in water, if necessary. Just before removing from stove add sugar and wine. Let mixture come to a boil. Pour over rice, toast, waffles or an omelet, and garnish with fresh chopped parsley and sliced lemon.

## HELEN LEOPOLD'S CHICKEN SURPRISE
### *(For leftover chicken)* *(Quickie!)*
### *(6 servings)*

1 pod garlic
2 T hot chicken fat, olive oil, or margarine
½ lb. mushrooms
2 T chopped green pepper
1 bay leaf
Flour
1 t Worcestershire sauce
½ C white wine

2 C chicken gravy and beef consommé (Use all consommé if you have no leftover gravy; or 1 C consommé and 1 C cream)
Salt and pepper to taste
Dash paprika
2 C diced cooked chicken
2 T chopped parsley

Sauté garlic until brown in the hot chicken fat, olive oil or margarine. Remove. Sauté mushrooms for 5 minutes in the same fat. Add chopped green pepper, gravy or consommé, or consommé and cream. Add white wine, bay leaf, salt and pepper to taste, and paprika. Cook 5 minutes more. Thicken with a little flour if necessary, so that sauce has the consistency of cream. Correct the seasoning, adding Worcestershire sauce, and if wine is dry, add a little sugar. Add the diced cooked chicken (mixed with diced chicken dressing if any is left over). Keep over flame until thoroughly heated in sauce. Add chopped parsley. Serve over rice, waffles or omelet, or roll in French pancakes.

## COUNTRY CAPTAIN
*(A Georgia dish)*
*(4 servings)*

A 3-lb. chicken
4 T butter or chicken fat
1 green pepper, chopped
1 pod garlic, chopped
1 onion, chopped
1 C water, or more if necessary
6 peeled fresh tomatoes

1 T chopped parsley
¼ t thyme
¼ lb. blanched almonds
3 T dried currants
1½ t curry powder
4 slices crisp bacon

Dismember chicken (there should be about 10 pieces). Heat butter or chicken fat and brown the fowl (this should take about 10 minutes). Remove fowl to roaster. To the fat in which chicken was fried add pepper, garlic and onion, and cook 5 minutes longer, stirring constantly. Add water mixed with curry powder, tomatoes, parsley and thyme. Pour this mixture over the chicken. Cover pan and bake in the oven until chicken is very tender (about 2 hours). Now add the almonds, which have been fried in butter or margarine and are golden-brown. The currants come next. Place chicken on a dish and pour the gravy over it. Garnish with bacon slices. Serve with chutney, Bombay duck and all the trimmings that usually accompany a curry.

## FRIED SPRING CHICKENS (Kentucky Style)
*(6 servings)*

2 young spring chickens, weigh-
    ing just 2 lbs. when dressed
Milk in which to soak chickens
Salt and pepper

2 lbs. lard, vegetable shortening
    or salad oil to fry chickens
Flour in which to roll chickens

Disjoint the chickens, separating the legs and the breasts into 2 sections each, cutting off both wings and leaving backs intact. Place in a bowl and soak from 20 to 30 minutes in milk. Drain but do not dry. Sprinkle with salt and pepper and roll in flour, or shake each piece of chicken in a bag in which 1 cup of flour has been placed—this is said to coat the chicken evenly. I just dump some flour on a plate and roll the pieces in that. If you like an extra-crunchy jacket on your chicken, dip it in cream after it has been floured once, then dip again in flour and fry at once. Dip one piece at a time. Have the fat smoking hot in a deep iron chicken fryer or Dutch oven (375°). Put in a few pieces of chicken at a time and lower the flame. When the pieces are golden-brown all over, remove them from the pan and put in a few more pieces to fry until all have browned. It will take 1 pound of lard or 2 cups of melted fat to fry each chicken, although there will be some left over when you are through. When all the pieces have browned, pour off all but 2 tablespoons of the fat. Return the chickens to the pot and cover, having a very low flame under the pot. Cook 20 to 30 minutes longer, or until chickens seem done—cut a piece to test. Serve with Hardin County Chicken Biscuits (page 56). Top with

## Brown Crumb Gravy

| | |
|---|---|
| 1 C milk | 2 T fat, and brown crumbs |
| 1 T flour | from pan in which chicken |
| Salt and pepper to taste | was fried |

After removing chicken to a serving platter, pour off all but 2 tablespoons of fat, but save all the brown crumbs and drippings. Return the pan to the flame. Add the flour and stir until brown. Add milk slowly, stirring to prevent lumping. Add salt and pepper to taste. Do not cook too thick. Serve hot. Save the fat in which the chickens were fried; it can be used again.

## SPANISH CHICKEN
### *(From the Florida Keys)*

| | |
|---|---|
| A 5-lb. hen | ½ t powdered saffron |
| 1 pimento, chopped | 1 bay leaf |
| 1 qt. tomatoes, fresh or canned | ¼ t marjoram |
| 2 large onions, chopped | 2 T chopped parsley |
| 1 green or sweet red pepper, chopped | 2 C canned artichokes |
| | Flour to thicken gravy |
| 1 tiny hot red pepper | Salt, pepper, tabasco to taste |
| 6 C water | 2 C cooked rice |
| ½ lb. mushrooms | 1 t sugar |
| 3 stalks celery, chopped | 1 pt. cooked buttered peas |
| ¼ t dried thyme | 1 pod garlic |

Wash chicken, disjoint, season with salt and pepper, roll in flour, and fry in deep fat until golden-brown. Remove chicken and pour off all but 4 tablespoons of fat. Add onions, garlic, and green pepper, and brown. Return chicken to the pot. Add water, tomatoes, pimento, seasoning and herbs and cook slowly until chicken is tender (about 2 hours). Put the boiled rice in a mound on a large platter, and put the pieces of chicken over this. Surround with the artichokes and the green peas in homemade timbales or small paper cups. Pass the gravy separately.

To make the gravy, sauté mushrooms in 2 tablespoons of olive oil or chicken fat for 10 minutes. Add slowly 2 cups of strained broth in which the chicken was cooked. If too thick, thin this sauce with a little water.

If too thin, add a flour paste made with 1 tablespoon of flour mixed with 2 tablespoons of water for every cup of broth.

## STEWED CHICKEN AND DUMPLINGS
### *(8 servings)*

| | |
|---|---|
| 1 baking hen, disjointed (4 or 5 lbs.) | 1 onion |
| 1 T salt or more to taste | 1 bunch celery tops or 3 stalks celery |
| 2 qts. water | 2 T chopped parsley |
| ¼ t black pepper | 1 carrot |
| ¼ t M.S.G. powder (optional) | |

Put chicken in a Dutch oven or covered iron pot with water, salt, pepper, carrot, onion, and celery tops (or stalks). Cook until chicken is tender enough to fall from bones (about 3 hours). Remove chicken and strain broth. Skim off all fat. Add dumplings (page 52) to broth and cook until done (about 15 minutes). Add chicken and parsley and let boil once. Place chicken on platter, surrounded by dumplings. Serve sauce separately. If too thin, thicken with 1 tablespoon (or more) of flour mixed with 2 tablespoons of cold water to form a smooth paste.

## TARRAGON CHICKEN
### *(6 servings)*

| | |
|---|---|
| 3 chickens weighing about 1¾ lb. each | 1 onion |
| Salt and pepper | 1 stalk celery |
| Salad oil, chicken fat or olive oil | 1 sprig each of parsley, thyme and tarragon |
| 2 carrots | 2 C water |

Allow ½ chicken for each person. Split down the back, salt and pepper and rub with salad oil, chicken fat or olive oil. Set the chickens under the flame to brown until golden-brown (see Broiled Spring Chicken, page 98). Place in a casserole, with carrots, onion, celery, parsley, thyme, and tarragon and any juice left from the broiling, plus the water. Set in moderate oven (350°) in a covered roaster and cook until chickens are done, about 1 hour.

To make the sauce:

| | |
|---|---|
| 4 egg yolks | ½ C thick cream |
| 1 T flour | 1 t fresh chopped tarragon or |
| 1 C chicken broth | ¼ t of the dried herb |
| 2 T chicken fat or butter | 2 T chopped parsley |

Beat the egg yolks with the flour. Add chicken broth and cook in double boiler with the chicken fat or butter until thick. Add cream, tarragon and chopped parsley. Stir while cooking. If sauce does not have enough body, add a chicken bouillon cube, tabasco, Maggi sauce, etc.

# *Duck*

## DUCKS GARNISHED WITH OLIVES

| | |
|---|---|
| 1 young duck weighing about 3 lbs. | ¼ C butter |
| 1 pod garlic | Salt and black pepper to taste |
| ¼ t powdered ginger | 1½ C water |
| ½ C sauterne or white wine | 2 T catsup |
| 1 small bunch celery leaves | 1 onion |
| Flour in which to roll duck | ½ C sliced olives |

Clean duck and wash well, removing all pinfeathers. Crush a pod of garlic with a teaspoon of salt and the ginger and black pepper and rub the fowl inside and out. Wrap in wax paper and let stand overnight in the icebox. Next morning rub the duck well with softened butter and dust with flour. Brown under the flame. Transfer to a roasting pan. Place onion and celery in the duck, season again with salt and pepper. Add water, wine and catsup and cook in a covered pan in a moderate oven (375°) until duck becomes tender—1½ to 2 hours. Then skim off all fat from gravy and add olives. If gravy is too thick, thin with a bit of wine or water. If too thin, add a flour-and-water paste, allowing 1 tablespoon of flour mixed with 3 of water to each cup of broth. Simmer a few moments to blend and place duck on a platter surrounded with pickled peaches or baked apples stuffed with chutney.

# *Goose*

## RAGOUT OF GOOSE

This is a wonderful way to use any leftover roast goose.

| | |
|---|---|
| 2 C cooked diced goose meat | 2 onions |
| 3 T goose grease or melted butter or bacon fat | 1 pod garlic |
| | 1 No. 1 can tomatoes (optional) |
| 1 T flour or more to make sauce the proper consistency | ½ C chopped celery |
| 2 C gravy or consommé or 2 C water plus 3 bouillon cubes | ¼ t paprika |
| | ½ t caraway seeds |
| Salt and pepper to taste | 2 T chopped parsley or chives |

Sauté onions, garlic and chopped celery in melted fat in a Dutch oven or deep heavy metal skillet. Add gravy, consommé or bouillon cubes dissolved in water, tomatoes, and salt and pepper to taste. Add paprika and caraway seeds, cover pot, and let simmer slowly 25 to 30 minutes, or until sauce is well blended. Thicken with a flour-and-water paste. Add goose meat and let cook until thoroughly heated—4 to 5 minutes. The sauce should be the consistency of cream sauce; if it is not, more thickening may be needed. Pour into a dish and garnish with chopped chives or parsley. Serve with boiled noodles.

## ROAST GOOSE

After the goose has been well cleaned and washed, it should be rubbed with the following mixture the night before it is to be used:

### Rubbing Mixture for Goose

| | |
|---|---|
| 1 T salt | 1 crushed garlic pod |
| 1 t black pepper | ½ t powdered ginger |

Mash all these ingredients with a fork until they are well blended. Rub goose well with this, both inside and outside.

Put the goose in the icebox in a hydrator and keep until ready to stuff next day. If very fat, prick the breast all over with a sharp fork before baking. Put breast side up in the pan and cook with the top off in a moderate oven (350°) until goose browns. Pour off all excess fat, add 2 cups of water, cover the pan, and cook until goose is done (see paragraph below).

### Roasting the Goose

An 8- to 12-pound goose will take about 30 minutes to the pound in a 350° oven. Some people stuff the goose and some do not. We belong to the latter school. We put 1 whole onion with only the brown skin removed and 1 whole bunch of celery tops in the goose when it is put in the stove. This really improves the flavor. If the stuffing is preferred, use any one of the suggested stuffings given in this book. Do not fill the cavity too full, for remember that the stuffing expands when cooking. Sew the stuffing into the goose or lace in. Loop a string around the legs and tie together about 3 inches apart if the legs will not fit into the cavity just below the hole where the bird was drawn. When ready to serve, add 1 tablespoon of flour mixed to a paste with 2 or 3 tablespoons of water for every cup of broth. We find that 1 tablespoon of chopped parsley is a fine addition to this gravy. Serve with barley (page 154).

# *Guinea*

Guinea may be substituted for chicken in any recipe given in this book. It has a gamy taste and the meat is a little drier than chicken meat, but there is no difference in the method of preparation.

# Squabs

Follow any of the recipes for Doves or Quail in the Game Bird section of this chapter, substituting squabs for doves or quail. If the jumbo squabs are used, cook a little longer and add a little more liquid.

# Turkey

## BARBECUED TURKEY

Wash the turkey and dry well. Rub with olive oil or salad oil and sprinkle with salt and pepper. Set in a roasting pan with the lid off and put in a moderate oven (350°). Baste every 15 minutes until turkey browns—2 to 3 hours. Drain off excess fat. Add more salt and pepper if needed. Add Barbecue Sauce (2 to 3 cups, see recipe below) and put the lid on the roasting pan. Return pan to oven and continue cooking until turkey seems done. Allow 25 to 30 minutes' cooking time per pound for a turkey over 10 pounds, 20 to 25 minutes per pound for a bird up to 10 pounds. The toughness of the birds will vary, though, and they should be cooked until they stick tender when pierced with a fork. The bird must be basted with the sauce every 20 minutes or so. If the sauce cooks too low, add a little water from time to time.

### Barbecue Sauce

| | |
|---|---|
| 1 No. 1 can of tomatoes | 1 t sugar |
| 1 bay leaf | 1 pod of garlic |
| ⅛ t thyme | 1 onion, sliced |
| ⅛ t basil | Bunch of celery tops |
| ¼ t paprika | ¼ t chili powder |
| Salt to taste | 1 chopped onion |
| 2 T olive oil or chicken fat | 1 chopped green pepper |
| 1 T flour | ½ sweet red pepper, or use a |
| Tabasco or pepper sauce | canned pimento |
| ⅛ t M.S.G. powder (optional) | Dash of soy sauce |

In a saucepan, put the can of tomatoes, bay leaf, thyme, basil, sugar, garlic, sliced onion, celery tops, paprika, chili powder, and salt to taste. When the mixture boils, cover the pot and let simmer for 25 minutes or until the vegetables seem done. Put the mixture through a food mill, or press through a coarse strainer. In a skillet melt the chicken fat or olive oil. Brown chopped onion, chopped green pepper, and sweet red pepper or canned pimento. If the canned pimento is used, do not add it until ready to serve. When the vegetables seem yellow and done— about 5 minutes—add flour. Mix well and add the strained seasoned tomato pulp. Taste for seasoning, adding tabasco, more salt, or any condiment desired.

## TURKEY À LA KING
### (serves 25)

Meat from 1 baked turkey (10 to 12 lbs.) chopped in 1 or 1½-inch pieces (8 C chopped turkey)
2 T flour (heaping)
2 lbs. mushrooms
2 C turkey broth
2 C cream
2 T Worcestershire sauce
¼ t M.S.G. powder (optional)
¼ t soy sauce

1 green pepper, chopped
3 pimentos, chopped
1 large onion, chopped
2 C celery, chopped
1 C sherry
½ lb. butter (or use half margarine)
6 egg yolks
½ t paprika
Salt, pepper to taste

Bake turkey until tender, saving broth. Remove skin, and dice meat into 1 to 1½-inch cubes. (There should be about 8 cups of turkey meat.) Cut mushrooms into quarters and sauté in melted butter 5 minutes. Add celery, green pepper and onion and cook 10 minutes longer. Add broth, M.S.G. powder and soy sauce and mix with turkey. Cook 5 minutes. Beat egg yolks well, add cream mixed with 2 tablespoons of flour and made into a smooth paste. Combine mixtures. Add salt, pepper, paprika, and Worcestershire sauce and sherry. If too thick, thin to desired consistency with more broth or cream. Add pimentos. Let simmer all together and serve in patty shells, on toast, or over rice or noodles.

# Dressings for Game and Poultry

## EMILY DAVENPORT'S DRESSING FOR ROAST GOOSE OR DUCK

Mrs. Davenport is one of Louisville's most distinguished residents, and a leader in the cultural and civic life of the town. She is noted for her excellent table; any recipe of hers is well worth treasuring. Here's her favorite stuffing for roast goose. Use half of the recipe for roast duck.

½ C seeded raisins
½ C currants
1 C soft bread crumbs (freshly made)
1 C sour apples, chopped fine

1 mealy potato, riced
2 lbs. Italian chestnuts
4 T butter
Salt and pepper to taste

The apples are peeled and diced. The chestnuts are boiled until tender, and the skins are removed, but the chestnuts are left whole. The potato is boiled, peeled, and riced. Then all the ingredients are mixed together and stuffed into the well-seasoned fowl, before roasting. When goose is the piece de résistance, Mrs. Davenport serves the following menu: Clear soup; goose flanked by dishes of red cabbage and wild rice; Colcombet or some red wine; avocado and grapefruit salad with French dressing; orange and cream mousse.

## OUR POULTRY DRESSING FOR CAPON, TURKEY, ETC.

Cut recipe in half for smaller fowl.

½ C melted chicken fat, butter or margarine
4 large onions, chopped
6 stalks celery with leaves, chopped
4 eggs, well beaten
⅛ t ginger
⅛ t grated nutmeg
⅛ t poultry seasoning

⅛ t dried thyme
⅛ t dried powdered sage leaves
⅛ C minced parsley
12 slices bought white bread cut ½ inch thick
2 C broth, consommé, or 2 C water mixed with 4 chicken bouillon cubes
Salt and black pepper to taste

Melt fat in skillet. Add onions and celery and cook until soft and yellow but not brown. Tear the bread in pieces and pour the broth or consommé over it. Mash with the hands to form a paste. Add celery and onions and all other ingredients. Mix well. Put the mixture back on the stove and cook in a large skillet or Dutch oven until it holds together and seems to leave the sides of the pan. It should not be dry, but just stiff enough not to run.

## VARIATIONS OF OUR POULTRY DRESSING
### Sausage Stuffing for Capon, Turkey, etc.

Follow the recipe for Our Poultry Dressing for Capon, Turkey, etc., adding ½ pound highly-seasoned sausage meat, sautéed until most of the fat has cooked away, then drained. In this recipe the sausage fat could be substituted for the fat listed in the basic recipe.

## Oyster Dressing for Capon, Turkey, etc.

Omit the thyme and sage from above basic recipe for Our Poultry Dressing and add 12 drained chopped oysters to the mixture before stuffing in fowl.

## PEANUT OR PECAN STUFFING
### *(For wild duck or quail or doves)*

½ C shelled peanuts or pecans run through food chopper
½ C bread crumbs
1 T melted butter
¼ C heavy cream

1 t salt, or more to taste
¼ t freshly ground black pepper
½ t onion juice

Pour butter over crumbs and peanuts or pecans. Add cream and seasoning. Mix well together. Double this recipe for pheasants.

## WILD RICE DRESSING FOR QUAIL OR DOVES

1 small onion, minced
1 stalk celery, minced
1 T parsley, minced
½ t M.S.G. powder (optional)
1 C cooked wild rice
2 T butter, margarine or chicken fat

⅛ t crumbled dried thyme, or ½ t fresh herb, minced (optional)
½ C slivered mushrooms sautéed in 2 t melted butter (optional)

Melt the 2 tablespoons of fat, and brown onion and celery slightly, but do not burn. Add all other ingredients. Leftover wild rice may be used, and if it has been cooked with mushrooms, so much the better. Even if melted butter has been poured on the rice, it will not matter. If the ½ cup of slivered mushrooms is being used, sauté for 3 minutes in the butter before adding. Stuff dressing into quail or doves before roasting.

## RICE DRESSING FOR GAME OR FOWL

1 C rice (polished or wild)
1 onion, grated
1 egg, well beaten
Salt, black pepper to taste

4 T butter or chicken fat, melted
1 T parsley, chopped
Cream or broth to make a soft mixture (about 2 T)

Boil rice in salted water until tender (about 30 minutes) and drain. Add all other ingredients and mix well. If mixture is too stiff, add more cream or broth. Stuff into fowl before roasting.

## RICE-NUT DRESSING

Add 1 cup of chopped pecans, walnuts or lightly toasted peanuts to the above dressing before stuffing game or fowl.

# *Gravy or Sauces for Game and Poultry*

## EGG AND GIBLET SAUCE FOR BAKED FOWL
### *(Quickie!)*

| | |
|---|---|
| 1 C gravy in which fowl was cooked | 2 chopped, hard-boiled eggs |
| 1 T flour | Cooked liver, chopped |
| 1 T chopped parsley | Cooked gizzard, chopped |
| | Salt, black pepper to taste |

If gravy is not thick enough, add a flour-and-water paste (1 tablespoon of flour mixed with 2 tablespoons of water) and cook until it is the consistency of cream sauce. Add all other ingredients and serve. This sauce is fine with roast turkey, chicken or capon.

## SAUCE FOR REHEATING COLD FOWL OR MEAT
### *(Quickie!)*

| | |
|---|---|
| 1 C water, gravy or stock | 2 T butter |
| 1 small onion, diced | 1 T flour |
| 4 T catsup | Salt, pepper to taste |
| 2 bay leaves | |

Brown an onion in butter. Add flour and brown. Add water, gravy or stock, then other ingredients, stirring to make a smooth sauce. Put meat in baking dish. Cover with the sauce. Bake for 20 minutes. This is especially nice with duck.

# Meats and Meat Sauces

❖❖❖❖❖❖❖❖❖❖❖❖❖❖❖❖❖❖❖❖❖❖❖❖❖❖❖❖❖❖❖❖❖❖❖❖❖❖❖❖❖❖❖❖❖❖❖❖

## Beef

### BROILED PORTERHOUSE OR SIRLOIN STEAK WITH SHERRY SAUCE *(Quickie!)*
#### *(4 to 5 servings)*

1 porterhouse or sirloin steak,
   cut 1½ to 2 inches thick
Juice of 1 lemon
½ C consommé
1 T butter

½ C sherry
1 pod garlic (optional)
Salt, black pepper to taste
2 T chopped parsley (optional)

Rub the steak with pepper and the juice from ½ lemon. Put in a biscuit pan in which butter has been melted, and, with a brush, rubbed over the bottom of the pan. Rub garlic over the steak and drop the pod into the pan, if you wish. Put steak just 3 inches from the flame in a hot broiler. Cook 4 minutes. Salt well. Turn the meat and cook 6 to 8 minutes on the other side, or until steak is done to your liking. Remove steak from pan to a platter and keep warm. Remove garlic from juice in pan (if you have used garlic) and add consommé, sherry, the remainder of the lemon juice, and more salt. Let the mixture bubble well. Skim off the excess fat and serve the gravy plain or thickened with a flour-and-water paste, letting it come to a boil before serving. I add 2 tablespoons of chopped parsley to the gravy.

### LEFTOVER STEAK IN PAPRIKA MUSHROOM SAUCE *(Quickie!)*

Cut 2 cups of leftover cooked beef in finger-length slivers. Make up the recipe for Paprika Mushrooms (page 153). Add meat to the sauce, heat and serve over boiled rice or noodles.

## EMILY RUSH'S CHIPPED BEEF DE LUXE

### *(4 to 6 servings)*     *(Quickie!)*

| | |
|---|---|
| 1 T browned flour * (rounded) | ¼ lb. chipped beef |
| 1 C milk | ½ lb. mushrooms |
| 1 C cream or top milk | 4 T butter or margarine |
| 1 T Worcestershire sauce | 1 diced pimento |
| 1 t Kitchen Bouquet | Salt and pepper to taste |
| 3 hard-boiled eggs | ⅓ C sherry (optional) |

Make a paste of browned flour with ¼ cup milk. Add ¾ cup milk, 2 T melted butter or margarine and the cream or top milk (gradually), the Worcestershire sauce and Kitchen Bouquet. Add chipped beef (shredded). Cook until thick, stirring to prevent lumping. Sauté the mushrooms in the rest of the butter or margarine and cook 5 minutes. Add to the creamed beef. Add pimento and hard-boiled eggs, and correct the seasoning. Let cook 5 minutes, add sherry and serve at once on rounds of toast or in patty shells.

## FILET MIGNON WITH ORANGE AND
## MUSHROOM SAUCE     *(Quickie!)*

| | |
|---|---|
| 2 T olive oil or melted butter | 1 bay leaf |
| 1 whole beef filet | Salt and black pepper |
| 1 T flour | ½ lb. mushrooms |
| Juice of 2 oranges | 2 T butter |

Melt 2 tablespoons of butter, add chopped mushrooms, and cook 5 minutes, stirring occasionally. Add flour, and brown. Add orange juice, salt, pepper and bay leaf. Cover and let simmer until sauce seems the consistency of a thin cream sauce. Meanwhile rub the filet with the 2 tablespoons of olive oil or melted butter, and pepper. Broil under flame until only half done, about 5 minutes on each side. Salt and add to the mushroom-orange sauce and continue cooking until filet is as done as you wish it. Pour any meat drippings into the gravy and serve. Pass the gravy separately.

---

* See recipe for browned flour on page 231.

# IRON POT BEEF OR BEEF À LA MODE
### (An old Kentucky recipe)
### (8 servings)

| | |
|---|---|
| A 4-lb. pot roast (top round) | 1 blade mace |
| ½ t black pepper | ½ t mixed herbs (marjoram, |
| ¼ C mild vinegar | thyme, basil) |
| ¾ C red wine | ½ lemon, sliced thin |
| 1 pod garlic, sliced | Salt |
| 1 onion, sliced | Water-wine, mixed to make 2 C |
| 2 bay leaves | 4 carrots |
| 4 cloves | 2 onions |
| Fat for browning roast | Flour for dusting roast |
| 2 allspice berries | |

Rub roast with black pepper and put in a bowl. Let stand overnight with the vinegar, red wine, garlic, onion, bay leaves, spices, mixed herbs and lemon. This must soak at least 24 hours, but 2 or 3 days would be even better. Turn the roast occasionally so that marinade goes through it. To cook roast, dust with flour and brown in fat. Pour off excess grease and salt the meat well. Add the marinade in which meat was soaked and enough water and wine mixed to make 2 cups. Add carrots and onions. Cover and simmer slowly until meat is done—about 4 hours. More water may have to be added from time to time. If desired, 30 minutes before serving add 4 whole onions and 4 whole carrots. Serve on a platter surrounded with vegetables and pass the gravy separately. We serve Noodles in Brown Sauce with this (page 159). Do not make this recipe for a small family, as a small roast is not satisfactory prepared this way. This meat is delicious, sliced cold.

# JOCKEY CLUB STEAKS          (Quickie!)
### (4 servings)

This is the way you would be served club steaks at the famous Jockey Club restaurant at Churchill Downs, home of the Kentucky Derby.

| | |
|---|---|
| 4 club steaks cut 1 inch thick | 1 pod garlic |
| Salt and pepper to taste | 2 T butter |

Melt butter in skillet. Add garlic. Sprinkle steaks with pepper. Sauté in butter for 4 to 6 minutes (depending on how well done you like your steaks) letting first one side brown, then the other. Salt as soon as meat is brown. Remove garlic. Serve meat at once while very hot. Henry Bane Sauce (page 139) often accompanies these steaks in Louisville.

## JOHNNIE MORZELLE or JOHNNIE MORZETTE
### *(6 servings)* *(Quickie!)*

This delectable dish is familiar fare in Kentucky, where it may have originated. No two people prepare it exactly the same way, but here is one recipe.

8 ounces broad egg noodles, boiled in salted water until tender, 15 to 20 minutes, then drained and placed in the bottom of a greased baking dish. Cover with a sauce made as follows:

| | |
|---|---|
| 4 T butter or margarine | ¼ t basil |
| 1 lb. round steak, ground | 1 can tomato purée |
| 3 stalks celery, diced | 1 C water |
| 2 medium onions, chopped | Salt and pepper to taste |
| 1 green pepper chopped | 1 bay leaf |
| ½ C bread crumbs | ½ C grated Cheddar cheese |

Melt fat in skillet. Add meat, celery, onions and green pepper and cook 10 minutes, stirring to prevent sticking. Add the tomato purée, salt, pepper, basil, bay leaf and water. Simmer 5 minutes. Pour over noodles in dish and sprinkle with the cheese and bread crumbs. Bake until top browns in a moderate oven (375°). This takes from 20 to 30 minutes.

## OSCAR HEIMS' MEAT LOAF

Oscar was my husband's barber for many years. He loved to cook, and once gave me this recipe which he said had been taught to him by a French "chief." I really think it is about the best meat loaf I ever tasted. It is just as delicious cold as hot, especially when the cold left-over loaf is sliced thin and put between equally thin slices of white bread spread with mayonnaise and crisp lettuce leaves. It's good on the cold meat platter too.

| | |
|---|---|
| 1 lb. ground beef or veal | ¾ C bread crumbs |
| ½ lb. pork sausage (sage fla-vored) | 1½ C canned tomatoes |
| | 1 small pod garlic, chopped fine |
| 1 onion, chopped fine | 2 T parsley, chopped |
| ½ C water | ½ green pepper, chopped |
| 1 carrot, chopped fine | Salt, pepper to taste |
| 2 stalks celery, chopped fine | 2 t Worcestershire sauce |
| 1 egg | |

Mix all ingredients together, except tomatoes and water. Form into a loaf. Put in roaster. Pour tomatoes and water over meat and cover pan. Set in a moderate oven (375°) for 2 to 3 hours. Serve hot, with the gravy in the pan poured over the loaf. Thicken gravy if desired.

## POTTED ROUND STEAK WITH RED DEVIL GRAVY
### *(6 servings)*

1½ lb. steak
Flour
¼ C butter
4 sliced onions
1 C catsup

1 C water
1 t Kitchen Bouquet
1 T Worcestershire sauce
Salt and pepper

Roll the steak in seasoned flour and pound thin with a wooden mallet. If necessary, cut in pieces. Melt butter and fry steak brown. Remove meat and fry onions brown. Add to the onions the catsup, water, Kitchen Bouquet, Worcestershire sauce; salt and pepper to taste. Put steak back in pot. The old iron pot is the best utensil for this dish, though the Dutch oven is almost as satisfactory. Cover pot and cook steak 1½ to 2 hours or until tender. Add a little more water if gravy cooks too thick.

## MILDRED NEFF'S RED GATES FARM GOULASH
### *(8 to 10 servings)*

Mildred Neff, Director of the Nutrition Program of the Kentucky State Health Department, gave me this treasured recipe. She and Alexandra Matheson, Director of the Visiting Nurse Association, serve it often at their charming hundred-year-old farmhouse on Lovers Lane, just on the outskirts of Louisville.

1 large mild onion cut in rings
3 T butter
1 green pepper, chopped
3 C tomatoes (fresh or canned)
½ lb. top round steak,
   cubed
½ lb. fresh pork, cubed
½ lb. veal, cubed
1 t salt or more to taste

5 black peppercorns or ¼ t
   ground black pepper
1 t caraway seeds
2 bay leaves
½ t capers
1 T paprika
1½ C water, or more if needed
2½ lbs. sauerkraut
1½ C sour cream

We use a Bermuda onion when we can get one for this delectable dish. The onion is sautéed in butter for about 8 minutes, or until soft but not brown. Then the green pepper is added and cooked a few minutes before the strained or puréed tomato juice and pulp is added. This is simmered 10 minutes. Then the meat and all other seasonings except the salt and the sour cream are put into the pot. The sauerkraut may be salty enough, but let the mixture cook a while to be certain, then add salt to your taste. Cover the pot—we use a Dutch oven with a tight-fitting lid—and let the goulash simmer 1 to 1½ hours or until it is tender and the whole mixture is done. Just before serving, add 1 cup of the sour cream. Let the goulash cook until the cream is hot, but do not let it boil. Pour the mixture into a large serving dish or soup tureen and spread the remaining ½ cup of sour cream over the top. Dust with paprika. With this we also serve raw-potato pancakes, rye bread rolls and butter, chocolate cake, and large cups of steaming black coffee.

## ROAST BEEF DE LUXE WITH YORKSHIRE PUDDING

| | |
|---|---|
| 6 to 8 lbs. prime ribs of beef | 1 pod garlic |
| 2 onions, previously charred in | 1 C water |
| the oven* | Salt, pepper to taste |
| 1 t Kitchen Bouquet | 1 T Worcestershire sauce |

Rub the roast with pepper and garlic. Place in roaster on top of stove and brown on all sides. Then add salt to the meat, sprinkling it generously over the entire surface. If Yorkshire Pudding is to be made, the drippings should be poured into a 9- or 10-inch skillet. Add the previously charred onions to the roaster. Set the uncovered roaster in a hot oven (500°) for 20 minutes. Then reduce the heat to 400° for the remaining time. Fifteen minutes to the pound is a safe rule for roasting moderately rare or medium-done beef. If you like the meat very, very rare, cook 12 minutes to the pound. Twenty minutes before removing meat from oven, pour off excess grease and add water, Worcestershire, Kitchen Bouquet, and more salt and pepper, if necessary. Rub the sides of the pan with the spoon to dissolve all the brown dried gravy. When meat is removed from pan, strain, skim, and serve the gravy without thickening. This should make a rich, black gravy. We like Horse-radish and Sour Cream Sauce with our roast beef:

### Horse-Radish and Sour Cream Sauce for Roast Beef

| | |
|---|---|
| 4 T prepared horse-radish | ½ t salt, or more to taste |
| 1 t sugar (optional) | 4 T thick sour cream |
| ¼ t black pepper | 2 t vinegar (cider vinegar) |

Mix all ingredients together, adding more sugar, vinegar or cream as needed. Serve cold with leftover meat. We like it cold with hot meat also, although you can heat it if you wish. It keeps well in a covered jar in the icebox.

---

*To char onions: wipe them with a dry cloth but do not wash. Leave on the outer skin—do not peel. Set in a container in a moderate oven (375°). Let onions roast until dark brown outside and soft inside—it will not matter if they burn a little on the outside.

## YORKSHIRE PUDDING FOR ROAST BEEF
*(6 servings)*

We always accompany our beef roast with Yorkshire Pudding, a recipe I once brought back from England and have treasured ever since. There are many versions of this traditional British dish, but the genuine article is a thin pancakish affair, crisp and crunchy on the outside, and inside the consistency of baked custard or egg soufflé. In the old days, the batter was poured in a skillet or pan and placed under the roast, which was probably being turned on a spit in the open fireplace over a bed of glowing embers. The drippings constantly basted the Yorkshire Pudding, making it brown on top. Then it was turned with a pancake turner and when that side had also browned, it was put on a hot plate and sent to the table immediately. Today we put the fat in the bottom of a 9- or 10-inch skillet, pour in our batter and bake the pudding in the oven. It must be rushed to the table as soon as it is done, for it is at the peak of deliciousness only when it is very hot. Cut into 6 pie-shaped wedges and douse with beef gravy or jelly. *To make the Yorkshire Pudding:* When the beef is browned before it is put in the oven, pour the drippings into a 9- or 10-inch skillet, There should be ½ cup; if not, add enough melted margarine, butter, or beef suet to make that amount. Set this pan of fat aside. Meanwhile, make the pudding thus:

| | |
|---|---|
| ¼ C flour | 1 C milk |
| 2 eggs | ½ t salt |

Beat eggs, milk, flour and salt (I use an electric mixer) for 3 minutes by the clock. Let stand 20 minutes to ½ hour. Just before cooking, beat for 3 minutes longer. Pour into a *hot* skillet containing the hot fat and set in a hot oven (400°) along with the roast. Cook until thoroughly brown and done. It will take 40 to 45 minutes. Serve at once.

## ROLLED STUFFED STEAKS WITH MUSHROOM DRESSING
*(8 servings)*

| | |
|---|---|
| 2½ lbs. round steak, cut very thin | 2 charred onions |
| 1 lb. mushrooms | 2 onions, chopped |
| 2 carrots | 1 pod garlic |
| 4 C water | 8 T butter or substitute |
| 1 t Kitchen Bouquet | Few drops of Maggi sauce |
| 2 T Worcestershire sauce | Flour to roll steak |
| | Salt, pepper to taste |

Steak should be cut into 8 pieces and beaten with a wooden mallet. Wash and scrape carrots well. Chop fine. Wash mushrooms and separate caps from stems. Add chopped stems to the carrots. Add 1 onion chopped fine and mix together with salt and pepper. Place 1 tablespoon of the vegetable mixture on each piece of steak (the steak squares should be about 4 inches square) and roll each square like a jelly roll. Secure the edges of the steak rolls with toothpicks or tie with strings. Salt and pepper outside of rolls. Roll in flour. Melt butter in skillet. Add steak and brown. Add 1 onion cut fine, and the garlic, also chopped fine. When steak is brown, remove to roasting pan. Add water, mushrooms, and all other ingredients, including the charred onions. (For charring onions, see page 119.) Place the lid on the roaster and bake the steaks in a rather hot oven (450°) for 30 minutes. Then reduce the heat to 400° and cook the steaks for 1½ hours. Remove the lid about 30 minutes before serving, to be sure the gravy will cook down and the meat be browned. If gravy cooks too low, add a little more water. It must *not* cook away. Cut strings before serving if the rolls have been tied. The toothpicks may be taken out at the table. Serve gravy over steaks or pass separately.

## SWEET AND SOUR TONGUE
### *(6 servings)*

A great many Germans settled in Kentucky. Here is a recipe they undoubtedly brought from the Old Country.

| | |
|---|---|
| 2 lbs. beef tongue or | 1 onion stuck with 6 cloves |
| 8 small lambs' tongues | Small bunch celery tops |
| 2 t salt | 2 C tongue liquor |
| 2 sprigs parsley | ½ lemon, sliced into thin rings, |
| 2 T butter | without peeling (remove |
| 1 small onion | seeds) |
| 1 T flour | More salt and pepper if neces- |
| ¼ C raisins | sary |
| ¼ C brown sugar | 1 to 2 T wine vinegar or cider |
| ⅛ t black pepper | vinegar |
| 2 bay leaves | |

Put meat into a soup kettle with the salt, pepper, 1 bay leaf, the onion stuck with 6 cloves, the sprigs of parsley, and the celery tops. Add 2 quarts of water, cover and let boil until tongue is tender, which will depend on the size. A large beef tongue takes from 4 to 6 hours, the small ones, 2 to 3 hours. If tongue is cooked in a pressure cooker, 1 hour will do for the large tongue, ½ hour for the small ones. (Use only 1 quart of water in pressure cooker.) Peel off the tough skin and put the tongue back into the broth to simmer until very soft and tender. Remove from broth, trim, and set aside for the moment. To make the gravy: Strain the broth. Only 2 cups will be required, but the rest may be used in soups, gravies, etc. Melt the butter in a skillet or Dutch oven and grate the small onion into this. When it begins to brown, add flour and let that brown also. Now slowly add the tongue liquor. Stir to keep from lumping, but if lumps appear, strain. To the gravy add the sliced lemon without peeling (remove seeds), 1 bay leaf, raisins, brown sugar, and wine vinegar or cider vinegar (taste to see how acid the sauce should be). Add more salt and pepper if necessary. Now add the skinned, trimmed tongue, either whole or cut into slices. Cover the skillet or pot and let simmer 15 minutes. Serve with boiled cabbage and buttered noodles, with apple strudel or pie and coffee for dessert.

## VARIATIONS OF LEFTOVER COOKED BEEF
### Ground Beef Hash
#### (6 servings)

2 C ground cooked beef (from the roast or sirloin steak if possible)

2 C finely diced, cooked, Irish potatoes

2 T butter or drippings from meat

½ C consommé, gravy, or cream to make hash stiff enough to hold together

2 T chopped parsley

¼ C bread crumbs, freshly ground

1 egg

2 medium-sized onions, grated

Salt and black pepper to taste

1 T Worcestershire sauce

Dash soy or Maggi sauce

Pinch M.S.G. (optional)

Melt butter or drippings and add grated onions—both juice and pulp. Brown. Pour over meat and potatoes in a bowl. Add all other ingredients, pouring in the consommé, gravy, or cream last of all. Return to stove and cook in skillet until mixture becomes mushy and the right consistency to mold easily—it should not be dry, however. Stir constantly. When mixture is soft and seems to leave the sides of the pan set aside to cool. If too runny to mold into patties, add a few more crumbs; if too thick, add a little consommé, but remember it thickens considerably when chilled. Pour into a bowl, cover, and set in icebox until firm. Form into flat, round cakes, a little larger and thicker than hamburgers. Brown in skillet in melted butter or roast beef drippings. Serve plain or with a poached egg on top of each patty. Pass homemade Chili Sauce or Tomato Catsup with this—I like to top my catsup with a dab of French or Creole mustard. This same hash mixture can be put in a greased casserole or baking dish and cooked in a moderate oven (375°) ½ hour, or until meat browns on top. Cut into squares or pie-shaped wedges (depending on the shape of your baking dish) and serve.

### Old-Fashioned Chopped Southern Beef Hash
#### *(6 servings)* *(Quickie!)*

| | |
|---|---|
| 3 C leftover steak, roast, etc. | 3 T butter |
| 4 medium-sized onions, chopped | 3 C stock, gravy, consommé, etc. |
| 3 medium-sized raw potatoes, peeled and cubed | 1 t Kitchen Bouquet |
| 1 T Worcestershire sauce | Salt, pepper to taste |

Melt butter. Add onions and meat. Cook 5 minutes, but do not let onions burn. Add potatoes and all other ingredients. Simmer until gravy is thick and potatoes done—25 to 30 minutes. Serve on split buttered hot biscuits, toast, rice, noodles or what you will.

# *Lamb*

NOTE: To remove a strong odor from lamb or mutton, rub with lemon juice and let stand about 2 hours before baking. Juice from half a lemon will be needed for a lamb shoulder and a whole lemon for a large leg.

## JULIA DUKE HENNING'S
## BREADED LAMB CHOPS EN PAPILLON
### *(4 lamb chops)*

This recipe was given me by Mrs. Samuel Henning, daughter of the famous Civil War general, Basil Duke, brother-in-law of the daring Confederate raider, General Morgan.

| | |
|---|---|
| 4 lamb chops | 1 hard-boiled egg yolk, riced |
| Grated rind ½ lemon | 2 T finely diced parsley |
| 1 T lemon juice | 2 to 3 T bread crumbs or more if needed |
| 2 T sherry | Salt and pepper to taste |
| 2 T melted butter | |
| 1 t onion juice and pulp | |

Mix melted butter, onion juice and lemon juice. Combine the dry ingredients—hard-boiled egg yolk, parsley, lemon rind and bread crumbs. Dip chops in the butter mixture, then in the crumb mixture. Then sprinkle each chop with salt and pepper. Cut 4 squares of parchment paper large enough to fold around chops and lap over edges, and brush both sides with sherry. Wrap each chop securely in the wet paper, tying it with string. Place chops in a baking dish in a moderate oven (375°) and leave 25 to 30 minutes. Chops should be done by then. Use large single chops. If double chops are used, they will need a longer time to cook.

## CROWN ROAST OF LAMB

Follow recipe for Crown Roast of Pork (page 127), substituting lamb for pork and filling the center of the roast with highly seasoned ground lamb to which has been added ground onion and chopped parsley. Serve mint sauce or mint jelly, or any tart jelly (plum, currant, etc.) with this roast.

## ROAST LAMB
### *(6 servings)*

| | |
|---|---|
| A 4- or 5-lb. leg or shoulder of spring lamb | 2 C water |
| Olive or salad oil | 1 T Worcestershire sauce |
| 1 garlic pod, crushed | 1 t Kitchen Bouquet |
| 1 diced onion | Extra salt and pepper |
| Salt and black pepper | 1 T flour |

Rub the leg of lamb with olive or salad oil, a crushed garlic pod, salt and black pepper (freshly ground if possible). Put in an uncovered roaster and place in a moderate oven (350°). Turn occasionally, but let remain until the lamb is crisp and brown all over. This takes about 2 hours. Pour off excess fat but do not discard any brown particles of meat or gravy. Add water, into which the Worcestershire sauce and Kitchen Bouquet have been stirred. Add the extra salt and pepper and the diced onion. Put the lid on the roaster, return it to the oven and continue to cook the lamb for another hour or two until it sticks tender. Strain the gravy. There should be about a cupful; if not, add enough water to make that amount. To thicken gravy, allow 1 tablespoon of flour and 2 tablespoons of water for every cup of gravy. Make a paste of the flour and water and add to the gravy.

## VARIATIONS OF ROAST LAMB
### Roast Lamb with Ben Buckner's Sauce

This is the recipe of my friend, Marion Green, of the Louisville *Times*. Marion got it from her cousin, Ben Buckner, and Ben got it from the old colored woman who made it famous in Kentucky, and she got it from Paris. Here's the story: Some few years after the Civil War, when Kentucky's General William Preston was American Minister to Spain, he took along his colored cook. But while she could prepare an excellent dinner, her food lacked a continental flavor, so the General sent her to Paris where he apprenticed her to an internationally known French chef. She was an apt pupil and a credit to her patron. When he died she returned to Lexington to become a cateress in her own right. The society ladies refused to pay her price ($20.00 to cook a meal, then considered exorbitant) but she served the local bachelors some of those delightful dishes that had made the General's dinners so famous. A few of her recipes she never would disclose, but here is one that was teased out of her:

| | |
|---|---|
| 1 C lamb gravy (unthickened) | Salt |
| ¼ C catsup | Red and black pepper |
| 2 t flour | ⅛ t allspice |
| ¼ C acid jelly | ½ C claret |
| 1 t brown sugar | |

To the unthickened gravy add the catsup mixed with the flour, jelly, brown sugar, salt, red and black pepper, and allspice. If the gravy has already been thickened, omit flour. Stir the mixture well, pour into a small skillet or saucepan and set over a low flame on top of the stove. When the mixture comes to a boil, add claret and heat once more. Serve at once.

## Sour Cream and Chive Sauce for Cold Lamb

| | |
|---|---|
| ½ C sour cream | 1 T finely minced parsley |
| ¼ C mayonnaise (homemade) | ¼ t prepared yellow mustard, |
| 1 T minced shallots | or more to taste |
| Salt, pepper, tabasco to taste | Paprika for dusting over sauce |
| 1 T minced chives or green onion tops | |

Mix all ingredients together. Put in a sauceboat or bowl. Dust with paprika. Serve with cold sliced lamb.

## Roast Lamb with Rosemary

Follow the recipe for Roast Lamb (page 124), adding 1 teaspoon of freshly minced rosemary or ½ teaspoon of the dried herb to the meat when it is put in the oven and substituting 1 cup of white wine for one of the cups of water.

## MARLEY MARTIN'S SHEESH-KABAB
### *(8 servings)*

A 5- or 6-lb. leg of lamb cut in
1½-inch squares
2 C Burgundy wine
½ C vinegar
⅓ C olive oil
2 medium-sized onions, sliced
Salt to taste
3 crushed garlic cloves (the original recipe called for 6)

12 whole cloves
1 t rosemary
3 bay leaves
1 scraped, sliced carrot
Pepper to taste
¼ C diced celery
Mushroom caps and tomato
slices or wedges for skewer-
ing

Trim lamb. Cut into steaks and then cut the steaks in 1½-inch squares. Place all the above ingredients, except mushroom caps, tomato slices, salt and pepper, in a bowl. Add the lamb and marinate at least 24 hours —48, Mrs. Martin says, is better. When ready to prepare the lamb, drain but do not wipe dry. Place on skewers, alternating a slice of lamb with a washed mushroom cap and a slice of firm tomato. Put at least 4 slices of lamb on each skewer. Brush the lamb, mushrooms, and tomatoes with olive oil; salt and pepper freely, and broil over charcoal about 25 minutes, turning constantly. That is the way to prepare the lamb out-of-doors. For indoors, Mrs. Martin puts the mushrooms, tomatoes, and lamb on very long skewers (I had some made especially, 2 feet long). She lets the wood logs in her living-room grate burn low, then puts a green log behind them and slants the skewers over the grate, resting the ends on the green log. She turns the meat constantly until it seems done. She serves one or two skewers to each person along with cooked barley, green salad, cheese, crackers and fruit, and lots of coffee.

# *Pork*

"May you always eat high on the hog."—(Old Kentucky saying.)

## BAKED PORK CHOPS WITH APPLES
### *(6 servings)*

6 chops, cut 1½ inches thick
Flour
1 T Worcestershire sauce
3 apples, peeled, cored, and cut
in half
Salt, pepper to taste

2 T fat
2 T cream
1 t Kitchen Bouquet
Sugar
1 C water

Season chops with salt and pepper and dip in flour. Fry in fat until golden-brown, then set aside in baking dish. Add 2 tablespoons of flour to fat in skillet and let brown. Add cream, Worcestershire sauce, Kitchen Bouquet and water, stir until smooth, and pour over chops. Put half an apple on each chop, sprinkling each half with sugar. Cook 45 minutes to 1 hour in moderate oven. Baste often. If gravy is not thick enough, thicken with a paste made of 1 tablespoon of flour and 2 of water for every cup of gravy.

## BOILED SPARERIBS WITH ONION GRAVY
### *(6 servings)*

This was a typical Sunday morning breakfast dish in Alabama when I was a child. It is equally good today for a weekday supper.

| | |
|---|---|
| 2 lbs. spareribs, cut in servings | ⅛ t pepper, or more to taste |
| Water | 1 T Worcestershire sauce |
| 1 large onion | 1 t Kitchen Bouquet |
| 1 pod garlic | 2 C broth |
| 1 bunch celery tops | 2 T flour (for paste) |
| 2 t salt | |

Boil the spareribs in a Dutch oven, covering with water and adding chopped onion, chopped pod of garlic, bunch of celery tops, tied together (remove when done), salt, black pepper, Worcestershire sauce and Kitchen Bouquet. Simmer 2 hours or until done. Strain the liquor (there should be about 2 C) and skim off excess grease. Thicken with a paste made of flour and 2 tablespoons of water. Cook until thick. Pour back over spareribs and let heat. Serve with boiled hominy grits (see recipe on box), hot coffee, waffles and honey.

VARIATION: The ribs can be browned under the flame of the grill after boiling, and Barbecue Sauce (page 139), substituted for the onion gravy.

## CROWN ROAST OF PORK WITH SAUSAGE STUFFING OR CHESTNUT AND PRUNE STUFFING

| | |
|---|---|
| 2 pork rib roasts | 1 T Worcestershire sauce |
| 1 lb. pork sausage | 1 t Kitchen Bouquet |
| 1 C water | Salt, pepper to taste |

Have the butcher skewer the roasts together. Salt and pepper to taste, and fill the center of the roast with pork sausage (page 132). Place roast in pan. Mix together the water, Kitchen Bouquet and Worcestershire sauce and pour this over the roast. Cook in a very hot oven until the roast begins to brown. Reduce the heat to 375° and cook 3 to 3½ hours, or until meat is thoroughly done. Do not cover the pan. When roast is done, place it on a large platter and fit a paper frill on bone end of each chop. Thicken the gravy with flour and water paste, using 1 tablespoon of flour and 2 tablespoons of water to each cup of broth. Garnish roast with parsley and surround with browned whole potatoes. This roast is always served with applesauce.

### Chestnut and Prune Stuffing

Prepare the roast as above, omitting the sausage filling. Half an hour before the roast is to be removed from the oven, fill the cavity with chestnuts and prunes prepared according to the recipe on page 152.

# *Ham*

## BAKED TENDERIZED HAM IN CHAMPAGNE OR GINGER ALE

| | |
|---|---|
| 1 qt. champagne or ginger ale | 1 ham weighing 12 to 20 lbs. |
| 1 qt. water | 1½ C dark brown sugar |
| 1 pt. sorghum or Southern mo- | 1 T prepared mustard |
|    lasses | Whole cloves |

Just before baking, weigh the ham. Place it in the roaster. Pour over it the molasses, water, and champagne or ginger ale. Cover the roaster and bake the ham in a moderate oven (350°), allowing 15 minutes to each pound and turning the meat every hour. If the liquor evaporates, it will be necessary to add more water from time to time. When ham is tender, remove it from the stove and with a knife peel off the top skin (do not throw it away, it gives a fine flavor to beans, greens, or cabbage). Dice the ham fat but do not cut through to the meat. Into each little square of fat place 1 whole clove. Smear the mustard over the surface of the fat. Pat on brown sugar and place the ham under grill until the sugar melts and the ham is glazed. If the ham is to be served hot, it should be cooked the day it is used, but if it is to be sliced cold, it may be cooked the day before. The hot ham is often accompanied by the following:

## Jelly Sauce

1 glass tart jelly (plum, grape,     1 t prepared mustard (heaping)
   currant, etc.)

Mix jelly and mustard in a saucepan. Place over a burner and when jelly
melts and comes to a boil the sauce is ready to serve.

# VARIATIONS OF BAKED TENDERIZED HAM

## Hambalaya                              *(Quickie!)*
### *(12 servings)*

1 lb. cooked ham, diced fine     2 medium-sized onions, chopped
1 lb. pork sausage, (links)      1 clove garlic, chopped
1 small can tomatoes             1 pt. cooked shrimp
1 C rice, uncooked               1 T flour
1 pt. oysters                    1 T chopped parsley
2 C water                        Salt, black pepper to taste
1 green pepper, chopped

Into a large iron pot or heavy aluminum pan place the sausage. Brown
on top of the stove. Remove to a platter and cut each link in half. Add
the ham to the sausage fat and brown. Remove it to the platter with
the sausage. Pour off all but 4 tablespoons of the sausage and ham fat.
Add the flour, and brown. Add water slowly to make a thin sauce, then
add tomatoes, rice, green pepper, garlic, onions, parsley, salt, pepper,
ham and sausage. Cover the pot and allow the mixture to simmer until
the rice is done—20 to 30 minutes, stirring constantly to prevent sticking. Add the boiled shrimp and the oysters. Heat through. Serve at once.
This is a meal in itself.

## Ham Loaf with Cider and Raisin Sauce
### *(6 servings)*

2 C ground cooked ham          2 T tomato catsup
2 T butter                     2 t Worcestershire sauce
2 eggs, well beaten            ¼ t prepared mustard
1 small onion, chopped         Salt and pepper to taste
½ C bread crumbs

Melt butter in frying pan. When hot, add chopped onion. Fry until not
quite brown. Add to ham, which has been mixed with all the remaining
ingredients, blend, and shape into a loaf. Place in a well-greased baking
pan in a moderate oven (350°) for about 40 minutes. Turn out on a
hot platter and serve with raisin sauce, given below. Or serve with
Horse-Radish and Sour Cream Sauce (page 119).

## Cider and Raisin Sauce

| | |
|---|---|
| 1 C apple cider | 1 T prepared horse-radish |
| 1 T flour | 2 T butter |
| Pinch salt | ¼ C seeded raisins |

Melt butter in saucepan. Add flour and salt, and brown slightly. Add cider gradually, stirring constantly to make a smooth paste. Add horse-radish and raisins and serve hot.

# KENTUCKY COUNTRY HAM

There is something about the flavor of a Kentucky cured ham that cannot be found in any other. It is richer, more nut-like and delicate than those of Virginia, Indiana, or any other State. Perhaps this flavor is due to the way the meat is cured. Perhaps the Kentucky hickory smoke is more fragrant than in other States, or perhaps the secret lies in the cooking. At any rate, hickory-smoked old country ham is perhaps Kentucky's most distinctive entry for the Culinary Hall of Fame. Prize specimens weigh from 18 to 25 pounds and, in the opinion of most experts, have been aged 2 or 3 years, but I like mine just 1 to 1½ years old, as I think the meat is juicier.

Before these hams are cooked, they should be scrubbed with mild soap-suds and a stiff brush to remove all mold, and inspected carefully for "skippers." * If any soft spots are present they should be cut away. Then the ham should be placed in a pan under running water and left for 30 hours. (Allow the water to run continuously in a thin stream).

After trying numerous recipes, I have come to the conclusion that the best way to cook these old hams is to boil them. Not having a large enough boiler, we have cleaned our copper clothes-boiler, and use it successfully. Put the ham into the boiler—the pan half-filled with water. Cover and set on top of the stove where 2 burners can be turned on under it. When the water boils turn the burners very low and let the ham simmer 15 to 20 minutes per pound, depending on the age and hardness of the meat. Add more water if necessary, but never fill the boiler more than half full. Turn the ham from side to side ever so often. To test it, pull out the tiny end bones with your fingers. When you can

---

* About "Skippers": After you buy a country ham, especially one that has been hanging in a country store, it is essential to dip it in a large pot of boiling water for a period of 3 to 5 minutes in order to kill the flies' eggs or larvae which may be in it. If allowed to develop, the larvae become "skippers" and may penetrate the ham and spoil it. After taking the ham out of the boiling water dry it well by hanging on a peg or wiping with a towel. Roll the dry ham in either red or strong black pepper and tie it up in a clean cloth or a paper sack. Hang the ham in a cool dry room until you are ready to use it. Only hams that are to be kept for several months require this drastic treatment.

do that, you will know that your ham is ready to be taken off the stove. Another method of testing is to stick the ham through to the bone with a long-pronged fork. When it sticks tender, it is done. Old mammy-cooks insist that the ham must cool in the liquor in which it was boiled but I take mine out as soon as it is cooked, on occasions—especially when I am going to serve it hot.

Just before serving, place the ham in a flat pan with 1½-inch sides, trim off the top skin and enough of the fat to make a smooth surface. Then with a sharp knife mark the fat into squares, being careful not to cut through to the meat. Insert a whole clove in each square, dust the surface with powdered cloves, then spread a thin layer of prepared mustard over this. Next, pat a cupful of soft, medium-brown sugar over the mustard. In some parts of Kentucky, a tablespoon of water-ground corn meal is previously mixed with the sugar, but this is not essential. Place the ham in the grill or broiler, then light the broiler and close the door. Let the ham remain until the sugar bubbles and the whole surface seems glazed, but peek in every now and then to see that it does not burn. Remove the ham to a platter and bring it to the table. When sliced the meat will be of a dark reddish-brown color, flecked with white. (Strangers have thought such hams spoiled, and refused to eat them. But they were wrong, for the white specks are medals of merit. By them you can tell the genuine article.)

## FRIED COUNTRY HAM (Trigg County Way)
### *(Quickie!)*

Down in Trigg County, in Cadiz, Kentucky, are said to be found the best country hams in the world. Many have graced the White House table and even some crowned heads of Europe have ordered them from this little town. We stopped for lunch one day last spring at the hotel in Cadiz, and as long as I live I shall remember that meal—fried country ham with wonderful red gravy, black-eye peas, corn bread, greens, and strawberry shortcake topped by rich vanilla ice cream.

For weeks, in Allan Trout's column in the *Courier-Journal*, there was a heated discussion on how to make or "raise" the gravy that always accompanies fried ham. Some of his fans insisted that the only way to achieve a perfect result was to use coffee, others said plain tap water was good enough. Well, try them both and see which you prefer.

Cut a large country ham into ¼-inch-thick steaks. If the meat is thin enough, the steaks will not have to be parboiled; otherwise, they will need some preliminary cooking. Put just enough ham fat into the skillet to keep the meat from sticking. Have the skillet very hot. Add the ham steak or steaks and sear on both sides. Add a cup of coffee or water and when the mixture begins to boil put a top on the skillet, lower the heat, and let the ham simmer for 15 or 20 minutes or until the meat sticks tender when pierced with a fork. Most of the gravy will have cooked away but enough should be left to moisten the ham. This gravy is often reddish-brown in color.

If you like thicker steaks, cut them ½ inch thick and simmer in a covered Dutch oven with a cup of water until they are tender. I use a pressure cooker and the meat is ready after 10 minutes at 15 pounds pressure. Remove the steaks from the pan in which they were boiled and put them into a hot skillet. Brown on both sides rapidly and serve. No gravy accompanies them, as the water in which the meat was boiled does not seem to substitute for the gravy made the other way.

## NOEL RUSH'S PORK SAUSAGE
### *(6 lbs. of pork sausage)*

No book on Kentucky food would be complete without a recipe for pork sausage. Here's one I've always liked. It was given me by my friend Noel Rush, president of the Lincoln Bank in Louisville. Mr. Rush makes his sausage out of pork tenderloins, and I must admit I do, too. We also use what is known as "backbone fat." But any good pork fat will do.

4 lbs. pork tenderloin or lean pork
6 t salt (or more to taste)
6 t pulverized sage leaves
3 t ground black pepper

2 lbs. pork fat (backbone fat preferred)
¾ t ground red pepper
2 t nutmeg
2 t coriander seeds, powdered or ground

Grind the meat and fat together, then mix with the other ingredients, kneading with the hands. Test a small cake by cooking and tasting. Add more seasoning, if necessary. Form into loaves. Wrap in wax paper and keep in icebox. Cut into ½-inch slices or form into cakes or patties. Cook in a hot skillet on top of stove. When brown on one side, turn and brown on the other. When meat has cooked through, it is ready to serve. It is delicious with fried apples, and corn cakes or waffles with maple syrup, etc.

## SAVORY PORK TENDERLOINS
### *(6 servings)*

6 pork tenderloin slices cut 1 inch thick
1 C water
½ C cream (sweet or sour)
Salt and pepper to taste
4 T butter or margarine

1 small button of garlic
¼ t dried thyme or a few sprigs of fresh thyme
Flour in which to roll tenderloins

Salt and pepper meat and roll in flour. Melt butter or margarine in a deep skillet or Dutch oven. Add garlic and meat. Brown meat on both sides, adding more salt and pepper. Remove garlic if desired. Add water and thyme. Cover the pot and let meat simmer slowly one hour or until meat is tender. Do not let cook dry; add a little more water from time to time if necessary. Add cream. Heat but do not boil. If necessary, thicken the gravy with a flour-and-water paste—1 tablespoon of flour and 2 of water for every cup of gravy. Pork or veal chops are also delicious prepared according to this recipe.

# *Veal*

## NICK MARLOWE'S BRAISED VEAL CHOPS IN CASSEROLE

Nick Marlowe was my mother's houseman and general factotum in Montgomery, Alabama. He has had many jobs since then, including one as chef on a dining car of the L. & N. R. R. He is now working for Ruth and Charlie Morris and the last time we were at the Morris's for dinner he served us these chops and presented me with the recipe.

4 veal chops, cut ¾ to 1 inch thick

Salt, pepper, paprika, flour in which to roll the chops

3 T bacon grease, drippings, margarine, butter, or what have you

Dust chops with salt, pepper, and paprika and roll in flour. Brown in a skillet in melted fat. When both sides are brown, transfer the chops to a pottery or glass casserole with a lid, and cook 1 hour in a moderate oven (375°) in the following sauce:

2 T drippings in which chops were fried (Save all the browned flour particles)

1 T flour

1 C meat stock (or 1 C water mixed with 2 bouillon cubes or 2 t meat extract)

2 T catsup

1 pod minced garlic

1 T butter

2 T minced stuffed olives or minced canned mushrooms, or 1 T of each

2 t Worcestershire sauce

Pour off all but 2 tablespoons of drippings in the skillet in which the chops were browned. Add butter and flour and stir until it browns. Add the meat stock and all other ingredients and mix well. Pour over chops in casserole, put on the lid, and cook until chops are tender (about 1 hour). If sauce is too thick, thin with a little stock or water. If too thin, thicken with the flour-and-water paste.

# Veal Sweetbreads

### BOILED SWEETBREADS      (Quickie!)
#### (2 servings)

1 lb. sweetbreads (large thymus  1 small onion
   gland sweetbreads)              ⅛ t black pepper
1 bunch celery leaves            1 t salt, or more to taste
3 C water

Put all ingredients in the Dutch oven or chicken frier. Cover and boil until sweetbreads are tender—45 minutes to 1 hour. Strain broth and save for gravy or soup.

### SAUTÉED SWEETBREADS

Roll boiled sweetbreads in flour. Salt and pepper. Melt ¼ cup butter or margarine in a skillet. Add sweetbreads and cook until brown all over. Serve at once with or without crisp bacon.

### AUNT MENA'S CASSEROLE OF SWEETBREADS IN HERBED WINE SAUCE
#### (8 servings)

My father's sister got this recipe years ago from her Hungarian cook, and we have blessed both of them many times since. It is one of our specialties for party luncheons or Sunday night suppers.

6 sweetbreads (about 2½ lbs.)   1 bay leaf
6 C water                       4 whole allspice berries
Bunch of celery tops            ¼ t dried thyme
6 T margarine or butter         2 sprigs parsley
½ lb. fresh mushrooms           2 stalks celery, diced
6 carrots, scraped and cut in   1 C green peas, fresh or frozen
   rings                        1 T Worcestershire sauce
4 T flour                       ¼ C sherry, or more to taste
2 C strained sweetbread broth   2 whole cloves
1 onion                         1 T chopped parsley or chervil
1 t salt                        1 t sugar, if wine is dry
⅛ t black pepper

Prepare Boiled Sweetbreads (see above). Strain off liquor, saving it for sauce, and set sweetbreads aside to cool. When sufficiently cool to handle, remove skin from sweetbreads and separate in pieces. Do not mince them; they should be chunky in size. Place in the bottom of a casserole or baking dish. Meanwhile, melt the margarine or butter in a skillet and add the fresh mushrooms cut in quarters. Braise for 5 minutes. Add the diced celery stalks, carrots, scraped and cut in rings, the green peas, and more salt and black pepper. Cook 10 minutes longer. Mix the flour with the strained sweetbread broth and pour over the vegetables. Add the Worcestershire sauce, sherry to taste, bay leaf, allspice berries, cloves, chopped parsley or chervil, dried thyme, and sugar if wine is dry. Add more salt and pepper to taste and pour this mixture over the sweetbreads. Bake 30 minutes in a moderate oven set at 375°.

## SWEETBREADS MORRIS FLEXNER
### (4 servings)

My husband often complains that I use so many condiments, herbs and spices, he misses the flavor of the main ingredients. So, to placate him, I once concocted this mixture, which he devoured with zest and has since requested from time to time.

3 sweetbreads  
3 C water  
2 stalks celery (tops included)  
Bunch of shallots with green tops  
½ lb. mushrooms  
2 T butter  
1½ C sweetbread broth  
¼ C thick cream  
Couple of sprigs of parsley  

1 small onion, quartered  
¼ t peppercorns or freshly ground black pepper  
1 t salt  
1 C cooked fresh or frozen peas  
2 hard-boiled eggs, diced not too small  
2 T chopped parsley  
Dash of paprika  
2 scant T flour  

Boil the sweetbreads with the water, celery, parsley, and onion. Add peppercorns or black pepper, salt, and shallots. When mixture comes to a boil, put a top on the pot, turn the flame low and let cook 45 minutes or until the sweetbreads are tender. Strain liquor and set aside. Meanwhile, sauté the fresh mushrooms in the butter for 10 minutes. Add the peas and hard-boiled eggs. Add the sweetbreads cut in chunks. (Remove any veins or skin and discard.) Add the sweetbread broth, and thick cream mixed to a paste with flour. Stir to make a smooth sauce. Taste for seasoning, adding more salt and pepper if needed. Pour into a serving dish, sprinkle the surface with the chopped parsley and dash of paprika. Serve on toast or buttered hot biscuits. This is also good over rice or in patty shells.

## SWEETBREADS WITH PAPRIKA MUSHROOMS

Add 1 pound of boiled tender sweetbreads to the Paprika Mushrooms (page 153) just before serving, and let simmer to heat thoroughly.

## SWEETBREADS WITH ROSEMARY

Prepare Boiled Sweetbreads (page 134), adding ½ teaspoon of rosemary and 1 clove of garlic to the water in which the sweetbreads are cooked. Strain the liquor and set aside. Roll the sweetbreads in flour, after salting and peppering to taste, and brown in 4 tablespoons of olive oil. Add 2 tablespoons of flour to the sweetbreads in the skillet and stir the flour until it is smooth. Then add the liquor from the sweetbreads, slowly stirring to prevent lumping. Let the liquid come to a boil and serve over boiled noodles or rice. One tablespoon of minced parsley and extra fresh chopped rosemary (a few sprigs) may be added to the sauce just before serving, if desired.

## VEAL BREAST WITH CARAWAY DRESSING
### *(6 servings)*

Have the butcher cut a pocket in a 3- or 4-pound breast of veal. Season with salt and pepper, roll in flour, and fill with the following stuffing:

| | |
|---|---|
| 2 C rye bread crumbs moistened to a paste with | 2 T chopped parsley |
| 1 C consommé or gravy | 1 chopped onion |
| 2 eggs beaten stiff | 1 t caraway seeds |
| 1 pod chopped garlic | Salt, pepper to taste |

Mix well and stuff into veal pocket. If mixture is too runny, cook in a skillet in which 2 tablespoons of butter have been melted, until enough moisture has cooked away to make a rather stiff dressing, but not an entirely dry one. Put stuffed breast in roaster and add:

| | |
|---|---|
| 2 C water | Salt, pepper to taste |
| 1 T Worcestershire sauce | ¼ t M.S.G. powder (optional) |
| 1 t Kitchen Bouquet | |

Cook 2 hours or until meat is tender. If gravy is too thin, thicken with 1 tablespoon of flour made into a paste with 2 tablespoons of water. If gravy is too thick, add a little water.

## VEAL CUTLET AU VIN EN CASSEROLE
### *(4 servings)*

This is a simple dish to prepare and one you can serve to any company. Have a 1½-pound veal cutlet ½ inch thick cut from the leg. Cut it into 4 pieces. Salt and pepper the pieces and flour each side.

4 T olive oil, or 2 T butter and  
    2 T olive oil  
Pod of garlic  
½ lb. mushrooms  
¾ C water  
½ t sugar

2 sprigs fresh thyme, or a pinch  
    of the dried herb  
1 bay leaf  
Salt and pepper to taste  
¾ C white wine  
Flour to thicken gravy

Melt olive oil, or butter and olive oil, in a heavy metal skillet. Add garlic and the 4 pieces of veal cutlet. Brown quickly on each side, but do not attempt to cook through. Transfer the veal pieces to a casserole, adding the garlic or not, as you wish. Add thyme and bay leaf. Toss the mushrooms into the skillet in which the veal was cooked. Light the flame again and stir the mushrooms a few moments. Add salt and black pepper to taste, then add the water and cook until all the brown particles from the meat have been absorbed, about 3 minutes. Pour the mushrooms over the veal. Now also pour over it the white wine and the sugar. Put the top on the casserole, set it in a moderate oven (375°), and let cook 1 hour. Remove casserole and thicken gravy if necessary, adding more salt and pepper, if desired. Veal chops are delicious prepared this way. Use 4 of them. Frogs' legs can also be prepared by this recipe. Cook ½ hour in the oven instead of an hour and allow 2 small or 1 large pair to each serving.

## VEAL CROQUETTES

Follow the recipe for Solger's Chicken Croquettes (page 100), substituting roast veal for chicken. Mr. Solger is said to have preferred veal to chicken in making these most delicious of all croquettes.

## VEAL ROAST WITH ANCHOVIES
### *(As served at Louisville's Old Vienna Restaurant)*

There was once a restaurant in Louisville famous all over the country for its gourmet Viennese recipes. It was called the Old Vienna, and closed soon after I came to Louisville to live. Someone told me about this Veal Roast recipe (one of their specialties) and when I talked to my butcher about it he said, "You don't have to tell me how to prepare that—I used to do it for the Old Vienna!" Don't let the ingredients put you off—the stuffing completely disintegrates while cooking and there is left only a solid slice of the most deliciously flavored meat you will taste in a long time. This is just as good cold as hot. Slice very thin. It makes wonderful sandwiches, too. You had better not try to prepare this yourself for roasting—let your butcher do it, sewing or tying the anchovies and kidneys into the roll. That's what I do.

A 4- or 5-lb. veal roast, cut from the leg
1 whole can anchovy fillets (12 to 18)

1 or 2 veal kidneys, depending on size of the roast. Be sure the pelvis or white part in the center has been removed. You must use only the outside lumps of meat, free from fat.

The anchovies and kidneys should be tied securely in the meat before it is rolled. When ready to cook it, you will also need the following ingredients:

2 T olive oil, bacon fat, or butter
1 pod garlic
2 onions, 1 peeled, 1 charred*
2 T chopped parsley
2 carrots

2 C white wine, or more if this cooks down
Pepper to taste
Do not add salt until meat is half-done—the anchovies are very salty and added salt may not be necessary

Rub the meat with pepper and oil and braise in the roasting pan in which it is to be cooked. The garlic browns with the roast. When meat is brown all over, add wine and let get hot, then add carrots and 1 whole onion, peeled, and put the top on the pan. Set in a moderate oven (375°) and let cook 30 to 40 minutes per pound, or until veal is done enough to cut with a fork. Taste every now and then to see whether or not the gravy is properly seasoned. Add the charred onion as soon as it is brown on the outside and soft inside. Mash into the gravy with the back of a spoon. When the meat is about half-done and the juices have had time to blend, I add the salt. Also, I never let the gravy cook away entirely. Add more wine from time to time if necessary. There should be about a cup of gravy when the meat is ready to serve, and sometimes I pour this off and add a little more wine to the meat, keeping the rich brown gravy to reheat when needed. This gravy thickens itself and is without a doubt one of the most delicious I have ever tasted. Add the chopped parsley to it before sending it to the table.

They tell an old joke in Kentucky about a man who stopped in a mountain home one evening and asked for hospitality, as he was too far away from any town to reach a hotel. The old couple said he could stop with them. When they put the food on the table, there were only two pork chops in a dish with lots of gravy. The woman took one chop, gave her husband the other, and said to the stranger, "You know, me and my husband is funny. We likes the meat—most folks likes the gravy." Well, if you are one of the folks "what likes the gravy," you'll have a field day with this gravy. It is just about the best I ever tasted.

---

* To char the onion, see page 119.

# Gravies and Sauces for Meat

## G. W. MUNZ'S CHARLESTON HOUSE BARBECUE SAUCE SANS GARLIC AND ONIONS
### (Quickie!)
### (For spareribs, pork shoulder, stuffed peppers, etc.)

This delicious sauce is a specialty of Charleston House, one of the really fine eating places near Louisville. It is just across the river in Charlestown, Indiana, only 20 minutes away by car. The House is run by Mr. and Mrs. Munz, who know good food and see that it is served to their patrons. I especially like this sauce because it is one of the few barbecue sauces free from onion and garlic, yet it has a tangy flavor just as satisfactory as the others. I add ½ cup of butter to my sauce when I make it, although Mr. Munz does not, and I cut down on some of the pepper, as this is a very hot sauce.

| | |
|---|---|
| A No. 2 can tomato purée | 1 T black pepper |
| 1 bottle chili sauce | 1 T salt |
| 2 T allspice | 1 T ground mustard |
| 1 C red wine vinegar or cider vinegar | 4 T sugar |
| 2 C ginger ale | 1 T mace |
| ½ C butter | 1 t cayenne pepper |

Mix thoroughly and cook 20 minutes over a slow flame. When done, it is the consistency of catsup.

Serve the above sauce on spareribs which have been washed, dried and baked in a slow oven (350°), allowing 20 minutes per pound. Or use with any recipe calling for Barbecue Sauce, such as Barbecued Turkey.

## HENRY BANE SAUCE FOR STEAKS OR ROAST BEEF
### (Quickie!)

Guests at Louisville's nationally-known Pendennis Club are served a distinctive, tangy, very peppery sauce with every order of broiled steak or roast beef. This wonderful condiment, which many prefer to any bottled meat sauce, was named in honor of its inventor, Henry Bane, for years the Club's dignified headwaiter. His masterpiece is still compounded in secrecy by some of his relatives. I have made my own version of it:

1 C Heinz's tomato catsup        ¼ bottle genuine tabasco
½ C Lea & Perrin's Worcester-    ½ C (Major Grey's) chutney
   shire sauce                   Salt to taste

Blend the tomato catsup with the Worcestershire sauce, the tabasco and the chutney. (I use Major Grey's Bombay Chutney when I can get it, although any good brand will do. The paste variety is best, but the other is satisfactory if the individual pieces are put through the finest blade of the meat grinder.) Stir well and salt to taste. Pour into a bottle and pass with steak or roast beef.

VARIATION: Since this sauce is so very hot, we often mix it with equal parts of homemade chili sauce before serving it.

## ANNE CLAY BEAUMONT'S MUSHROOM SAUCE
### *(With bouillon or consommé base) (Quickie!)*
### *(4 to 6 servings)*

2 T butter or margarine         1 rounded T flour
½ lb. fresh mushrooms           1 T chopped parsley
Salt and pepper to taste        1 T Worcestershire sauce
1 can beef bouillon

Brown butter or margarine in a skillet and add the mushrooms. Separate caps from stems. Add salt and pepper to taste and cover pan or skillet. Cook 7 to 10 minutes, depending on size and freshness. Stir into the mushrooms the beef bouillon mixed with the flour. Cook until it thickens, then correct the seasoning. Just before serving, add the chopped parsley and Worcestershire sauce. This is a most useful and delightful sauce to serve with meat, especially leftovers. Slivers of beef or veal added to it are good to serve on omelets or waffles. Boiled sweetbreads cut into it are delicious on rice or toast. Use it to heat over a cooked roast where no gravy has been left, and on similar occasions.

# Vegetables

No MATTER how scarce or expensive some articles of food may become, our supply of vegetables is apt to remain plentiful and comparatively cheap. Regardless of our partiality to certain favorites, we'll grow sick of the sight of them unless we find new and interesting ways to prepare them. Not long ago I saw a Dictionary of Recipes—a French publication, not yet translated into English. There were 3,000 ways to cook potatoes. Yes, 3,000, and that was not a misprint. How many of us know 30? One of my favorite summer vegetables is fried green tomatoes served with chili sauce, a dish I had never heard of until I came to Kentucky to live. Nor did we make green tomato chutney or pie in Alabama. Have you served cooked celery as a winter vegetable? It's good boiled and topped with Hollandaise sauce, braised in butter, stewed in chicken broth, chilled and served as a cold salad, or creamed. And what about cucumbers? Do you ever give them to your family in any form except the traditional pickles or in salads? Have you eaten stuffed baked cucumbers? Have you tasted the subtle delicacy of cucumber soup, or of boiled young cucumbers without skin and seeds, served with hot Sour Cream Sauce or Mock Hollandaise? And what about carrots? Did you ever eat them candied and spiced; made into a whipped cream ring filled with mushrooms; or mixed with a cheese sauce and baked as a soufflé?

In this chapter I have tried to give some of the unusual sauces and combinations of vegetables we have liked and have added to our files.

## Non-Starchy Vegetables

### ARTICHOKES BOILED, WITH MOCK OR SOUR CREAM HOLLANDAISE

Place artichokes (the French Globe variety) in a deep pot with a tight-fitting lid—we use the Dutch oven. Cover with water, add salt and a pod or two of garlic, if desired. Cover and let simmer until the hearts are tender. Cooking time will depend on the size and freshness of the artichokes—from 45 minutes to 3 hours. Drain them well, and serve with either of the Hollandaise sauces given in this chapter (page 162).

## ASPARAGUS IN TARRAGON BUTTER
*(3 servings)*                    *(Quickie!)*

Boil 12 stalks of fresh asparagus in salted water and drain; or, to cook, tie in bunches and stand upright in the bottom of a double boiler. Half fill the bottom of the boiler with salted water; if you want your asparagus to have a grass-green look, add ¼ teaspoon of soda. Yes, I know it destroys the vitamins, but get them some other way; the asparagus looks so tempting when green. Invert the top part of the double boiler over the bottom and put the boiler over a high flame on top of the stove. When the water begins to boil, lower the flame. Cook 20 minutes, or until the asparagus stalks stick tender. The tops will be steamed and the bottoms boiled. Remove bunches from water, cut strings, and serve with Tarragon Butter, made by browning ½ cup of butter and adding to it 3 tablespoons of tarragon vinegar and a dash of tabasco sauce. If fresh tarragon is available, use 2 tablespoons of the vinegar and 1 of minced fresh tarragon. This same sauce is also delicious on boiled or broiled fish.

## GRANDMOTHER FLEXNER'S GREEN BEANS
## WITH BROWN ROUX OR GRAVY
*(3 servings)*

1 lb. green beans, fresh or frozen
2 T bacon drippings, butter, or margarine
1 T flour, rounded
½ t sugar (optional)

2 C water
1 small onion, peeled and left whole
1 small onion, diced
Salt and black pepper to taste

Into a skillet put the bacon drippings, margarine or butter. Add the flour, and brown slightly. Add diced onion and cook until mixture is dark-brown, but not burned. Add the water slowly. Stir until slightly thickened and strain over the green beans, cut in 1-inch pieces. Add the whole onion (to lift out later). Salt and pepper to taste, add sugar, cover and simmer slowly 1 hour for fresh beans, ½ hour for frozen, or until beans are done. There should be a delicious dark-brown gravy the thickness of heavy cream. If beans cook dry, add a little more water.

## GRANDMOTHER FLEXNER'S GREEN BEANS
## WITH CORN
### *(6 servings)*

To the above recipe for Grandmother Flexner's Beans with Brown Roux or Gravy add a cup of fresh white corn, cut from the cob, and cook for the last 20 minutes before taking the beans from the fire. More salt, pepper, 1 teaspoon of sugar and ½ cup of water will be necessary. There should be a little thick gravy when the corn and beans are done, but the mixture should never be runny.

## GREEN BEANS WITH HAM HOCK
### *(6 servings)*

When baking a country ham, or a city one for that matter, cut off the hock and set it aside. It should weigh from 1 to 1½ pounds. This "end" meat, while full-flavored, is usually stringy and can be put to good use when cooked with vegetables.

| | |
|---|---|
| Ham hock weighing 1 to 1½ lbs. | A slice of very hot red pepper |
| 1 qt. water | or ⅛ t cayenne pepper |
| 2 lbs. green beans | 1 t sugar |
| More water if needed | Salt if needed later |
| | 1 onion, peeled but not diced |

Cover the hock with a quart of water, a slice of very hot pepper or the cayenne pepper, sugar, and onion. We use a Dutch oven for this, or a heavy aluminum pot with a tight-fitting lid. Simmer slowly for an hour or two or until the hock is almost done. Some of the water will have cooked away, and if you are using 2 pounds of beans, which is enough to serve 6 people, you will have to add more water to make up the original quart. Do not add salt at first as some hams are so salty that no other seasoning will be needed. Add the beans, put the top on the pan, and simmer slowly from 1½ to 2 hours, or until the beans are tender and have a glossy, almost transparent look. Taste and add salt and more pepper if necessary. By this time most of the liquor should have cooked away. That which remains is served with the beans. We call it "pot likker," and if you like to "dunk," crumble your corn pone into this and "smack yo' lips."

## GREEN BEANS WITH JOWL OR BACON

Follow the recipe for Green Beans with Ham Hock given above, substituting ½ pound of country-cured bacon or hog jowl for the ham hock.

## BRUSSELS SPROUTS WITH PECAN SAUCE
### (4 servings)                              (Quickie!)

1 pt. boiled, drained Brussels        ¼ C coarsely chopped pecans
  sprouts                             2 T butter
1 C cream sauce

To Brussels sprouts add cream sauce and mix well. Pour into a serving
dish and top with the chopped pecans, browned in butter.

## MRS. WIGGS' FRIED CABBAGE
### (4 servings)                              (Quickie!)

Who has not read about Mrs. Wiggs and the famous Cabbage Patch,
where she made her home? Alice Hegan Rice, who immortalized the
lovable Louisville heroine, is no more. But here is a dish to remind us of
Mrs. Wiggs and of the distinguished Louisville author who created her:

4 T bacon drippings or chicken        1 small head green cabbage,
  fat                                   shredded
1 onion, thinly sliced                1 C soup stock (or 2 bouillon
Slice of red hot pepper or a            cubes dissolved in 1 C water)
  dash of cayenne

Melt the bacon drippings or chicken fat in a deep, heavy iron pot—a
Dutch oven or Southern chicken fryer is best. Add the sliced onion and
the shredded cabbage. Add the soup stock or bouillon cubes and water.
Add slice of red hot pepper or dash of cayenne. Cover the pot and when
cabbage begins to sputter and boil, turn the heat low and simmer for ½
hour to 45 minutes. Serve with corn bread, of course. Spoon cabbage
and "pot likker" into saucers. Pass a cruet of cider vinegar with this
cabbage. "Dunk" your corn bread in the "pot likker" if you so wish—
it is in order when fried cabbage is on the menu.

## VIENNA RESTAURANT * SPICED CARROTS
### (4 servings)                              (Quickie!)

8 small carrots                       Juice ½ lemon
2 cloves                              1 T chopped parsley
1 bay leaf                            Carrot water
2 T flour                            2 T butter
1 t sugar, or more to taste          Pepper, salt

Boil carrots until done, in salted water, to which sugar, pepper, cloves
and bay leaf have been added. Melt butter in skillet, add flour and 2

* Note about the Vienna Restaurant under Veal Roast with Anchovies (page 137).

cups of the water in which carrots were cooked. Add lemon juice and allow carrots to cook a few moments in sauce before serving. Sprinkle with chopped parsley.

## CELERY LEAF SOUFFLÉ
### *(6 servings)*

This Kentucky dish may be served in place of a starchy vegetable with baked ham, and pinch-hits for chicken dressing. Only the celery leaves are used, leaving the stalks for salad or soup.

| | |
|---|---|
| ¼ C butter, bacon drippings or chicken fat | 1½ C tender celery leaves (chopped fine) |
| 1 medium-sized onion, grated | Salt and pepper to taste |
| 1 C bread crumbs | 1 C chicken broth or consommé |
| ¼ C cream | 4 eggs |

Melt fat in skillet, add onion, and fry to a golden-brown. Remove skillet from fire and add bread crumbs, chicken broth or consommé, cream, and celery leaves chopped fine. Fold in first the well-beaten egg yolks, then the whites beaten stiff. Season to taste. Pour into greased individual baking cups or a large round baking dish. Set in a pan one-fourth full of water and place in a moderate oven (375°). Bake 30 to 45 minutes, or until soufflé is set.

## CUCUMBERS WITH MOCK HOLLANDAISE SAUCE
### *(Quickie!)*

Peel large cucumbers and cut in halves lengthwise. With a silver spoon remove seeds and soft pulp and discard them. Cut each half in two. Put in boiling salted water and cook until tender when pierced with a fork—20 minutes. Drain. Serve 2 or 3 pieces to each person, with Mock Hollandaise Sauce. A nice change from the usual green vegetable. Cucumbers prepared this way have a very delicate flavor and are preferred by many to summer squash. For the Mock Hollandaise Sauce see page 162.

## HATTIE DICK'S STUFFED CUCUMBERS
### *(4 servings)*

| | |
|---|---|
| 2 medium-sized cucumbers, as fresh as possible | Salt and pepper to taste |
| 1 T green pepper, seeded | Dash of nutmeg |
| 1 small onion, peeled | 4 T bread crumbs for sprinkling on top of cucumbers |
| 1 T chopped parsley | 2 T butter |

Cut the cucumbers in halves lengthwise, allowing a half to each person. Do not peel. Using a silver spoon, scoop out the centers of the cucumbers, leaving the shells. Grind the scooped-out pulp with the green pepper, onion and parsley and add the seasonings. Stuff this filling back into the cucumber shells. Sprinkle 1 tablespoon of bread crumbs over each half. Dot each half with 1 teaspoon or a little more of butter. Set the cucumbers in a greased pyrex baking dish. Put ½ cup of water in the pan to keep the cucumber shells from sticking. Bake in a moderate oven (350°) for 35 minutes to 1 hour, or until cucumbers are tender and crumbs brown and crisp. Serve with fried chicken, country ham, or any other meat.

## EGGPLANT STUFFED WITH HAM, PECANS, OR SHRIMP
### *(6 servings)*

| | |
|---|---|
| 1 large eggplant | 2 eggs, well beaten |
| Salt and pepper to taste | 2 T catsup |
| 1 t sugar | 1 t Worcestershire sauce |
| 1 onion, grated | ½ C chopped ham, pecans, or |
| 4 T butter, margarine or other fat | shrimp |
| | ½ C bread crumbs |

Boil eggplant 15 minutes. Cut in half lengthwise and remove shells from inside pulp with a sharp knife. Place shells side by side in a greased baking dish. Cut the remaining inside pulp into chunks and boil in salted water 15 minutes, or until tender enough to be mashed to a paste with a potato masher or a fork. Add salt, pepper and sugar to this paste, and the onion browned in 2 tablespoons of the butter or margarine. Add well-beaten eggs, catsup, Worcestershire sauce, and more salt, if necessary. Fold in the nuts, shrimp, or ham. Place the filling in the shells and sprinkle each with ¼ cup of bread crumbs. Dot each with 1 tablespoon of butter or margarine and cook in a moderate oven (375°) until the crust has browned—15 to 20 minutes.

## OKRA, CORN, AND TOMATO MÉLANGE
### *(6 servings)*

This is a veritable chameleon of a recipe. It may be served plain as a vegetable, and very delectable it is, too! If a pound of cooked shrimp is added to the mixture and it is poured over a mound of boiled rice, it becomes the main dish for a luncheon or Sunday night supper. One cup of leftover meat or freshly ground beef, ham or veal may be substituted for the shrimp, and the mixture stuffed into green peppers or tomatoes, covered with bread crumbs and dabs of butter or margarine, and baked until brown.

| | |
|---|---|
| 4 strips bacon, fried crisp | 3 peeled, diced tomatoes (large) |
| 4 T bacon drippings, butter or chicken fat | 1 small green pepper, chopped |
| 1 onion, chopped fine | 1 t sugar |
| 1 pt. okra | Salt and pepper to taste |
| 4 ears corn | Dash tabasco or cayenne pepper |

Fry bacon until brown. Set aside to "crispen," as they say in the South. Measure bacon drippings and if there are not enough, make up the difference with butter or chicken fat, or simply use 4 tablespoons of the fat on hand. Now add onion and okra cut into ¼-inch rings. (Be sure the okra is small and tender, for hard, tough okra will never cook tender.) Add corn cut from the cob and cook 10 minutes, stirring constantly to prevent sticking. Now add tomatoes, green pepper and seasoning. Put a top on skillet or pot and simmer until all vegetables are done (about 25 minutes longer). This mixture is not cooked dry but is always a little runny. Stir from time to time to prevent sticking and add more seasonings if necessary. Pour into a serving dish and sprinkle with crumbled bacon or toasted bread crumbs.

## LOUIS SMITH'S SOUTHERN FRIED ONIONS
### *(4 servings)*

Louis Smith, our houseman, fries food better, we think, than anyone else south of the Mason and Dixon Line. We always serve his onions with fried calves' liver, over hamburgers or potato kläse, or use them as a vegetable in their own right. We like gigantic portions of this truly Southern dish, but if you aren't a fried-onion addict, cut the recipe in half.

| | |
|---|---|
| 3 C thinly sliced onions | Salt |
| ¼ C bacon drippings, chicken fat, or lard | Freshly ground black pepper to taste |

Peel the onions and cut in slices about ¼ inch thick, but do not soak in water. Place them in a 10- or 11-inch skillet containing the hot melted fat. Have the flame high at first, then as the onions begin to brown, lower the flame and let them simmer until done, stirring them occasionally to prevent burning or sticking. Salt and pepper them as soon as they are put in the skillet, seasoning to taste when they are done. When onions are brown and soft they are done. Watch carefully to see that they do not burn. We use a heavy iron skillet, but any heavy metal will do. The skillet is not covered while the onions are cooking. Put them over the meat, or serve separately in a bowl or dish. This is one of those word-of-mouth recipes every Southern child knows how to prepare, and yet you won't find it in many cook books.

## LETTUCE-STEAMED GREEN PEAS
### (4 servings)

2 C shelled green peas, fresh or frozen*
1 medium-sized onion or 6 tiny ones (we use onion sets)
1 small head leaf lettuce or enough to cover top of peas
⅛ t black pepper

1 C water
3 T butter
2 t sugar (scant)
1 t salt, or more to taste
3 T thick cream mixed to a paste with 1 t flour

Wash peas well. Place in the bottom of a saucepan. Add the whole peeled onion, or tiny ones, butter, sugar, salt, pepper, and water. Cover top of peas completely with the washed lettuce, sealing them in. (Iceberg lettuce may be substituted if no leaf lettuce is on the market.) Put a cover on the saucepan and let simmer 1 hour or until peas are tender. Remove lettuce. Add cream and simmer a few moments longer. If the sauce is too thin, thicken it with a teaspoonful of flour mixed with 2 tablespoons of cream.

## ELIZABETH PLEUS'S
## BAKED STUFFED YELLOW SQUASH
### (As served at the Old Stone Inn near Simpsonville, Kentucky)
### (6 servings)

One of the oldest and most delightful inns in the State is the Old Stone Inn, an 18th-century coaching hostelry on the road between Louisville and Lexington. Run by Mrs. Elizabeth Pleus, it is noted for its delicious meals. Besides the usual fried chicken and chicken livers with rich cream gravy, Mrs. Pleus serves most unusual vegetable dishes. With her permission I give one of them.

Allow ½ a squash for a serving. For six persons you will need:

3 tender small yellow squash
¼ lb. highly seasoned pork sausage
¼ cup uncooked rice
1 medium-sized onion, chopped
Salt and black pepper to taste
2 T chopped parsley

2 T butter or margarine
6 t butter or margarine (for tops of squash)
6 T freshly rolled Ritz or butter cracker crumbs (for tops of squash)

* If peas in the pod are used, buy 2 pounds to make 2 cups of shelled peas.

Boil rice in salt water until tender—about 25 minutes. Drain and set aside. Fry pork sausage in a hot skillet until done but not brown. Pour off all grease, and combine rice and sausage. Meanwhile prepare the squash by boiling them 10 minutes in salt water or until they seem tender outside. Cut in half, placing the halves side by side in a biscuit pan or rectangular baking dish, greased with margarine or butter. Remove the center portions of the squash halves gently with a sharp knife and a silver spoon, leaving a ½-inch shell. If the center pulp is not done, boil again in salted water. If the squash are young and tender the seeds can be used and mashed with the rest of the pulp, but if the seeds are large and tough they must be discarded and the pulp strained or put through the food mill. Combine the cooked squash pulp with the rice and sausage, and add the parsley and onion, the latter cooked until soft and golden in the 2 tablespoons of butter or margarine. Season highly with salt and pepper. Pile into squash shells, pour thick tomato sauce over the tops of each squash (sauce recipe given below), then sprinkle the top of each stuffed squash with a tablespoon of cracker crumbs, dot each with a teaspoonful of butter or margarine, and bake ½ hour in a moderate oven (375°). Serve with fried chicken or broiled steak.

### Tomato Sauce for Baked Stuffed Yellow Squash

Simmer in a covered saucepan a No. 2 can of tomatoes or 2 cups of peeled, quartered, fresh tomatoes until the mixture is sufficiently thick to suit you—it should not be as thick as a cream sauce, but should not be runny, either. Stir occasionally to keep from sticking. Season with salt, pepper, pinch of sugar, and, if you like the flavor, a diced button of garlic. Mrs. Pleus says she sometimes adds a 4-oz. can of mushrooms, or ½ cup of slivered fresh mushrooms, but this is not necessary. Ten to 20 minutes should be sufficient to cook the sauce.

### MINN-ELL MANDEVILLE'S   *(Quickie!)*
### FAMOUS SPINACH FARMERS' SPECIAL
#### *(6 servings)*

| | |
|---|---|
| 3 lbs. tender young spinach | 2 T olive oil or butter |
| Salted water | 1 onion, cut fine |
| Salt and pepper | 1 garlic clove, cut fine |
| 4 slices crisp bacon | ¼ C vinegar |
| Bacon drippings | Salt, pepper, cayenne |

Wash spinach and cook in boiling salted water. When tender, drain and put through meat grinder. Season with salt and pepper and cook in the olive oil or butter 5 minutes. Serve with sauce made of the onion, garlic, vinegar, bacon drippings, salt, pepper and cayenne. Heat sauce and pour over hot spinach. Garnish spinach with bacon.

## LENA TACHAU'S TOMATOES AU CARAMEL
### *(6 servings)*

**6 firm, ripe, medium-sized tomatoes, peeled (allow one to each person)**

(Here is the best and easiest way I have found to peel tomatoes: Hold each tomato on a long-handled fork over a high flame, turning constantly until skin begins to break. Plunge into cold water, then peel. Drain.) Sprinkle with salt and pepper. Remove the hard core and put 1 teaspoon butter in each tomato. Bake 20 minutes in a moderate oven (375°). Pour off all excess liquor and save for soups or gravies, or use in the sauce below. Then pour the following sauce over the tomatoes and send them to the table:

### Sauce au Caramel

| | |
|---|---|
| 2 stalks celery | 1 C water, or juice from baked |
| ⅓ green pepper | tomatoes |
| 1½ C dark brown sugar | 1 T flour (rounded) |
| Salt, pepper to taste | Juice of ½ lemon |
| ½ onion | |

Grind celery, pepper and onion. Mix water or juice from the tomatoes baked as above with ground vegetables and thin juices in a skillet or saucepan. Add lemon juice. Cover and simmer until vegetables are tender (about 20 minutes). Add sugar, salt and pepper and the flour mixed to a paste with a little cold water (about 2 tablespoons). Cook until sauce is thick, and pour some of it over each tomato. Serve in separate saucers.

## FRIED GREEN TOMATOES

Slice ¼ inch thick the large, firm, green, unpeeled tomatoes (green throughout)—discard end and stem slices. Sprinkle with salt, pepper and sugar. Dip in corn meal or flour and fry in a skillet containing enough bacon drippings or melted butter to be ¼ inch deep in the skillet. Have the fat hot when the tomatoes are added, then reduce the flame and brown on one side. Turn with a pancake turner and brown on the other. Serve with hot homemade chili sauce. These are delicious with roasts, fried chicken, sausage or what you will.

## FRIED RED TOMATOES

These are sliced a little thicker than the green tomatoes but the method of preparation is the same. They make a nice luncheon dish with crisp bacon and scrambled eggs or a plain parsley omelet. We also serve them with broiled chops or steak.

## TURNIP SALAD GREENS

The tops of the turnip, or the greens, used to be called salad tops. Here's how they are prepared in the South—*have been* for generations, and probably *will be* for some years to come.

1 peck tender young turnip greens, tough stems removed (about 2 lbs.)

½ lb. jowl bacon or country-cured bacon, salt pork, or a ham hock

1 slice hot red pepper (optional) or cayenne to taste

2 qts. water or more, enough to barely cover greens

2 medium-sized onions

1 large onion, peeled and sliced (Bermuda preferred) for garnishing

Salt to taste (Do not add until meat is cooked—some cured meat is very salty)

Poached or hard-boiled eggs for garnishings

In a preserving kettle with a lid put the water, 2 medium-sized onions, pepper, and meat and simmer 2 to 3 hours, or until meat is tender. If salt pork is used, it should be thoroughly rinsed and the salt washed off the surface. When the meat sticks tender, taste liquid for seasoning, adding salt and pepper as needed. Add the greens, which have been well washed in running water and thoroughly rinsed free of all sand or grit. Use a dishpan or some other large bowl where the greens can be "swished" around in the water until every leaf has been hand-washed. Drain and add to meat and broth. There should be enough water so that greens will wilt down and be almost covered. Cook for a few minutes and then add more water if necessary. The greens are allowed to come to a hard boil; then they are covered and simmered at a reduced temperature from 1½ to 2 hours or until very, very tender. To serve greens, place in a deep bowl or soup tureen, pouring some of the "pot likker" over the greens. Cover top of greens with the onion slices; place either a poached egg (4 minutes) or 2 hard-boiled egg halves on each slice, allowing 1 egg for each person. Everyone helps himself generously, spooning greens, egg and onion, and "pot likker" into his soup plate or deep bowl. A cruet of cider vinegar is handed round the table and each person mixes the desired amount with the "pot likker." Corn bread always accompanies these greens. Serve the pones, skillet corn bread, or corn sticks. Don't tell me that the vitamins have cooked out of the greens or that the fat makes them indigestible—Southerners consider this food for the gods—their gods, anyway.

Kale and mustard greens are prepared by this same recipe.

## CHESTNUTS

An easy way to prepare chestnuts: It isn't really much more time-consuming to cook and hull a pound of large Italian, Portuguese or Japanese chestnuts, than to peel a pot of those delectable marble-sized new potatoes. The following method is much simpler than the old-fashioned one where the nuts were split, roasted, peeled, scraped and then boiled. Put as many nuts as desired into a saucepan (about 25 nuts will be needed to make a cup of purée), cover with water, and, when it begins to boil, cook for 30 minutes. Remove from stove, drain the chestnuts and plunge them into a bowl of cold water. The hulls and skins can then easily be removed with a paring knife, and the nuts are sufficiently tender to be pressed through a ricer or strainer. If, by any chance, they are not thoroughly done, cover them with water again and cook until tender.

## CHESTNUTS AND PRUNES
### (6 servings)

2 C boiled, peeled chestnuts (for preparing, see above)
1 lb. prunes
2 T sugar, or more to taste

1 stick cinnamon
1 slice lemon ½ inch thick
2 T butter
1 T flour

Soak prunes overnight in 2 cups of cold water. Next morning, put in a saucepan with cinnamon and lemon, and the water in which prunes were soaked. Cook until prunes are tender. Add butter, sugar and chestnuts. Mix flour with the remaining liquor (if any is left) to make a paste and thicken mixture. Add salt if necessary and more sugar to taste. Remove lemon and cinnamon. Serve as a vegetable with fowl, or stuff into cavity of crown pork roast, ½ hour before serving. To use as stuffing, you can seed the prunes if you wish, but we do not.

## CHESTNUTS AND RAISINS IN WINE SAUCE
### (6 servings)

2 C boiled peeled chestnuts, 1 qt., uncooked (for preparing, see above).
1 C seeded raisins
1 stick cinnamon
1 t vinegar
2 t butter

½ lemon, juice and rind
2 bay leaves
¼ C sherry or Madeira wine
1½ C water
F. G. salt
2 T sugar

Boil together the raisins, lemon cut in quarters, cinnamon, bay leaves, and water. Cook 10 minutes. Add chestnuts and vinegar and cook 10 to 20 minutes longer. Add wine, butter and sugar to taste. Simmer 3 minutes, and if sauce is too thin, thicken with a flour-and-water paste (2 teaspoons flour and 2 tablespoons water should be enough). If too much of the water cooks away as the mixture boils, add a bit more from time to time. Serve with game, poultry, ham or pork, instead of a starchy vegetable and a compote.

## MUSHROOMS

Note on the preparation of fresh mushrooms: There is some controversy about the advisability of washing mushrooms before cooking them. However, I am of the school that believes in giving them a quick bath in cold water. Don't soak them or they will get mushy, but put them in a bowl of cold water and swish them around, then drain well before using. You will be amazed at the amount of dirt in the bottom of the bowl. We don't peel hothouse mushrooms when they are very fresh, but if they seem old and dry, peeling helps. Wild mushrooms usually need peeling if they are over a day old, as they dry out very quickly.

## PAPRIKA MUSHROOMS

| | |
|---|---|
| 4 T butter or chicken fat | 1 C chicken broth or sweetbread |
| 1 lb. mushrooms | broth |
| 1 T Worcestershire sauce | ½ C milk |
| 1 t Kitchen Bouquet | ½ C cream |
| 1 T flour | 1 t paprika |
| | Salt, pepper to taste |

Brown butter or fat in a skillet. Add mushrooms (caps separated from stems), salt and pepper. Cover the pan. Simmer until mushrooms are done—10 minutes should cook them. Stir occasionally. Add milk mixed with flour, and all other ingredients. Serve in patty shells or over noodles or rice.

# Starchy Vegetables and
# Cereals Served as Vegetables

## BARLEY FOR ROAST GOOSE OR DUCK

Barley makes a wonderful substitute for potatoes when roast goose or duck is on the menu. It is also served with skewered lamb. Here's how we prepare it:

| | |
|---|---|
| 1 C uncooked pearl barley | Salt and pepper to taste |
| 3 stalks celery, chopped fine | Wings, neck, gizzard of goose or |
| 1 qt. water, or more as needed | duck |
| Dash ginger (optional) | Bunch celery tops tied together |
| 1 onion, diced | or 2 stalks celery, diced |
| 1 small clove garlic, diced | |

Put all ingredients into a Dutch oven or heavy iron pot with a lid, and let simmer until barley is thoroughly done and water has evaporated. (This should take from 1½ to 2 hours.) It should be rather mushy but not runny. It may be necessary to add more water from time to time. Stir constantly to prevent scorching. Remove celery tops, wings, neck and gizzard before serving.

## BLACK-EYE PEAS, CORNFIELD PEAS,
## COWPEAS (dried)

(There is an old Southern superstition that if you eat black-eye peas and pork on New Year's Day, you will have good luck throughout the coming year.)

Soak peas overnight in water to cover. The next day drain them, and to prepare them follow the recipe for fresh black-eye peas. They may have to be simmered longer than the fresh peas, but the taste is very similar. Add more water also if the liquid evaporates too much.

## BLACK-EYE PEAS, CORNFIELD PEAS,
## COWPEAS (fresh)

No, there isn't a mistake in the spelling of the title; this is a black-eye pea in the South, not a black-eyed one! I am convinced that to like them you have to be born where these peas are a part of the family's weekly menu or else cultivate a taste for them. My son thinks they "taste like dirt," but his mother and thousands of Southerners do not agree with him. To cook them, follow the recipe for Hoppin' John given on page 158, omitting rice and using 2 cups of black-eye peas. Here is a recipe for cooking cowpeas from an 1874 book called *Housekeeping in Old Virginia*, which I think might amuse you:

## MOZIS ADDAMS'
## "RESIPEE FOR CUKIN KON-FEEL PEES"

"Gether your peas 'bout sun-down. The folrin day, 'bout 'leven o'clock, gowge out your pees with your thum nale, like gowgin' out a man's eyeball at a kote house. Rense your pees, parbile them, then fry 'em with som several slices uv streekt middlin (Bacon), incouragin uv the gravy to seep out and intermarry with your pees. When modritly brown, but not scorcht, empty into a dish. Mash 'em gently with a spune, mix with raw tomarters sprinkled with a little brown shugar and the immortal dish ar quite ready. Eat a hepe. Eat mo and mo. It is good for your genral helth uv mind and body. It fattens you up, makes you sassy, goes throo and throo your very soul. But why don't you eat? Eat on. By Jings. Eat. *Stop!* Never, while thar is a pee in the dish.—Mozis Addums."

## CORN PUDDING
### *(4 to 5 servings)*

This is the Southern Corn Pudding recipe you will find throughout Kentucky and the whole South. Young field corn is much better for this recipe than sugar or yellow corn. After the tender young ears have been shucked and the silk removed, they are washed and dried and the very tip ends of the grains cut off with a sharp knife. Then the ear of corn is held upright over a bowl and the tender inside kernels scraped out with the back edge of a dull knife. None of the husks are supposed to be scraped off the cob.

| | |
|---|---|
| 4 ears of corn | 3 T melted butter |
| 2 eggs | ¼ t salt, or more to taste |
| 1 C whole milk | ⅛ t black pepper, or more to |
| 2 T sugar | taste |

Prepare corn kernels according to directions given above. Beat eggs and milk. Add corn, sugar, melted butter, salt and pepper. Pour into a greased baking dish and bake in a moderate oven (375°) until pudding is just set. When it does not shake when moved, it is ready. Do not cook too long. It takes from 35 to 45 minutes.

# FRIED CORN
## (6 servings)

8 ears corn (young field corn      2 T bacon drippings or lard or
   preferred)                                      butter
4 T butter                                     1 diced green pepper (optional)
Salt and pepper to taste

Cut corn kernels from cobs. Melt butter in skillet. Add corn and seasoning and cook until the corn is tender—about 10 minutes. Stir occasionally. Do not have the flame too high, as the corn may burn. If mixture begins to brown before corn is done, add ½ cup of milk or cream.
Keep the lid on while cooking and stir occasionally to keep from sticking.
We often add a diced green pepper when the corn is put in the skillet.


# HASHED BROWN POTATOES WITH CARAWAY SEEDS
## (6 servings)

4 medium-sized potatoes            2 T finely chopped parsley
3 T olive oil                                  1 t caraway seeds
3 T butter                                     1 small pod crushed or sliced
Salt, pepper to taste                            garlic
1 T chopped chives or green
   onion tops

Boil potatoes. Peel and slice about ¼ inch thick while still hot. Add salt
and pepper. Melt butter and olive oil in skillet. Add garlic and brown
lightly. Pour over potatoes in a bowl. Add caraway seeds, parsley and
chives or onions. Mix well. Pack potatoes in a 6- or 7-inch skillet and
smooth with the top of a spoon. Brown on one side but do not stir again.
Instead, place the skillet under the broiler flame and brown the top side.
Turn out on a platter and serve at once. Delicious with grilled steak or
chops. We serve this dish often in the summer for our backyard picnics,
especially when barbecued or grilled meats are on the menu.


# POTATO KLÄSE OR MASHED POTATO CAKES
# FOR SAUERKRAUT
## (6 servings)

4 medium-sized potatoes            1 egg
Salt, black pepper to taste        4 T flour

Boil the potatoes with jackets on. Peel and put through ricer or food
mill. Add salt, pepper, egg and flour. Set in icebox to cool. Form into
balls. Return to icebox. Just before cooking, put a saucepan of salted

water on stove to boil. When kicking vigorously add potato balls and lower heat. Cook slowly until balls are fluffy and done (15 to 20 minutes). Or flatten balls and sauté until brown on both sides in skillet with melted butter or margarine. We prefer this latter method. Serve on a platter around sauerkraut, barbecued spareribs, roast pork, etc., with fried onions on top of each ball.

## RAW POTATO PANCAKES    *(Quickie!)*
### *(6 servings)*

You need 1 pound of grated potatoes to make this recipe, usually 3 average-sized ones, or one large one. Use old potatoes.

| | |
|---|---|
| 1 small onion, grated | 1 t baking powder |
| 1 medium-sized apple, grated | 1 t salt |
| 3 medium-sized raw potatoes, grated (1 lb. grated potatoes) | 1/8 t black pepper |
| | 1/2 t sugar |
| 2 to 4 T flour (or more if needed) | Bacon drippings, vegetable shortening or lard to fry pancakes. |
| 1 egg, well beaten | |

Peel and grate onion, apple and potatoes. Add flour, well-beaten egg, baking powder and all other ingredients. Mix well. Drop by tablespoonfuls onto a 10-inch skillet containing 2 tablespoons of melted grease, and fry 4 or 5 cakes, as you would pancakes or corn fritters, letting the fritter brown on one side, turning, and adding more fat as needed. They must not be cooked too quickly over too high a flame, but browned and cooked thoroughly over a low flame. It is well to make a test fritter. If mixture is too thick, thin with a little milk; if too thin, add a bit more flour. Do not be alarmed if the potato batter turns blackish. Raw potatoes always change color when they stand. The flavor of the pancake is not harmed one bit. Serve with sauerkraut, roast pork, veal or lamb. These pancakes are especially good with Red Gates Farm Goulash (page 118).

## GREEN RICE
### *(4 servings)*

Boil 1/2 cup rice in salt water until tender. Drain and add:

| | |
|---|---|
| 1 well-beaten egg | 1/2 t grated onion |
| 1/3 C milk | 2 T minced parsley |
| 2 T melted butter | 1/3 C ground or minced raw spinach |
| 2 T grated cheese | |
| Salt and pepper to taste | 2 T Worcestershire sauce |

Beat all ingredients to blend with rice. Pour into a greased baking dish and set in a pan ¼ full of water. Bake 35 to 40 minutes in a moderate oven (375°). Serve with Mushroom or Tomato Sauce. This makes a nice Sunday night supper or luncheon dish. Green rice can also be baked in a greased ring mold and filled with creole or curried shrimps.

## HOPPIN' JOHN (Rice and Peas)
### (An old Carolina recipe)
### (6 servings)

| | |
|---|---|
| ½ lb. bacon or salt pork | 1 qt. water (or more if needed) |
| 1 C black-eye peas | 1 C uncooked rice |
| 1 slice hot red pepper | Salt and black pepper to taste |

Wash bacon or salt pork. Put in a Dutch oven or heavy metal pot with a tight-fitting lid. Put all ingredients in pot except salt—the meat is so salty that this seasoning is added later. Cover the pot and let come to a boil, then reduce heat and let peas simmer until tender—this takes about 1½ hours or longer. Add salt to taste. Add rice and cook until it too is tender—about 30 minutes. If liquid evaporates add more from time to time. Put rice and peas in a serving dish and place the bacon on top of them. If dried peas are used, soak overnight before cooking.

## RICE FRITTERS
### (4 to 6 servings)                    (Quickie!)

| | |
|---|---|
| 1 C cooked rice | 1 egg white mixed with 1 T |
| 1 T butter | cold water, in which to roll |
| 2 t sugar | fritters |
| 1 whole egg | Bread crumbs in which to roll |
| 2 or 3 T cream | fritters |
| Salt to taste | |

Beat the whole egg well. Add cream and rice. Put in a stewpan or skillet and cook until mixture is quite thick, stirring constantly. Add butter, salt to taste, and sugar. Set aside to cool. Form into flat round cakes, roll first in the egg white slightly beaten with the water, then in the bread crumbs. Fry in a basket in deep hot fat. Serve with jelly or syrup for breakfast or dessert. To serve these cakes as a starchy vegetable or an accompaniment to game or meat, omit sugar and add 2 tablespoons of minced parsley and a teaspoon or more of curry powder to taste.

## YELLOW RICE
### *(A recipe from the Florida Keys)*
### *(6 servings)*

| | |
|---|---|
| 1 C white rice, well washed | 2 onions, chopped |
| 1 oz. salt pork | ½ green pepper, chopped |
| 2 T olive oil | 2½ C chicken broth |
| ½ C tomato juice | ½ t powdered saffron * |
| 1 pod garlic, crushed | ⅛ t thyme |
| ½ t sugar | ⅛ t oregano (Spanish sage) |
| 1 bay leaf | Salt and black pepper to taste |

Wash salt pork and chop fine. Fry out in a skillet, putting aside crisp pieces to use later. Add olive oil to the salt pork fat in the skillet. Add onions, garlic and green pepper. Cook 10 minutes, but do not allow to become too brown. Add broth, tomato juice and rice, and cook 5 minutes. Add crisp salt pork, saffron, herbs and sugar. Season with salt and pepper to taste. Pour mixture into a greased baking dish and bake in a moderate oven (375°) 1½ hours, or until rice is well done. Stir every 15 minutes to keep from sticking. Serve this rice with Creole, Spanish or Italian dishes. It is delicious with baked fowl or sea food.

VARIATION: Sometimes ½ cup chopped ripe olives is added to the above mixture just before taking it from the stove. If a stronger tomato flavor is liked, substitute 2 tablespoons of imported tomato paste for the tomato juice. The rice can also be cooked on top of the stove in a covered Dutch oven or chicken frier. Accompanied by a green salad it makes a nice luncheon dish.

## NOODLES IN BROWN CRUNCH SAUCE
### *(6 servings)*

This is a Flexner specialty and I had not tasted it before my marriage. It is particularly good with veal, although it is at home with almost any roasted meat or fowl.

---

*Note on saffron: All recipes in this book calling for saffron refer to the powdered Spanish saffron made from the stigma of the crocus and not from the dried leaves. You can purchase good saffron from any Spanish or Italian importing house. Saffron made from the leaves of the crocus always tastes like carbolic acid to me and is far better left out of any recipe. These leaves are dark bronze in color. The powdered saffron has a delicious spicy odor and is a bright copper color.

½ lb. broad egg noodles            Salt and cayenne pepper to taste
½ C butter (or ¼ C butter and
  ¼ C of margarine)

Remove a cup of noodles from the half-pound package and set aside.
Cook the remainder of the noodles in boiling salt water until tender.
Drain thoroughly and serve with a sauce made as follows: Crush the cup
of raw noodles into tiny particles (I do this by putting them on a biscuit
board or marble table on a piece of wax paper, and rolling them into
bits with my rolling pin); melt the butter or butter and margarine in a
skillet; add the noodle bits and brown, stirring constantly to prevent
burning; add salt to taste and a dash of cayenne pepper. Mix the cooked
noodles with the Brown Crunch Sauce and serve at once.

## DR. ARNOLD GRISWOLD'S ITALIAN SPAGHETTI
### (8 servings)

Dr. Arnold Griswold, the noted surgeon, now professor of surgery at the
University of Louisville, was assigned to the Italian army in World
War I. He got this recipe from a confrere and has concocted it on occa-
sions ever since, to the delight of his friends.

| | |
|---|---|
| 3 lbs. ground beef | 2 cloves garlic |
| 3 medium-sized onions | 1 lb. mushrooms |
| 1 t salt, or more to taste | 3 cans tomato purée (small) |
| 1 t black pepper | 3 cans tomato paste |
| 1 t ground mustard | (Italian style) |
| 1 T Worcestershire sauce | 6 cans water (to wash out cans) |
| Herbs to taste (basil, oregano, | ⅓ C olive oil (no substitutes) |
| thyme, marjoram, rosemary, | 1 or 2 bay leaves |
| etc.) | 2 lbs. long, unbroken spaghetti |

In the bottom of a Dutch oven or heavy metal pot with a lid sauté
onions and garlic in olive oil for 3 or 4 minutes. Add meat and stir, break-
ing it up into small chunks, until meat browns lightly. Add mushrooms
and let brown slightly, then pour off excess grease (if any). Add tomato paste and purée, washing out each can with some of the water
and adding it. Put in the rest of the water, the salt, pepper, Worcestershire and herbs. "This is a fine opportunity to experiment with herb seasoning," said the good doctor. Let the mixture come to a hard boil,
stirring to prevent sticking, then cover and turn the heat low. Let simmer
2 to 3 hours or until all vegetables and meat and sauce blend to make a
smooth, pastelike sauce. If the mixture is watery at the end of 2 hours,
remove top from kettle and cook until thick. The mixture should be
the consistency of thin cream sauce. Stir every 20 minutes or so to be

sure the meat does not stick to the bottom of the pan and scorch the sauce. This sauce may be made the day before, Dr. Griswold says; in fact, he thinks it tastes better if made one day and reheated the next.

To serve, have a large kettle of boiling water on the stove. Add the unbroken spaghetti, stirring to separate it. If at first the spaghetti will not go into the kettle, stick the ends in and gradually, as they become limp, the remainder can be pushed in. After 5 minutes, add salt, then cook 10 minutes longer. Drain. Put in a colander and let cold water run over this. Replace the spaghetti in another kettle of boiling water. Cook 5 minutes. Drain once more. Put a mass of the spaghetti on a large dinner plate or soup plate. Cover with a generous portion of the sauce. Dust with grated Parmesan cheese. Pass each portion thus prepared. With this the Griswolds serve garlic bread or Italian bread sticks, grapefruit and Bibb lettuce salad and a tart French dressing, and, of course, lots of strong coffee.

## SAUCES AND TOPPINGS FOR VEGETABLES

NOTE on mixing flour-and-water paste for sauces: To make a smooth flour-and-water paste free from lumps, put the flour in a bowl or cup and add cold water (usually the proportions are twice as much water as flour). Beat hard with a fork instead of a spoon. Don't ask me why this should make a difference—I don't know—but it does.

## GRANDMOTHER FLEXNER'S ASPARAGUS SAUCE
### (6 servings)

My husband's French grandmother brought this recipe with her when she came to this country from Paris in the 1840's, and it has been one of the specialties of the family ever since. The sauce is passed with boiled, fresh, green, or quick-frozen asparagus.

| | |
|---|---|
| 3 T butter or margarine | ¼ t salt, or more to taste |
| 1 T flour (rounded) | 1 to 2 T sugar (to taste) |
| 1 C water or milk | 1 T cream |
| 2 egg yolks | ¼ t cinnamon |
| 2 T lemon juice, or more to taste | |

Melt butter in skillet. Add flour and stir to make a smooth paste. Add water (or milk, if preferred) stirring constantly until mixture is free from lumps. Turn off flame. If mixture is lumpy, strain. Add well-beaten yolks, lemon juice, salt and sugar. Stir until blended. Add cream. Heat once more, but do not boil, and pour into a sauceboat. Dust with powdered cinnamon. The sauce should be the consistency of cream sauce.

## MOCK HOLLANDAISE SAUCE FOR
## ALL BOILED GREEN VEGETABLES
*(Quickie!)*

2 T butter  
¾ C boiling water  
1 T flour  
¼ t dry mustard  

2 T lemon juice, or more to taste  
2 egg yolks  
½ t salt  
⅛ t cayenne pepper  

Melt butter in skillet but do not brown. Stir in flour. Add boiling water slowly, stirring to keep mixture from lumping. Remove skillet from stove. Add egg yolks well beaten, and mix well. Then add lemon juice mixed with mustard, salt, and pepper. Put back on stove and cook 1 minute. Stir constantly. Serve at once or pour into double boiler and set aside until ready to use. To reheat, beat 1 tablespoon of cream into the sauce, put in a double boiler and warm. One tablespoon of chopped parsley may be added to the sauce before .pouring over boiled cauliflower, stewed celery, or white asparagus.

## SOUR CREAM HOLLANDAISE
*(For artichokes or asparagus)*

2 egg yolks  
¾ t salt  
1 T lime or lemon juice, or more to taste  
¼ t dry mustard  

¼ t sugar  
Dash cayenne or tabasco  
1 C sour cream  
Paprika for garnishing  

Beat eggs and cream. Add lemon juice mixed with salt, sugar, mustard, and cayenne or tabasco. Pour into a double boiler and cook until mixture thickens. It should just coat the spoon as a boiled custard does. Do not cook too long, and stir constantly to prevent lumping or curdling. Pour into a sauceboat or individual saucers and dust with paprika.

# Salads and Salad Dressings

✦✦✦✦✦✦✦✦✦✦✦✦✦✦✦✦✦✦✦✦✦✦✦✦✦✦✦✦✦✦✦✦✦✦✦✦✦✦✦✦✦✦✦✦✦✦✦✦✦✦✦

## Green Salads and Vegetable Salads

### MARY HELEN BYCK'S *(Quickie!)*
### AVOCADO COCKTAIL IN FOAM DRESSING
#### *(6 to 8 servings)*

Dice 3 large avocados in ½-inch pieces. Mix with Foam Dressing and marinate ½ hour before serving in cocktail glasses surrounded by crushed ice. With crisp crackers, this is a delicious first course or salad course.

#### Foam Dressing

1 C homemade oil mayonnaise (see Foolproof Mayonnaise, page 171)
¼ C catsup

¼ C chili sauce
1 C whipped cream (measured after whipping)
Salt, pepper to taste

Strain the chili sauce. Mix with the catsup and mayonnaise. Fold in whipped cream gradually. Salt and pepper to taste. Pour over avocados. This dressing is also very good with crab meat or other sea food.

### CAULIFLOWER, ONION, AND *(Quickie!)*
### FRESH MUSHROOM TOSSED SALAD

For a slightly different tossed salad, try this one:

1 crushed garlic pod
1 small head cauliflower separated into flowerets
1 Bermuda onion, cut in rings
3 large fresh hothouse mushrooms, washed and slivered
1 green pepper, diced
1 pimento, diced

½ C sliced green olives (*not* stuffed)
1 head iceberg lettuce, shredded
½ C blue, Roquefort or Gorgonzola cheese
⅔ to 1 C French dressing to moisten

Mix vegetables well in a wooden bowl previously rubbed with garlic. Salt and pepper the whole, using freshly ground black pepper. Add enough dressing to moisten well but do not have the salad swimming in it. Serve as soon as mixed.

## COMBINATION SALAD (Southern style)
### *(without oil)*                                    *(Quickie!)*

1 small head cabbage, shredded
    fine
1 green pepper, chopped
1 pimento, diced
2 stalks celery, diced

1 onion, grated, or
    6 spring onions, diced
2 tomatoes, diced
1 cucumber, diced
Chopped whites of 2 hard-boiled
    eggs

Mix above ingredients with Sour Cream Dressing (page 175) or use this

### Sweet Vinegar Dressing for Combination Salad

⅔ C cider vinegar
⅓ C sugar
1 t celery seed
⅛ t pepper
⅓ C water

2 t dry mustard
1 t salt
⅛ t paprika
2 hard-boiled egg yolks, mashed

Blend vinegar with egg yolks and add all other ingredients. Beat well. Pour over salad and serve at once.

## CUCUMBER BOATS

Peel and cut medium-sized cucumbers in halves lengthwise. Scoop out seeds with a silver spoon.* Soak 1 hour in a bowl of French dressing. Drain and fill with Kentucky Coleslaw or boiled shrimps topped with Pickwick Café Cocktail Sauce or Salad Dressing (page 173). Allow ½ cucumber for each portion.

## DRESSED CUCUMBERS

In our own family there is a treasured recipe known as "dressed cucumbers." This requires no fat or oil of any kind. The cucumbers keep a week in a covered jar in the icebox.

---

* If the seeds are not large, the cucumber pulp can be used for Benedictine Spread (page 30).

2 medium-sized cucumbers, peeled, scored * and sliced thin
6 spring onions, diced or 1 small onion, sliced
½ C apple cider vinegar

2 T sugar, or more to taste
2 T chopped parsley
1 chopped green pepper
½ C water
1½ t salt, or more to taste
¼ t black pepper

With a fork mix green pepper, finely diced onions, cucumbers and parsley. Pour over them the vinegar and water mixed with the other ingredients. Correct the seasoning. Put in a glass jar with a tight-fitting lid and set on ice to chill thoroughly before using (2 hours). The cucumbers will keep several days in the ice-box.

## VARIATIONS OF DRESSED CUCUMBERS

### Dressed Cucumbers in Sour Cream

Drain the marinated or "dressed" cucumbers. Mix with 1 cup thick sour cream before serving. These cucumbers are a nice side dish with thick soups, stews or roasts, especially with Pot Roast.

### Dressed Herbed Cucumbers

Add 1 tablespoon of freshly chopped dill to the dressed cucumbers before chilling, or use any preferred combination of herbs. Chives, thyme and marjoram are nice; tarragon, parsley and chives are exceptionally good; thyme and summer savory are also fine for a change. If dried herbs are used, do not add more than ½ teaspoonful altogether. These cucumbers are wonderful with fish.

## HOT SLAW

For Hot Slaw follow recipe for Old-fashioned Wilted Lettuce or Spinach Salad (page 166) substituting 2 cups of shredded cabbage for lettuce or spinach.

---

* To score cucumbers: Scored cucumber slices look as if they were fluted. To make them, peel the whole cucumber and cut off each end down to the seeds. Wash and dry. Take a fork and drag it the length of the cucumber, pressing about ⅛ inch deep, making "scratches." When the whole cucumber is covered with these fork lines, slice the cucumbers into ¼-inch rounds or chips. The slices have a "different" look which is very effective.

## KENTUCKY COLESLAW
### (With boiled mayonnaise)
### (4 to 6 servings)

In the Deep South a boiled mayonnaise made of eggs, butter, vinegar, cream, etc., is often preferred to that with an oil foundation. This mayonnaise is especially delightful with sliced cold tomatoes, in potato salad, used with fresh fruits in frozen salads or aspics, or mixed with shredded cabbage to make this delectable Kentucky Coleslaw.

Shred 1 small head of green cabbage very, very fine. There should be about 2 cupfuls. Put in a bowl of ice water and let stand 20 minutes. Drain, pat dry in a towel, and mix with a dressing made as follows:

| | |
|---|---|
| 2 well-beaten eggs | 1 t salt, or more to taste |
| 1 T flour (rounded) | 1 or 2 T sugar (to taste) |
| ¼ C apple cider vinegar | 1 T butter or olive oil |
| 3 T sweet or sour cream | ¼ C water |
| ½ t dry mustard | |

To the well-beaten eggs add flour, mustard, salt and sugar. Beat until smooth and creamy. Slowly add water mixed with vinegar. Pour into saucepan, add butter and set over a low flame, stirring constantly. Let cook until thick. The mixture will lump, but do not be discouraged. Remove pan from stove and *beat* and *beat* and *beat* the mixture until smooth once more. Add cream and correct the seasoning. Cool. Mix with the shredded cabbage. Serve with fish, ham, roast pork, or any dish where slaw is indicated. This slaw should be a moist one.

To serve this slaw for buffet suppers we often scoop out the heart of the largest cabbage we can find, leaving the shell and outer green leaves intact. We make our slaw out of this center portion, preparing it according to the recipe given above, but doubling the dressing recipe as many times as necessary. Then, just before serving we pile the slaw and boiled mayonnaise into the cabbage shell, put it on a platter and serve the slaw from the cabbage.

## OLD-FASHIONED WILTED LETTUCE, HOT POTATO OR SPINACH SALAD WITH BACON AND VINEGAR DRESSING
### (4 servings)

| | |
|---|---|
| ½ lb. leaf lettuce, spinach or sliced hot potatoes | Salt and black pepper to taste |
| 1 small onion, grated | 2 hard-boiled egg whites, chopped |

Be sure the lettuce or spinach has been well washed and picked over and all tough stems removed. Potatoes should be boiled in their jackets until tender, then peeled and sliced thin while hot. Mix the greens or potatoes, depending on which salad you are making, with the other ingredients listed above. Then just before serving pour the following dressing over the mixture:

### Bacon and Vinegar Dressing

4 thin slices breakfast bacon
⅓ C apple cider vinegar
1 t salt or more to taste
1 T sugar or more to taste

⅛ t red pepper
⅛ t black pepper
2 hard-boiled egg yolks
2 T water

Fry bacon in a skillet. Remove to absorbent paper and set aside until crisp. Crumble. To the hot fat in the skillet add the yolks and water. Mash with a fork and stir until yolks make a smooth paste. Add dry ingredients and blend. Add vinegar. Heat once more, pour over greens or potatoes in salad bowl, sprinkle the top with bacon, taste for seasoning and serve at once.

## *Aspic, Egg, Meat, Poultry and Fish Salads*

### ALENE BURGER'S AVOCADOS STUFFED WITH DEVILED EGGS AND TOPPED WITH WATER CRESS DRESSING
#### *(6 servings)*

Alene Burger serves this salad as a luncheon dish or as a first course at formal dinners.

3 ripe avocados
6 hard-boiled eggs, riced
1 small can of anchovy fillets
6 slices green pepper
6 slices pimento or ripe sweet red pepper

1 C French Dressing, via Alabama (page 171)
1 C chili sauce
1 C finely minced fresh water cress firmly packed (about ¼ lb.)

Allow half a peeled avocado for each person. Place each avocado half on a bed of shredded lettuce and fill with a minced egg preparation made as follows: Take 6 anchovy fillets out of the can and set aside; mince the others and add them, with their oil, to the eggs; add pepper to taste,

and salt, if necessary, although anchovies usually furnish sufficient salt.
Divide this mixture into 6 portions and fill the avocado cavities with it.
Decorate the top of each avocado with a strip of anchovy, another of red
pepper or pimento, and another of green pepper. To make the Water
Cress Dressing, mix all the remaining listed ingredients. Pass separately,
allowing about ½ cup for each serving. This is delicious and excellent on
a hot summer day or for a Lenten lunch.

## CHICKEN LIVER ASPIC
### *(6 servings)*

| | |
|---|---|
| 12 chicken livers | 4 T parsley, cut fine |
| 6 T celery, cut fine | 2 T grated onion |
| 2 T butter | 1 t salt |
| 2 T gelatin | 2 C chicken broth or water |
| 3 drops tabasco sauce | Cayenne pepper to taste |

Brown livers and onions in butter. Mash to a paste or put through the
strainer or food mill. Add gelatin dissolved in water or broth as follows:
Mix gelatin with ½ cup of the cold liquid in a pyrex cup or bowl; set in
a small skillet ¼ full of water; put over a flame on top of the stove and
let cook until gelatin melts and becomes the consistency of liquid glue;
add to the rest of the broth or water which is at room temperature.
After pouring the gelatin broth into the liver mixture, add all other ingredients and stir well. Pour into a small ring mold lightly greased with
salad oil, or into 6 individual lightly greased molds, and set in the icebox until aspic becomes firm. Unmold on a bed of shredded lettuce or
water cress and serve with mayonnaise. A delicious first course at a formal
dinner, or a nice luncheon or supper dish.

## JANE McFERRAN'S CHICKEN SALAD SPECIAL
## WITH BOILED DRESSING
### *(20 servings)*

This recipe is a family heirloom and came, says Jane, from her Grandmother Tyler about 1860. The McFerrans make the salad for parties and
this recipe will serve 20. It can be cut down for smaller servings.

| | |
|---|---|
| 6 celery hearts, or | Two 4-lb. chickens (or capons) |
| 1 large bunch celery | boiled (Stewed Chicken, page 106) |

Remove skin and bones from the cold boiled chicken and dice into inch
pieces. Place in a bowl with celery, which has been cut into ⅓-inch
pieces. Add the dressing made as follows:

6 eggs
1 dessert spoon dry mustard
1 T salt, or more to taste
1 t freshly ground black pepper
An 8-oz. tumbler of wine vinegar

Butter size of an egg (about 2 T rounded)
Pinch of cayenne (about ⅛ t)
½ tumbler (4 oz.) pure olive oil

Beat eggs well—I use an electric beater. Add salt, pepper and mustard and continue beating. Add a little of the vinegar at a time until all has been used. Put the butter in the top of a double boiler and place the pan over boiling water. Set on top of the high flame and when the butter has melted, add the egg-vinegar mixture and lower flame. Stir and stir until mixture thickens—it may lump, but keep on stirring. When it has thickened to the consistency of thick cream sauce, remove from the stove and beat furiously—you can return it to the electric beater if you wish. This is a tricky sauce to make and is apt to curdle unless some flour is added. If you aren't an experienced cook, you'd better slip in 1 tablespoon of flour when you are beating the eggs, to be sure that you will have a smooth paste and the mixture won't separate or curdle. When cool, add the olive oil, a little at a time, beating until all is incorporated. Pour over chicken and celery and mix with 2 forks. Taste for seasoning, adding more salt and pepper if needed. Pile into a cut glass dish or silver bowl lined with lettuce leaves. Dust with paprika and set in the icebox to chill for several hours before serving. If you like a sweet boiled dressing, you can add 1 tablespoon or more of sugar to your dressing before blending with the chicken, but the original recipe does not call for it.

## DOROTHY CLARK'S CRAB-MEAT SLAW WITH TOMATO JUICE DRESSING   *(Quickie!)*

2 C finely shredded cabbage
1 chopped pimento
1 onion, grated
1 small cucumber, peeled and diced

1 chopped green pepper
½ C finely cut celery
1 can crab meat picked over and flaked, or 1 C fresh crab flakes

Mix all together and add:

### Tomato Juice Dressing for Crab-Meat Slaw

¾ C tomato juice
1 t dry mustard
1 t Worcestershire sauce
1 T lime or lemon juice
1 T mayonnaise

¼ C vinegar
1 t sugar
1 t salt, or more to taste
⅛ t black pepper
Few drops tabasco sauce

Mix all above ingredients and pour over Crab-meat Slaw served in Cucumber Boats (page 164) or individual salad bowls.

## EGG SALAD WITH GARLIC AND ANCHOVY DRESSING
### *(A most unusual dressing and a treat for garlic-lovers)*
### *(4 servings)*

4 hard-boiled eggs
6 pods garlic
1 C water
8 anchovies
1 T capers
1 lb. water cress or
   1 head lettuce, shredded

6 T olive oil, or salad oil
   (including oil from anchovy
   can)
2 T vinegar
3 drops tabasco or a dash of
   cayenne pepper

Slice the eggs in quarters. Place on a flat dish. Surround with water cress or lettuce and just before serving pour the salad dressing over the whole. To make the dressing, boil the garlic in water for 15 minutes, or until garlic is thoroughly tender. If a small quantity of water remains, use it in the dressing, although by this time it usually evaporates. Mash the garlic with a fork until it forms a paste. Add chopped anchovies and all other ingredients. Should there be too little liquid for the amount of hard-boiled eggs or salad greens, add 3 tablespoons of salad oil to every 1 of vinegar, and more salt and pepper to taste. Mix well and pour over the eggs.

VARIATION: This same Garlic Dressing is wonderful on a Spring Salad or Tossed Salad composed of cooked green peas, slivered green beans, fresh diced shallots, green peppers, tomatoes and cucumbers with a small amount of fresh chives or tarragon well minced. Should there be too little dressing for the amount of vegetables, add 3 tablespoons of salad oil to every one of vinegar, and more salt and pepper to taste.

## COUNTRY HAM AND          *(Quickie!)*
## COTTAGE CHEESE CROQUETTE SALAD
### *(A Kentucky specialty)*

2 C creamed cottage cheese
2 T chives
1 t onion juice
1 t Worcestershire sauce or
   more to taste

1 C cooked ground ham
2 T chopped parsley
Salt, pepper and tabasco to taste
Chopped nuts in which to roll
   croquettes

Mix all ingredients, except nuts, and shape into balls or croquettes. Roll in chopped nuts (we prefer pecans). Serve on lettuce with tart mayonnaise.

# Salad Dressings

## AÏOLI                    (Quickie!)
### (A garlic mayonnaise to serve with cold fish)

This is dear to the Frenchman's heart but we in this part of the country like our mayonnaise a little less strong. Here is the version of aïoli we use:

> 1 C highly seasoned homemade mayonnaise (see below)
> 2 medium-sized garlic buttons, pounded to a paste
> (I mash the garlic on the biscuit board with a wooden potato masher.)

Blend the garlic and mayonnaise and let stand at least 2 hours in a covered container in the icebox before using. Serve plain or mash the mayonnaise through a strainer, discarding the garlic shreds. The aïoli keeps fresh for a week or 10 days, but after that the garlic taste becomes too strong for us.

## FRENCH DRESSING, VIA ALABAMA
### (Quickie!)

½ C cider vinegar or malt vinegar diluted with 2 T warm water if vinegar is strong
1 C salad oil
½ C olive oil (no substitute)
1 t salt

¼ t black pepper (freshly ground, if possible)
1 pod garlic, crushed, or
1 t onion juice (or more to taste)

Put all ingredients except garlic or onion juice in a bowl, and beat in the electric mixer or with a Dover egg beater. Add a cube or a small piece of ice and beat with a spoon. This seems to make the mixture into an emulsion. Discard ice. Pour into a bottle or jar, add garlic or onion juice, and cover the bottle or container. Set in the refrigerator until needed. Shake well before using. If dressing is to be used for fruit salad, omit garlic or onion juice.

## FOOLPROOF MAYONNAISE       (Quickie!)
### (A basic oil mayonnaise)

1 whole egg
½ t salt
½ t dry mustard
⅔ C salad oil

⅓ C olive oil
Juice ½ lemon, or more to taste (2 to 3 T)

Beat egg with rotary beater or electric mixer (a small deep bowl is best). Add salt and mustard. Add oil, drop by drop at first, beating well between each addition; then gradually add the oil in larger amounts, still beating constantly. When mixture is smooth and thick, add the lemon juice a teaspoonful at a time, alternating it with the remainder of the oil until both have been used up. Lime juice may be substituted for lemon if desired. This mixture should not curdle, but if it does, beat a whole egg and add the curdled mixture to the egg, a tablespoonful at a time. However, if all ingredients are of the same temperature when mixed the mayonnaise is not likely to curdle.

## LIBERTY HALL MAPLE SYRUP SALAD DRESSING
### *(Quickie!)*

Some years ago I had an interview with old Sarah Parrant, the devoted colored cook who served the Scott family in Frankfort, Kentucky for over 30 years. The Scotts were descended from John Brown, who built beautiful Liberty Hall in 1796, a brick mansion many people consider the finest in Kentucky. It is now a museum where all can enjoy the treasures collected by that one family during the 150 years of their residence. Sarah Parrant showed me the notebooks in which the favorite recipes of seven generations had been recorded. In them was this salad dressing recipe from the private ledger of Miss Mary Mason Scott, last resident and owner of the historic mansion.

| | |
|---|---|
| 1 C malt vinegar | Juice and pulp of small onion, |
| 3 t salt | grated (about 1 T) |
| ¼ t paprika | ½ to ¾ C real maple syrup |
| Dash of tabasco, or more if you | 1 C real olive oil, or ½ C olive |
| prefer a hot dressing | oil and ½ C salad oil |

In a mixing bowl place the malt vinegar and add salt, paprika, tabasco sauce, onion juice and pulp. Mix well. Add maple syrup. Stir until blended then add olive oil. Pour into a bottle or jar and shake well. This dressing is especially good with pear or pineapple or any fruit salad, cheese and fruit aspics, or with any salad requiring a sweet dressing. This often accompanies Bibb lettuce, a tender yellow-green head lettuce first found in Frankfort, Kentucky.

VARIATION: Add ¼ teaspoon poultry seasoning and ¼ teaspoon dry mustard to above dressing, mixing these ingredients with the vinegar and proceeding as above. This gives a much spicier flavor.

# FRED RUDOLPHI'S PICKWICK CAFÉ SEA FOOD COCKTAIL SAUCE OR SALAD DRESSING
*(Quickie!)*

Mr. Fred Rudolphi used to run the Pickwick Café in Montgomery, Alabama—one of the most delightful restaurants in the South. Of its numerous fish dishes, none are more famous than its Crab Meat and Shrimp Cocktails, made with lumps of sweet fresh crab meat or with freshly boiled shrimp and this magnificent sauce. The sauce is equally good on lobster. Make it and keep in the icebox in a covered jar. The Pickwick Café is being run now by Mr. Rudolphi's son and he still serves this delicious dressing.

½ pt. homemade mayonnaise
½ pt. bought chili sauce
2 T tarragon vinegar
½ t tabasco sauce

2 T Worcestershire sauce
1 t anchovy paste, essence or chopped canned anchovy fillets

Blend vinegar and anchovy paste or anchovies, then add all other ingredients. Mix well. Keep in icebox in covered jar until needed. Stir well before serving.

# PICKWICK CAFÉ ROQUEFORT CHEESE DRESSING FOR HEARTS OF ICEBERG LETTUCE
*(Quickie!)*

1 C French Dressing, via Alabama (page 171)
1 C homemade mayonnaise
2 T Worcestershire sauce

2 T white vinegar (I use wine vinegar)
½ lb. imported Roquefort cheese or blue cheese
Salt and cayenne pepper to taste

Mash cheese with a fork in a bowl. Add mayonnaise slowly, beating to make a stiff paste. Add vinegar and all other ingredients, adding salt only if necessary. The mixture should be thick, but if a few lumps of cheese remain, it is all right. Spoon over sections of crisp iceberg lettuce.

# PIQUANT DRESSING          *(Quickie!)*
## *(Will keep for 30 years!)*

One of my friends has an old crockery teapot which she insists has not been washed during the past 30 years. It always contains French dressing, and she adds to it constantly, but never quite empties the pot. If you ask her for her recipe she says it is quite impossible to give it, since the original concoction was made by her grandmother. However, the following approaches it as closely as my taste buds and ingenuity can make it. This recipe makes about a pint of dressing.

¾ C salad oil (cottonseed, corn or peanut oil)
¼ C olive oil
½ C malt or apple cider vinegar
1 t dry mustard
¼ t paprika
1 T Worcestershire sauce
6 drops tabasco

2 t salt, or more to taste
1 t sugar, or more to taste
2 T catsup
¼ t black pepper
1 T grated onion juice and pulp, or 1 lump of sugar rubbed with a pod of garlic until all juice has been absorbed

Mix dry ingredients. Add vinegar, stirring to keep from lumping. Add remainder of ingredients and beat with a rotary egg beater until well blended. Correct seasoning, and bottle. This will keep indefinitely in the icebox.

## HERBED DRESSING FOR SHAKE-UP SALAD

Add to Piquant Dressing 1 tablespoon of mixed, freshly picked and chopped, or dried garden herbs—dill, tarragon, thyme, marjoram, basil, summer savory, sage or any preferred herbs. I usually use dill alone, since we like it, and it dominates the other herbs when used in a mixture. This dressing is especially nice with a stuffed egg salad or a "shake-up salad"—a green salad, that is.

## SALAD DRESSING WITH HENRY BANE SAUCE
### *(Quickie!)*

⅓ C cider vinegar
⅓ C olive oil
⅓ C salad oil
1 t salt, or more to taste
⅛ t paprika
1 t sugar (optional)
⅛ t black pepper

1 clove garlic, split
¼ C Henry Bane Sauce (page 139)
⅛ t dry mustard
1 T grated onion pulp and juice

Whip all ingredients with a Dover egg beater or an electric beater, except garlic. Put the pod of garlic (cut in half) in the salad jar or bottle and add the whipped dressing. Keep covered in the icebox. Shake well before using. Add more salt and pepper if necessary and more Henry Bane Sauce if you wish.

## SOUR CREAM DRESSING    *(Quickie!)*
### *(Without oil)*

⅔ C thick sour cream *
1 saltspoon salt, or more to
   taste
2 T catsup (optional)
Sugar to taste (about 1 level T)
Dash tabasco sauce

Juice 1 lemon or 4 T mild
   vinegar
1 to 1½ t prepared mustard
1 T chopped chives, parsley, or
   chervil

Mix the cream with the salt, tabasco, lemon juice, catsup (optional), and prepared mustard (amount depending on how hot it is). Add chives, parsley, or chervil. Pour this over the salad and mix well with two forks. Add sugar to taste. Use less than ı level tablespoon of sugar if you like a somewhat acid dressing. This is delicious over cucumbers, mixed green salad, or fish salad.

## TARRAGON ORANGE SALAD DRESSING
### *(A Louisville original)*    *(Quickie!)*

2 T tarragon vinegar
2 T apple cider vinegar
1 small bud garlic
1 lump sugar
Juice 1 lemon
Juice 1 orange

1 t salt
½ C tomato catsup
½ C olive oil
1 t Worcestershire sauce
¼ t paprika
3 drops tabasco sauce

Rub garlic into sugar until all juice has been absorbed. Mix sugar with other ingredients. Pour into a pint bottle or jar and keep on ice. Shake well before using. This recipe makes ı pint. It is a most unusual dressing, delightful on fruit salad or mixed vegetable salad.

### For Other Dressings See the Following

Foam Dressing (page 163), Sweet Vinegar Dressing for Combination Salad (page 164), Bacon and Vinegar Dressing (page 167), Boiled Dressing (page 168), Tomato Juice Dressing (page 169), Boiled Mayonnaise (page 166), Garlic and Anchovy Dressing (page 170) and Watercress Dressing (page 167).

---

* Thick sweet cream may be used instead of sour but will require an extra tablespoon of lemon juice.

# Fruits, Fresh and Cooked

❋❋❋❋❋❋❋❋❋❋❋❋❋❋❋❋❋❋❋❋❋❋❋❋❋❋❋❋❋❋❋❋❋❋❋❋❋❋❋❋❋❋❋❋❋❋❋❋❋❋❋❋❋❋

## APPLES STUFFED WITH MINCEMEAT
### (6 servings)

6 large tart apples
2 T rum or whiskey
½ lemon, sliced thin
1 C cream, whipped
1 lb. mincemeat
¾ C sugar

1½ C water
2 T powdered sugar
   (to sweeten cream)
Cinnamon and nutmeg for
   sprinkling on top of apples
   (about 2 teaspoons of each)

Wash and core apples. Place in flat biscuit pan or pyrex baking dish. Put 1 tablespoon sugar in each. Fill centers with mincemeat to which has been added rum or whiskey. Sprinkle top of each with a pinch of cinnamon and nutmeg. Add remaining sugar and water. Add lemon and bake 1 hour in oven at 400°, or until apples are tender. Top with whipped cream flavored with rum and sweetened with powdered sugar.

## BAKED FRUIT IN WINE SAUCE
### (6 servings)

1 C sugar syrup (see recipe
   under Fruit Cup, page 180)
1 C Burgundy, claret, or any
   red wine
2 Bartlett pears, peeled, cut in
   half and cored or 2 peaches
   peeled, seeded and cut in
   half

2 apples, peeled, cored and
   quartered
¼ lemon cut in thin rings
1 C green seedless grapes
6 cloves
½ t coriander seeds
F. G. salt
6 allspice berries
1 stick cinnamon

Thoroughly mix the sugar syrup and wine. Put the fruit in a baking dish, sprinkle with the spices, and cover with the wine sauce. Add lemon slices. Bake for about 45 minutes in a moderate oven (375°) or until fruit is soft and transparent. Baste every 20 minutes. Five fresh peaches may be substituted for the apple, pear and grape combination. Chill fruit before serving.

## BAKED BANANAS AND GREEN GRAPES
### *(4 servings)* *(Quickie!)*

Serve this with baked ham, pork shoulder, green pork or pork tender-loin.

| | |
|---|---|
| 4 bananas | ¼ t nutmeg |
| ¼ C sugar | 2 T butter |
| ⅛ t salt | 4 T maple syrup |
| ½ lemon, juice and rind | ½ C seedless green grapes or |
| 1 t cinnamon | white seedless raisins |

Slice peeled bananas lengthwise and crosswise. Place a layer in the bottom of a glass or pottery baking dish. Add a few of the grapes. Sprinkle with some of the sugar and the spices. Add the remainder of the bananas in another layer, then the rest of the grapes and more sugar and spices. Dot with butter, add salt, pour syrup over this, and add the thinly sliced lemon. Bake in a moderate oven (375°) for 20 minutes. Serve with any roast. If no maple syrup is handy, brown sugar may be substituted, in which case add 1 tablespoon of water to the whole before baking.

## BANANAS FLAMBÉ *(Quickie!)*
### *(4 servings)*

| | |
|---|---|
| 4 bananas (one for each person) | ¼ C sugar |
| | 2 jiggers rum or brandy or |
| ¼ C butter or margarine | whiskey or 2 jiggers of any |
| Cream to serve with bananas | of these liquors combined |

Allow a banana for each person and use medium-ripe, medium-sized ones. Peel and remove strings. In a heavy iron or aluminum skillet melt the butter. Add the bananas, browning first on one side, then on the other, allowing about 3 to 5 minutes on each side. Sprinkle the top of each with ½ tablespoon sugar, then turn and let that sugar caramelize. Repeat until both sides are glazed; use the ¼ cup of sugar. Turn the flame low while this is going on and watch carefully to see that the sugar does not burn. Add the rum. I usually use 1 jigger of heavy rum, such as Lemon Heart, and 1 jigger of light rum, such as Barbados or Bacardi. Touch a match to the sauce and allow it to burn itself out, tilting the pan slightly to help it along. If desired, this may be done at the table. Serve from skillet in which the bananas were cooked. This makes a nice, easy and very impressive dessert to prepare at table, if you own a chafing dish or crêpe-maker. In order to burn, the liquor must be hot, but do not let it boil hard. Serve hot and pass sour cream or thick, unsweetened cream along with this.

## BRANDIED SOUR CHERRIES
### *(6 pints)*

This is a wonderful dessert by itself or is nice to serve with game, meat or roast fowl.

| | |
|---|---|
| 5 lbs. sour red cherries | 1 C kirsch or any other good |
| 5 C sugar | brandy |
| 2 C water | |

Stone cherries and put into a crockery or china bowl. Make a syrup of the sugar and water. Let this boil 12 minutes. Pour over cherries while it is still hot. Cover bowl and let stand 24 hours. Next morning boil cherries and juice for 15 minutes, counting boiling time after the whole is kicking vigorously. Remove from stove, add the kirsch or any other brandy and pour at once into sterile jars. Seal.

## MOTHER'S BRANDIED FRUIT MELANGE

| | |
|---|---|
| 1 pt. pure alcohol | 1 lb. granulated sugar to every |
| 1 lb. rock candy | pound of fruit in season |

Put alcohol and rock candy into a 3-gallon crock and stir until candy dissolves. Add a pound of granulated sugar to every pound of fruit in season—cherries, peaches, pears, pineapple, raspberries and strawberries. Use small fruits whole; peel peaches and pears and cut in eighths; peel and dice pineapple. Do not use bananas, grapes or apples. Fruit and sugar may be added from time to time. Each time that sugar is added, stir until it dissolves. Keep lid on the crock when not in use, and store in a cool, dark place. Do not use fruit until three weeks after the last batch has been added. This sauce is wonderful as a topping for ice creams, puddings and other desserts. It makes a company dessert out of a plain one.

## ISABEL McMEEKIN'S FILLED CANTALOUPE RINGS
### *(Quickie!)*

Peel a cantaloupe and cut into 1½-inch rings. Take out the seeds with a silver spoon. Place a ring on a dessert plate and fill the center with any one of the following:

1. Pineapple, raspberry, orange, lemon, lime or any preferred sherbet or water ice. Garnish with seedless green grapes, black cherries or what you will.

2. Fruit cup. (See recipe below.)

3. Frozen grapefruit or orange sections made by dumping the contents of a can of the grapefruit or orange sections or a mixture of the two into the freezing tray of the refrigerator and leaving until the mixture freezes. Garnish with a sprig of fresh mint.

## ORANGES AU CARAMEL    *(Quickie!)*

Pour French Caramel Sauce (page 199) over peeled, sliced navel oranges. Sprinkle with blanched, coarsely chopped almonds, previously browned in the oven.

## FRIED PEACHES    *(Quickie!)*
### *(An old Kentucky recipe)*
### *(4 servings)*

2 large freestone peaches (not    4 T sugar
   too ripe)    2 T butter

Peel and halve peaches, remove stones, and place the peaches cupside-down in a skillet of hot butter. When edges are nicely browned turn halves up, sprinkle half the sugar over top side and allow the other side to brown, then turn. Sprinkle the other side with remaining sugar. Cook until sugar caramelizes slightly, turning the peaches to coat them. Serve with fowl, game or roast or for dessert with rich cream.

## FRUIT CUPS OR CUT-UP FRUITS
### *(Quickie!)*

These are our favorite summer desserts and we serve them on many occasions. They do not require accompanying cake, but if you feel they should be thus chaperoned, use Dixie Tea Cake (page 247) or Bishop's Bread (page 244) to set them off. The actual fruit mixture will, of course, be composed of mixed fruits in season unless you wish to supplement them with frozen fruits.

To make the fruit cup, place the prepared fruits in a bowl and sweeten to taste with some of the sugar syrup (recipe given below). If allowed to stand ½ hour or so before serving, the flavor will be improved. Allow ½ to ¾ of a cup of mixed fruit for each serving.

## Sugar Syrup for Fruit Cup

1 C sugar                                    1 lemon, juice and rind
1 C water

Boil sugar and water 5 minutes, then add the juice of the lemon and drop the peels into the syrup and let the mixture cool. Remove peels, strain the syrup and pour it into a pint jar. Keep on ice to use for fruit cup or cooked baked fruit.

# FRUITS IN SPIRITS OR LIQUEURS
## (Quickie!)

Serve cold bananas with curaçao to taste.

Pour brandied peaches, cherries or any desired brandied fruit over vanilla ice cream.

Marrons soaked in a little rum make a wonderful topping for coffee or bisque ice cream.

A delicious dessert, quickly prepared, is made by soaking 1 package of frozen strawberries with a mixture of Cointreau, kirsch and rum—try a tablespoon of each of the liquors and add more to taste. Let stand in a covered bowl in the icebox. Then serve over vanilla or bisque ice cream. This has the royal title, Strawberries Romanoff.

Apricot liqueur is delicious poured over canned apricots and served over orange ice.

Serve chunks of sliced fresh pineapple in crème de menthe. Fill the dessert saucer with the fruit and add a few tablespoons of the liqueur. Both should be thoroughly chilled.

Kirsch (cherry brandy from Switzerland) is a natural for cold canned black cherries. It is equally delicious on pineapple.

One of our favorite winter desserts is canned pears, chilled, and soaked in claret or port. Add the wine to the fruit syrup and be sure there is enough to color it. Taste for proper amount.

B and B or Cointreau will take the curse off canned figs—they are too cloyingly sweet for me and the liqueur helps.

Boil apples in a sugar syrup (see above) until they can be stuck with a fork and are tender throughout. Then pour a few tablespoons of grenadine over them to color them red, or crème de menthe to color them green. Combine this liqueur with the syrup from the cooked fruit. To be certain the color penetrates, fortify it with a few drops of the red or green coloring, depending on what liqueur you have used. Drain and serve around baked ham or roast pork.

# Miscellaneous Desserts and Dessert Sauces

✠✠✠✠✠✠✠✠✠✠✠✠✠✠✠✠✠✠✠✠✠✠✠✠✠✠✠✠✠✠✠✠✠✠✠✠✠✠✠✠✠✠✠✠✠✠✠✠

## Custards

### CARAMEL ORANGE CUSTARD
#### (4 servings)

| | |
|---|---|
| 1 T butter | ¾ C orange juice (fresh or |
| ⅓ C sugar | frozen) |
| 2 T flour | Grated rind of medium-sized |
| 3 egg whites, stiffly beaten | orange |
| F. G. salt | ¼ C sugar |
| 3 egg yolks | |

Cream butter with the sugar. Add flour, egg yolks, orange juice—and grated rind (yellow part only) if freshly squeezed juice is used. (Frozen juice usually has enough of the oil of orange peel in it without adding more.) Fold into this mixture stiffly beaten egg whites previously mixed with a few grains of salt. Meanwhile, caramelize the ¼ cup sugar (see recipe for French Caramel Sauce, page 199) and pour while hot into 4 individual serving or custard cups. Turn them to spread the sauce evenly. Pour custard mixture into cups and set in a pan ¼ full of water. Bake in a moderate oven (375°) until custard sets—about ½ hour. As soon as it seems firm and the center is no longer runny, remove it from the oven, as it becomes tough and leathery if left in the stove too long. May be served warm or cold, although it will turn out of the cups nicely and the bottom will have a delightful caramel layer if left in the refrigerator overnight. This is especially good with Creole or Spanish food and we often serve it for dessert when Spanish Chicken (page 105) has been the main dish.

181

# FLAN, CRÊME AU CARAMEL,
## BAKED CUSTARD WITH CARAMEL SAUCE
### (6 servings)

| | |
|---|---|
| 1 C single cream | ⅓ C white sugar |
| 4 eggs | ½ C sugar (to caramelize) |
| 1 t vanilla | F. G. salt |
| 1 C milk (whole milk) | |

Beat eggs until light and lemon-colored. Add sugar, dash of salt, vanilla, milk and cream, and mix well. Meanwhile, caramelize ½ cup sugar (see recipe for French Caramel Sauce, page 199). Pour the caramel into 6 individual custard cups or into 1 large baking dish and coat bottom and sides of dishes, or dish. Pour the uncooked custard into this. Set in a pan ¼ full of water and bake in moderate oven (375°) until custard is set—about 30 minutes for the individual custards, 40 to 50 minutes for the large dish. Do not let cook too long, as it will become tough and leathery if overcooked. Chill. Loosen edges of custard with a dull knife and turn individual custards out of molds, inverting them on the saucer or dish on which they are to be served. Pour the caramel syrup over them. If the large mold is used, the custard will have to be served in the dish in which it was baked and not turned out at all. This is one of our standbys and one we serve on many occasions. It is at home at a simple luncheon or following a formal dinner.

## BRANDY AND RUM CUSTARD
### (As served at the Keeneland Club House)

Lexington, Kentucky, is a gourmet's paradise. Undoubtedly the first thing a visitor to that historic town will want to try is the Burgoo, and if he is lucky enough to get a card to the clubhouse at the Keeneland Race Track he can taste it at its best. Burgoo is filling and this Brandy and Rum Custard makes an excellent ending to your luncheon. I was too timid to ask the chef for his recipe, but here's mine which, to me at least, tastes a great deal like the original. Follow the recipe for the Flan (above), using ¾ cup of milk, 2 tablespoons of brandy and 2 tablespoons of rum instead of 1 cup of milk and 1 teaspoon of vanilla and omitting the caramel. When done, top with the French Caramel Sauce (page 199) to which 2 or 3 tablespoons of Jamaica rum have been added just before serving.

## WINE CUSTARD OR ZABAGLIONE
### (Quickie!)

I brought this recipe with me from Italy. As everyone who has seen the traditional recipe knows, it has no flour in it, but if the custard is made in the classic way, it should be eaten at once as it curdles easily. By adding a little flour, as I do, this Zabaglione not only can be made ahead of time, but any that is left over can be put in a covered dish in the icebox and used next day. The flavor is not affected at all, in my opinion. We serve this dessert following spaghetti, or any time a light dessert is indicated.

| | |
|---|---|
| 6 egg yolks | 2 T rum |
| 3 to 4 egg whites | 1 T flour (scant) |
| 1 C sugar | 3 T sugar (for egg whites) |
| ½ lemon (juice only, about | Nutmeg for sprinkling |
| 1½ to 2 T) | Grated peel 1 lemon (yellow |
| F. G. salt | part only) |
| ¾ C sherry | |

Beat egg yolks light. Add 1 cup of sugar and flour—use an electric mixer if you own one; if not, the Dover beater. Add sherry, rum and lemon juice. Beat to blend well. Add lemon rind. Cook in the top of a double boiler over boiling water as you would a custard. Use a wooden spoon if possible and continue to beat until custard is thick. Set aside to cool slightly. Beat the egg whites stiff with salt. Add the 3 tablespoons of sugar. Fold into the custard. Pile Zabaglione into sherbet or parfait glasses and dust each serving with a grating of nutmeg.

## JELLIED ZABAGLIONE

This is a delicious summer dessert and can be made the day before it is to be used, if desired. Follow the recipe for Zabaglione given above. Add to the hot, cooked Zabaglione, just when taking it from the stove:

**1 T granulated gelatin mixed with 2 T cold water**

Stir until well blended and free from strings or lumps. Spoon into individual salad molds lightly greased with salad oil or use a quart mold if desired. Set in the icebox until firm. To serve, loosen the edges of the Zabaglione with a dull knife and unmold on the plate on which it is to be served. Serve plain, or top with:

### Peach Purée for Jellied Zabaglione

| | |
|---|---|
| 2 C peeled, sliced ripe peaches | Few drops lemon juice |
| ½ C sugar | |

Mash peaches or put through strainer or food mill. Add sugar and lemon juice. Cover and chill before serving. Apricots, strawberries or red raspberries may be substituted for the peaches, if desired.

# *Frozen Desserts*

## GARNET RICHARDS' FRUIT CAKE CRUMB CREAM
### *(To be frozen in the refrigerator)*
### *(8 to 10 servings)*
### The Crumb Mixture:

Save the crumbs from a fruit cake as you cut it, or crumble enough to fill a pint jar. Add enough bourbon whiskey, rum or sherry to make a moist but not runny or sloppy mixture. Stir well, seal, and set in the icebox to mellow for a few days.

### The Cream Mixture:

| | |
|---|---|
| 4 to 6 egg yolks | ¾ C prepared fruit cake |
| 3 C milk, warmed | crumbs (see paragraph |
| ½ pt. double cream, whipped | above) |
| ½ C sugar | |

Make a custard by beating the egg yolks with the sugar and adding the warmed milk. Put in the top of a double boiler and stir with a wooden spoon until thick. Do not overcook or the mixture will curdle—just cook until the custard coats the spoon and no more. Remove from stove and add cake crumbs. Cool. Fold in whipped cream. Freeze in the tray or trays of the refrigerator. Stir every 20 minutes or until cream is stiff and frozen to your taste. The mixture can also be frozen in a crank freezer if desired.

## ICE CREAM GERTRUDE LAWRENCE
### *(As served at the Old House Restaurant)*
### *(1 serving)*

The Old House is one of Louisville's most distinguished town restaurants. Although it has not been in existence very long, already its fame has spread throughout the country. The house itself was built in 1836, and the old mantels and woodwork have been left intact wherever possible. The ground floor is paved with stone from the Ohio river bed, and the silver doorknob which, on the street level, is only three feet from the ground, carries a legend. Although three generations of dentists are said to have lived in the house, a family of dwarfs was also rumored to have inhabited it, and the front doorknob, so near the ground, was for their convenience. I recall with particular pleasure a memorable dessert I once had, a flaming chocolate sauce subtly blended with orange and rum and brandy and spooned over a scoop of vanilla ice cream—called Ice Cream Gertrude Lawrence. Here is the recipe, which is changed a little from the original but which I believe you will treasure as I do.

The first step is to make a chocolate paste which can be kept in the icebox and used as a base for the flaming sauce whenever needed. To make enough for 4 you will need

| | |
|---|---|
| **2 squares of bitter chocolate** | **¼ C cream** |
| **(2 oz.)** | **Grated rind (yellow part only)** |
| **Sugar to taste (I use ¼ C)** | **of 1 medium-sized orange** |

In the top of a double boiler melt the chocolate with the cream and stir to form a thick paste, adding sugar to taste. If you like a bitter sauce add 1 or 2 tablespoons of sugar; if you prefer a sweeter sauce add ¼ cup, as I do. Even this is not too sweet. Then add orange rind. In the original recipe the rind is not added at this point but is added later when the individual portions of the sauce are made; I find it more convenient to add the rind to the paste. Pour this mixture into a jar or small bowl, cover, and keep in the icebox.

When ready to make the flaming sauce you will need the following ingredients for each serving:

| | |
|---|---|
| **1 T of the prepared chocolate** | **3 T (1½ oz.) brandy** |
| **paste** | **1 T sugar (optional)** |
| **2 T (1 oz.) Myers or some sweet** | |
| **dark Jamaica rum (or use** | |
| **curaçao if preferred)** | |

This sauce should be prepared at the table in a chafing dish or crêpe-maker. However, I have made it on top of the stove in a small iron skillet. Place the chocolate paste in the chafing dish, crêpe-maker or skillet with rum or curaçao. Stir until paste is smooth. Heat slightly, but do not cook just yet. Add the sugar, if you are using it, and stir to blend. When the mixture is completely dissolved, light the flame beneath the pan and let the sauce bubble until it is the consistency of maple syrup. Now add the brandy and let this cook also for a moment until the sauce is hot again. Flame, tilting the pan back and forth until it no longer burns. If the sauce will not flame, cook for a moment longer. It must be hot and syrupy to burn, but if cooked too long the alcohol will evaporate. With practice you will soon know just when to apply the match. Pour the hot sauce over a large scoop of vanilla ice cream placed in a deep bowl or dish and serve at once.

## OLD-FASHIONED FROZEN OR ICED PUDDING
## OR PLOMBIÈRE

This is my own version of a very popular 1870 dessert for weddings, receptions and formal parties. "And very good it is, too," as Wanda Gag's "Funny Thing" is constantly remarking in one of my children's favorite nursery books. It deserves reintroducing into our menus. Pound cake, sliced thin, usually accompanies it, but it is so rich it doesn't need anything.

| | |
|---|---|
| 2 T currants | 1 pt. double cream |
| 2 T seeded raisins, cut in shreds | 1 C sugar (scant) |
| | 1 C water |
| 4 T marrons in vanilla syrup, or ground almonds | 4 egg yolks |
| | 4 egg whites |
| 2 T diced citron | F. G. salt |
| ¼ lb. crystallized cherries minced | 2 T light rum |
| | 2 T dark rum |
| ¼ lb. crystallized pineapple, minced | 4 T brandy or bourbon whiskey |

Put all nuts and fruits into a bowl or jar. They should all be minced fine; not ground, but cut into tiny bits. Add the rum, and brandy or bourbon. Seal the jar and let fruit stand overnight. Boil the sugar and water and after it comes to a boil let it cook 4 minutes longer. Put that also in a covered jar and let stand until cold. Put on ice until ready to use.

Next morning mix the sugar syrup with the fruit and stir well. (This mixture is delicious on not-too-sweet frozen ice creams or hot puddings such as sponge pudding. I call it Plombière Sauce.)

Beat the egg yolks and add the cream. Put in the top of a double boiler over boiling water and stir until mixture just coats the spoon. Do not cook too long or it will curdle—you want it to just coat the spoon, which it will do after the hot eggs and cream have cooked 1 minute. Remove from boiling water compartment. Set aside to cool. Fold the fruit mixture into the cooled custard. Add egg whites beaten stiff but not dry with the salt. Freeze in an ice cream freezer and serve, or, if you wish, pour into molds and pack in salt and ice for 4 hours.

## PEPPERMINT STICK CANDY ICE CREAM
### *(6 to 8 servings)*

This is an old Southern favorite. Serve it plain or topped with rich Hot Fudge Sauce (page 198).

| | |
|---|---|
| ½ lb. red-striped peppermint stick candy | 2 C single cream |
| 1 pt. double cream | F. G. salt |

Soak the crushed candy in the single cream overnight. If it does not dissolve, heat slightly. Cool. Combine the unbeaten double cream with the peppermint cream mixture and salt and freeze until stiff. We use an electric freezer or an old-fashioned crank freezer, but this ice cream will probably freeze in your automatic refrigerator.


# *Puddings*


## BISHOP WHIPPLE'S PUDDING

This recipe came from Montgomery, Alabama, and is a very good date pudding, easy to make and rather unusual. The original recipe specified that the baked pudding be broken up when cold and mixed with whipped cream. I see no reason for this, and make my pudding in a 2-quart pyrex or pottery baking dish; when it tests done, I brush the surface with sherry, and serve the pudding with sweetened whipped cream, also flavored with sherry. You can take your choice.

| | |
|---|---|
| 2 eggs | 1 C dates, seeded and chopped coarsely |
| ½ C sugar | |
| ⅔ C sifted flour | 2 T sherry, or more to taste |
| ½ t vanilla | 1 C double cream to whip for topping or to mix with pudding |
| 1 t baking powder | |
| 1 C pecans, coarsely chopped | |

Beat eggs well—I use an electric mixer. Add sugar and beat again. Fold in flour sifted with baking powder. Add vanilla, dates and nuts. Beat smooth. Pour into a greased baking dish and bake in a moderate oven (350°) until the pudding no longer shakes when the pan is moved. Do not cook hard. Serve warm with the whipped cream—1 cup double cream whipped is the amount we use.

## MOTHER'S DE LUXE CHERRY PUDDING
### *(8 to 10 servings)*

This is a dessert our old colored cook used to term "scrumptuous."

4 eggs, separated
1½ C freshly ground rye bread crumbs *
½ t cinnamon
2 T blanched toasted almonds (coarsely chopped)
F. G. salt
1½ C powdered sugar

1 T lemon juice
Grated rind 1 lemon (yellow part only)
1 qt. sour red cherries, measured before seeding, or use 1 quart of frozen cherries and juice

Toast bread and grind through finest blade of meat chopper. There should be enough to make 1½ cups of crumbs. Beat egg yolks light, add sugar, and beat again. I use an electric mixer, for the eggs and sugar must be a light sponge before the crumbs, lemon juice and rind, cinnamon and cherries are added to it. The egg whites, beaten stiff with the salt, are folded in last of all. Pour mixture into a lightly greased spring form, or a pottery or pyrex baking dish (butter is best for greasing the dish). Top the pudding with the coarsely chopped almonds and dust lightly with more powdered sugar. Place in moderate oven (375°) and bake for 40 to 50 minutes or until pudding just sets. It should not be runny, but it should be moist. Serve hot or warm with double cream, plain or whipped, or serve with:

### De Luxe Pudding Sauce for Cherry Pudding

1 egg, well beaten
2 T brandy, or more to taste

¼ C powdered sugar
1 C double cream

Beat egg well. Use an electric beater if you own one. Add sugar and beat again. Add brandy and fold in whipped cream just before serving.

## IROQUOIS PERSIMMON PUDDING
### *(6 to 8 servings)*

This is a delicious taste-treat and should be used for fall and winter desserts as an alternate for pumpkin or mincemeat pies.

Iroquois Park is one of Louisville's most beautiful, and it is full of persimmons. They can be gathered at will after the first frost. These are the wild native small persimmons, not the large Japanese ones.

---

* I find it an improvement to use ½ cup ground almonds and 1 cup rye bread crumbs instead of 1½ cups rye bread crumbs as suggested above.

To make the persimmon purée, wash the fruit well, picking off any dead leaves or dirt that may stick to it. Remove stems and put the fruit through a food mill or potato-ricer. A quart of persimmons makes 2 cups of purée. This will keep for some time in a covered bowl in the refrigerator, or it may be frozen if you own an electric freezing unit. Freeze plain, or mix 1 cup of sugar with each 2 cups of purée before freezing. It keeps well all winter in a frozen state. Here's the recipe for Persimmon Pudding:

| | |
|---|---|
| 1 C prepared unsweetened pulp | 1 C flour, measured after 1 sifting |
| 1 C sugar | ing |
| 1½ C buttermilk | ½ t soda |
| 2 T melted butter | 1 t baking powder |
| ½ t cinnamon | F. G. salt |
| 2 eggs, well beaten | ½ t freshly grated nutmeg |

Mix the pulp with the sugar. Add buttermilk, melted butter and eggs. Sift the flour with the soda, baking powder, salt, cinnamon and nutmeg. Combine the two mixtures, pouring the liquid slowly into the dry, and beating well. Pour into a pyrex baking dish with high sides, and set in a hot oven (450°) for 15 minutes, then reduce the heat to 400° and leave the pudding in the stove for 25 to 30 minutes longer, or until it no longer shakes in the middle. By that time it should begin to leave the sides of the pan and the top should be a lovely dark brown. Serve hot with your favorite caramel or wine sauce, or use half the Zabaglione recipe (page 182) as a sauce. Persimmon Pudding is also good cold. It is rather on the sweet side and I dribble about a teaspoonful of sherry on each cold portion and pass unsweetened double cream with it.

Some people omit spices from the Persimmon Pudding, claiming the flavor of the delicate persimmon is ruined by them. But almost all the recipes for this classic Kentucky pioneer dessert call for lots of spices.

If the sweetened frozen pulp is used in the above recipe add ½ cup of sugar to each cup of frozen pulp when making this dessert.

## SARAH BUCKNER'S POT DE CRÊME
### (French Chocolate Pudding)
### *(6 servings)*

Sarah Buckner gave me this recipe of her great-grandmother's when she showed me the tiny French porcelain chocolate cups and stand used a hundred years ago by Sarah Gibson Humphreys in serving her famous pot de crême. Mrs. Humphreys was known throughout the Bluegrass for her elaborate table, her delicious dishes. (See page 23, A Lavish Collation.) Here is her recipe:

½ lb. semi-sweet chocolate     2 T sugar, if necessary
4 egg yolks     Whipped double cream for gar-
1 C top milk or thin cream     nishing
1 t vanilla (optional)

This recipe sounds so very simple that it is hard to believe it is a company dessert of the first water. The secret lies in using the finest chocolate you can buy—Rosemarie or Maillard's would be my choice, but I have made it with Baker's German Sweet Chocolate plus a teaspoon of vanilla extract. Melt the chocolate and milk or cream in the top of a double boiler. Remove from the stove. Add the egg yolks, well beaten, and stir until mixture is thick—the consistency of boiled custard. It is not necessary to recook. It stiffens when chilled. Add sugar if necessary, and vanilla. Pour into custard cups or the real pot de crême cups if you are lucky enough to own any. Cover and set in the icebox until thoroughly chilled. Just before bringing to the table, top each portion with a heaping teaspoon of whipped double cream sweetened to taste and flavored with vanilla.

## MOUSSE AU CHOCOLAT

The egg whites beaten stiff with 2 tablespoons of sugar can be folded into the cooked pot de crême recipe before it is poured into cups. This is known as Mousse Au Chocolat. It is very delicious although not quite as stiff a mixture as the Pot De Crême. More sugar and vanilla may be needed. Use to taste.

WARNING: Do not make Pot De Crême with milk chocolate. Semisweet or French sweet chocolate is required for proper consistency and flavor.

## POT DE CRÊME AU CAFÉ
### (French Chocolate-Coffee Pudding)

Make up the recipe for Pot De Crême (French Chocolate Pudding), using 1 cup of very strong coffee instead of the top milk or thin cream. I use 1 cup of plain coffee mixed with an extra teaspoon of instant coffee. When the egg yolks are added, I mix them with 2 tablespoons of cream because no cream is in the pudding. Two tablespoons of brandy or whiskey may be substituted for the cream if desired. This gives a truly continental flavor. Omit extra vanilla, if brandy or whiskey is used.

## QUERY CLUB SPONGE PUDDING WITH WINE SAUCE

(For note on Louisville's Query Club, see Dr. Alice Pickett's Bishop's Bread, page 244.) This is a very old dessert, but one I was glad to meet. It is delicious with various pudding sauces or fruit toppings and is a worthy alternate for cottage pudding.

### Pudding

| | |
|---|---|
| 1 pt. milk | 1 C flour |
| ½ C butter | 4 egg yolks, well beaten |
| 1 t vanilla | 4 egg whites, well beaten |

Put half of the milk in a bowl and place in another bowl or basin of hot water. Add melted butter, the flour made into a paste with the rest of the milk, and the egg yolks. Then, just before baking, fold in the well-beaten egg whites and the vanilla. Pour into pudding dish and set in a pan ¼ full of hot water. Bake in a moderate oven (375°) ¾ of an hour or until pudding sets. I add a scant ⅓ cup of sugar to the pudding mixture before baking, but the original recipe does not call for any sugar.

### Wine Sauce

| | |
|---|---|
| 1 C butter | ½ C sherry, Madeira, or port |
| 1 C powdered sugar | wine |
| 1 C cream | |

Cream butter with powdered sugar. Add cream and wine. Beat well. Pour into a double boiler and set on the top of the stove over a low flame, stirring constantly. Heat to the boiling point. Serve at once with hot sponge pudding. This sauce can be used with any dessert requiring a wine sauce.

## SOUTHERN FRUIT OR BERRY PUDDING

*(4 servings)*          *(Quickie!)*

*(For sliced peaches, rhubarb, cherries (sour), huckleberries or blueberries, strawberries, red or black raspberries, blackberries or youngberries.)*

This is so good we often make it instead of pie when we are in a hurry. It's easy, too, and foolproof, a company dessert in a jiffy.

| | |
|---|---|
| 2 C berries or prepared fruit | ½ C sugar (or more if the fruit |
| ¼ t cinnamon | is tart) |
| ¼ C butter or margarine | ½ C flour |

Place the washed berries or peeled, sliced peaches or seeded cherries or whatever fruit you are using, into the bottom of a quart pyrex or pottery baking dish.* Dust with the cinnamon. Make crumbs of the sugar, flour and butter, crumbling with the fingers as for pie crust. Dump onto the fruit, smoothing evenly, then with a fork or spoon make 4 or 5 little holes in the topping to let the steam escape. Set the pan or dish in a hot oven and let remain 15 minutes—450° is about right. Reduce heat to 375° and let remain 20 to 30 minutes longer, or until fruit is done. Do not cook too long or the pudding will be too stiff to be good. It should have a wonderful thick sauce for the fruit, and a crunchy topping. Serve hot or warm with frozen or unfrozen whipped cream, flavored with vanilla and sweetened to taste. Vanilla ice cream is also delicious with this.

## FRUIT PUDDING WITH FROZEN FRUIT

Frozen fruit is delicious prepared by the above recipe. Dump the thawed fruit into a baking dish and proceed as above. I do not decrease the sugar for frozen fruit. This is one of our favorite family desserts and one we use constantly in winter and summer, for ourselves and for our friends.

## SWISS PUDDING
### *(6 to 8 servings)*

When my husband was a young medical student, this was his favorite dessert, but somehow the recipe was misplaced or lost and I could never find it. Then an old cousin of his died and in her treasury of family dishes we came across the formula for this wonderful pudding. It is a rich dessert, reminiscent of the Edward VII era, and should not follow a heavy meal. The pudding is only half-dressed without the Golden Lemon Sauce that should completely envelop it. It will be noticed that this pudding is not very sweet; that is because the sauce has ample sugar in it. If a less sweet sauce is substituted for this one, add a little more sugar to the pudding recipe.

| | |
|---|---|
| Grated rind of 1 lemon (yellow part only) | 5 T butter, softened |
| | 5 egg yolks |
| 1 pt. rich milk | 5 T sugar |
| 1 C flour | 5 egg whites |
| 2 T lemon juice | F. G. salt |

---

* If very tart or acid fruit (such as sour cherries or rhubarb) is used, add an extra ¼ cup of sugar to the fruit before putting it in the baking dish.

To make the Swiss Pudding, grate the rind of lemon into the milk and cook in the top of a double boiler until it reaches the boiling point. Meanwhile, mix the flour and butter with the fingers. Pour the hot milk over the flour-butter mixture and stir until smooth and well blended. Then return the mixture to the double boiler on top of the stove and cook until thick and free from lumps. Vigorous stirring all the time should prevent lumps, but if not, remove from the stove and continue beating. I sometimes have to dump the whole mixture into the electric mixer and let the electric beaters take over, but elbow grease was all that was used in the old days. Now, if you have used the electric mixer, add 5 egg yolks, one at a time, and the sugar. Otherwise, fold into the smooth mixture the egg yolks well beaten separately with the sugar. Cool. Fold into the pudding the egg whites, well beaten with the salt. Add the lemon juice to the whole, then pour into a well-buttered mold, being careful not to fill it over ⅔ full. A mold with a top will do if a regular steamer is used, or the top of the mold can be covered with parchment paper or 3 layers of heavy brown paper, securely tied with a string. Be sure that the covering is tight. Place in a steamer and cook 40 minutes. If a pressure cooker is used, place the mold on a rack in a 4-quart cooker. Add 1 quart of water. Put the lid on and cook 15 minutes with the petcock open. Then close it and cook 15 minutes longer at 15 pounds pressure. Turn out on a platter and serve with

## Old-Fashioned Lemon Sauce

This is the most delicious lemon sauce I ever tasted.

½ C butter, softened but not melted
1 C sugar
1 whole egg

Juice and grated rind of a lemon
¼ C boiling water

Cream butter with sugar. Add the egg and beat well. Use your electric mixer here, too, if you own one. Add boiling water, and beat again. Add the lemon juice and grated rind and stir well. Then pour into the top of a double boiler and set on the stove. Heat to the boiling point, stirring constantly. *Never let this sauce boil.* Serve at once, dousing each portion of pudding with a generous amount of sauce.

NOTE: If the pudding and sauce recipes are cut in half to serve 4, use 1 whole egg plus an extra white to make the pudding, and 1 egg yolk for the sauce. This sauce is equally good on leftover cake, cottage pudding, lemon soufflé, or with any recipe calling for lemon sauce.

## JUDGE H. H. TYE'S WOODFORD PUDDING
### *(6 servings)*

Judge H. H. Tye of Williamsburg, Kentucky, was one of the most charming gentlemen I've ever met. In his rambling Victorian house, with the able assistance of Arthur, his cook and family retainer, he offered a brand of hospitality reminiscent of his Scottish ancestors who came to this country so many generations ago. The Laird of Williamsburg, as we affectionately called him, was noted for his excellent table, as well as his witty conversation and his weekly newspaper column, *Broom Sedge Philosophy*. Dr. Lillian South (who was Mrs. Tye in private life) gave me some of the "Jedge's" famous recipes. Here's one I copied from a private ledger. This was a favorite Kentucky dessert for many generations and there are many versions of it. Certainly it is closely related to an old English jam pudding. Some top it with a meringue, but since the Judge's recipe did not call for it, I give it here as it was given to me.

½ C softened butter or margarine
1 C sugar
3 egg yolks
1½ C blackberry jam
1 C milk

1 C flour
2 t baking powder
1 t cinnamon, ½ t nutmeg, ¼ t cloves
3 egg whites, well beaten

Cream the butter or margarine with the sugar. Add egg yolks and blackberry jam. Sift flour with baking powder and spices. Add the milk and the butter mixture alternately to the flour mixture. Fold in the well-beaten egg whites. Pour into a greased mold or pyrex dish and bake in a moderate oven (375°) until pudding sets, ½ hour to 45 minutes. Serve hot, with:

### Pudding Sauce for Woodford Pudding

¼ C softened butter (no substitutes)
½ C sugar

1 well-beaten egg
¼ C brandy or whiskey, or more to taste

Cream the butter with the sugar. Add the egg. Put into a double boiler and stir until mixture thickens, *but do not boil*. Add the brandy or whiskey. Serve at once.

# *Soufflés*

## BANANA SOUFFLÉ
### *(6 servings)*

| | |
|---|---|
| 4 ripe bananas | Grated rind of ½ lemon |
| 2 well-beaten egg yolks | ¼ C sugar |
| 2 T melted butter | 2 egg whites |
| ½ C sweet or sour cream | F. G. salt |
| 1 T lemon juice | Cinnamon for dusting on soufflé |

### Meringue

| | |
|---|---|
| 2 egg whites | F. G. salt |
| 6 T brown sugar | |

Put bananas through a ricer or food mill. Add the well-beaten yolks, butter, cream, lemon juice and grated lemon rind. Fold in ¼ cup of the sugar and, last of all, the whites, well beaten with the salt. Pour into 6 individual ramekins or baking cups, greased with butter. Dust the top of each with cinnamon. Set in a pan ¼ full of water and put in a moderate oven (375°). After the raw soufflé mixture has been baking 15 minutes, remove from the stove and top with meringue made by beating the 2 egg whites with a few grains of salt and 6 tablespoons of brown sugar. Cook 10 to 15 minutes longer, or until meringue browns slightly. Serve warm or cold. The soufflé can, of course, be baked in one large dish, but will probably require a slightly longer time to set.

## CARAMEL SOUFFLÉ
### *(6 servings)*

We found this recipe in the notebook of one of my husband's cousins, 80 years old, who died a few years ago. She had written beside it the one word—Superb!

| | |
|---|---|
| 1 C sugar | ¼ C flour |
| ¼ C butter | 4 egg whites, beaten stiff |
| 1 C heavy cream | F. G. salt |
| 4 egg yolks, beaten | |

Caramelize the sugar. (See recipe for French Caramel Sauce, page 199.) Add butter and allow to brown. Mix well. Have the cream heating in a double boiler and pour into it the caramelized sugar mixture. Stir well and let cook until mixture is thoroughly smooth and blended. Set aside. Let cool to lukewarm. Beat the egg yolks and if there is an electric beater handy, use it. Slowly pour the cream-sugar mixture into the egg mixture, alternating with the flour, until all is used. Strain if lumpy. Beat the egg whites and salt until eggs are stiff enough to stand alone. Fold egg whites into other mixture and pour into a pyrex baking dish previously greased lightly with butter or margarine. Set pyrex dish in shallow pan ¼ full of water and bake in a moderate oven (375°) until soufflé just sets—45 minutes or longer. The mixture may also be poured into individual baking dishes, and in that case will take 25 to 30 minutes to set. Serve warm or hot with thick double cream, unsweetened. This is a delicious dessert, especially following a rather heavy meal.

## CHESTNUT SOUFFLÉ

Europeans have long known that a soufflé for dessert gives just the right sweet touch, especially after a heavy meal. Most Americans limit their menus to chocolate, lemon or prune soufflé—three old standbys of proven worth. But in my opinion none of them can compare with this Chestnut Soufflé, a gourmet's bit of heaven.

| | |
|---|---|
| 1 C cooked puréed chestnuts | 1 t vanilla |
| 4 eggs, separated | 1 to 2 T whiskey or rum or |
| ½ C sugar | kirsch, or more to taste |
| 1 T butter | F. G. salt |

Boil about 25 large chestnuts for half an hour. Peel, skin and put through the ricer or food mill. There should be 1 cup of purée. To this add the well-beaten egg yolks, sugar, melted butter, vanilla and liquor. Add egg whites beaten stiff, few grains of salt, and pour into a greased baking dish. Set in a pan ¼ full of water and put in a moderate oven (375°) until mixture sets. Do not cook stiff—the soufflé should be light, the consistency of baked custard. Serve hot, with Hot Fudge Sauce (page 198) and sweetened whipped cream flavored with whiskey, rum, kirsch, or vanilla, if preferred.

## SHERRIED PRUNE SOUFFLÉ
### *(6 to 8 servings)*

| | |
|---|---|
| 1 lb. prunes | 1 C sugar |
| 2 C water to cover | 1 T lemon juice |
| 4 egg whites | 1 t vanilla |
| F. G. salt | ¼ C sherry |

Soak prunes overnight. They need not be large ones. Next day put on to boil in the water in which they were soaked—20 minutes in a covered saucepan should be sufficient. Cool, stone, and put through a potato-ricer or food mill. (Do not use the juice in which the prunes were cooked. It may be used in desserts or mixed with lemon juice and sugar and served as a substitute for early-morning orange juice.) A pound of prunes when cooked, seeded and puréed should measure about 2 cups of pulp. Beat the whites of eggs with the salt. When stiff, add slowly, beating all the while, the sugar and lemon juice, and combine with the purée. Flavor with vanilla and sherry. Pour into a greased baking dish, set in a pan ¼ full of water, and bake in a moderate oven (375°) until set—45 minutes is the usual time. Individual custard cups may be used if desired. One half-hour usually is enough to cook these small soufflés. Serve warm or cold with whipped cream flavored with sherry or vanilla or with vanilla pudding reinforced with a couple of tablespoons of fine sherry. If kept in the refrigerator, the soufflé is good the next day.

# *Dessert Sauces*

## TO MAKE DOUBLE-STRENGTH COFFEE
### *(To use in desserts or sauces)*

Add 1 teaspoon instant coffee to every cup of hot coffee brewed just as you make it to drink for breakfast. Thus ¾ cup would take ¾ cup of regular coffee plus ¾ teaspoon instant coffee, etc.

## HINTS ON MIXING AND COOKING SAUCES

I prefer a wooden spoon with a long handle for stirring sauces. The spoon doesn't get hot and it is easier to use.

\* \* \*

When a recipe calls for a sauce to be cooked in a double boiler, put the sauce to be cooked in the top compartment. Have the bottom compartment just ½ full of water and set this on top of the stove over a flame. When the water begins to boil, put the top compartment over the bottom one. If the sauce you are preparing does not have to be constantly stirred and has to cook a long time, put the lid of a Mason jar in the bottom compartment and as the water cooks dangerously low, the lid will rattle. This is a warning to add more water. Never let the pans cook dry; it ruins them. As soon as the mixture begins to get hot, lower the flame; the sauce will continue to cook without danger of lumping or scorching.

*   *   *

Recipes calling for cream mean single cream. Where double cream is indicated, it will be mentioned.

## BROWNED-BUTTER AND BOURBON SAUCE
### (A pre-Civil War Kentucky recipe)

Excellent for gingerbread, cinnamon bread or plum pudding.

| | |
|---|---|
| 2 T butter | 1 C double cream |
| 1 C brown sugar | ⅛ t salt |
| 2 T bourbon whiskey or more to taste | |

Brown butter in a heavy metal skillet. Add sugar and salt. Heat until smooth. Set aside to cool. Add whiskey and whipped cream just before serving.

## CHOCOLATE FUDGE SAUCE

Serve this sauce hot or warm over ice cream, leftover cake, pudding or what you will. This is the original Southern hot fudge sauce, and in my opinion cannot be improved on. If any is left over, put in a covered jar and keep in the icebox. It will become granular but will become smooth again when heated. To heat, set the jar (top removed) in a pan of warm water and when the jar has warmed set the pan over a flame until chocolate sauce melts.

| | |
|---|---|
| ⅛ lb. bitter chocolate (2 squares) | F. G. salt |
| ½ C water or milk | 1 t vanilla |
| 1 C sugar | 1 T butter or margarine |

Into a double boiler put the chocolate with the water or milk. Cover and cook until chocolate melts. Stir well to make a smooth thick paste. Add the butter or margarine, sugar and salt. Stir to mix and let cook 15 minutes to 20 minutes or until mixture makes a thick syrup. Remove from stove and add the vanilla extract. Serve hot.

## HATTIE DICK'S EGGNOG SAUCE FOR
## ICE CREAM OR PUDDINGS

3 egg yolks  
3 T sugar  
1 C double cream

3 jiggers (3 oz. or 6 T) bourbon  
   whiskey  
F. G. salt  
Nutmeg, if desired

Beat yolks light. Add sugar and salt and beat again. Add whiskey and mix well. Fold in whipped cream. Dust with nutmeg if desired. This is also wonderful on steamed plum or fig pudding, gingerbread or, heated, over steamed fruit cake.

## FRENCH CARAMEL OR BURNT SUGAR SAUCE
### *(For ice cream, puddings, pancakes, fruit)*

1 C granulated sugar          ½ C water

Put the sugar into a heavy metal skillet and stir and stir until the mixture begins to lump. At first the flame should be high, but lower it as the lumps form. When the sugar is smooth and clear and resembles maple syrup, add ½ cup water. The mixture will lump again but it will cook smooth if allowed to simmer slowly over a very low flame. When mixture has once more reached the syrup consistency, remove from stove, as it is ready to serve. It is wonderful on puddings, over vanilla or bisque ice cream garnished with toasted chopped almonds, or used in the bottom of custard cups (see recipe for Flan, page 182).

CAUTION: Do not let the mixture burn, as the sauce will be bitter, and do not cook too thick, as it has a tendency to thicken when cold.

## HELEN EVERHARDT'S PUDDING SAUCE FOR SIX
### *(With brandy or whiskey)*
### *(For Sponge Pudding, Woodford Pudding,*
### *Plum Pudding, etc.)*

½ C butter  
1 C sugar  
1 C hot cream

4 egg yolks, well beaten  
1 glass brandy or whiskey (4 T)  
Pinch of salt

Cream butter and sugar. Add egg yolks. Add salt and hot cream. Stir well. Pour mixture into double boiler. Set over a flame and stir until mixture thickens. Do not let it boil. Add whiskey or brandy. Stir until hot. Serve warm.

## For Other Sauces See the Following

FLAMING CHOCOLATE SAUCE (page 185), DE LUXE SAUCE (page 188), WINE SAUCE (page 191), OLD-FASHIONED LEMON SAUCE (page 193), PUDDING SAUCE FOR WOODFORD PUDDING (page 194), BRANDIED FRUIT SAUCE FOR ICE CREAM (page 178), PLOMBIÈRE SAUCE (page 186).

# Pie Crust and Miscellaneous Pastries

❋❋❋❋❋❋❋❋❋❋❋❋❋❋❋❋❋❋❋❋❋❋❋❋❋❋❋❋❋❋❋❋❋❋❋❋❋❋❋❋❋❋❋❋❋❋❋❋❋❋❋❋❋❋❋

## Pie Crusts and Variations

### ALL-PURPOSE PIE CRUST FOR ONE PIE (One-crust)
#### *(Enough for a 9-inch pie pan)*     *(Quickie!)*

1 C flour, measured before sifting (¼ lb.)
¼ t salt
2 to 4 T ice water

4 rounded T lard or vegetable shortening (about ⅓ C) I use bland lard or Swiftning

Sift flour and salt. Add lard or shortening and blend with the fingers until thoroughly mixed—it resembles corn meal. Add enough ice water to make a paste just stiff enough to roll. The dough should handle easily. Toss onto a floured board or floured marble-top table or floured pastry square. Roll with a floured rolling pin until very thin—⅛ to ¼ inch. Fold in halves and then in fourths. Place in a 9-inch ungreased pie pan and open out. Fit the dough into the pan and press out all air bubbles from under it. Let it set a minute, then press the edges flat with a fork dipped in ice water. Trim the edges with the dull edge of a knife. This dough makes enough for a bottom crust. Roll the trimmings into a ball, then roll thin into a strip. Make into a coil, rolling between the hands. Press this coil onto the edge of the pan, joining it to the bottom crust, then press into crimps or flutings with the thumb and forefingers. This makes a nice finish for the pie when no strips or top crust are used. If the crust is to be precooked before adding filling, prick all over with a fork to prevent blistering when baking.

## BOTTOM CRUST AND STRIPS FOR TOPPING

1½ C flour, measured after sift-     6 rounded T lard or vegetable
  ing                                        shortening
⅓ t salt                                 3 to 5 T ice water

Sift flour and salt. Add fat and mix with the fingers until the concoction
resembles corn meal. Add water to make a paste stiff enough to roll. Toss
onto a floured board or marble-top table and roll with a floured rolling
pin. Fold in half and then in half again. Place in an ungreased pie pan,
open crust and fit the dough evenly into this. Press the edges down with
a floured fork, and trim. Add the filling. Roll the remaining dough and
cut into strips with a pastry wheel—I like ½-inch-wide strips. Place
diagonally over the top of the pie ½ inch apart. Top with another
layer of criss-cross strips. Press the edges down once more with the
floured or dampened fork. Trim with the edge of a dull knife. Bake
pie in a hot oven according to directions for the particular pie you are
baking. If you like a highly glazed crust, brush the surface with a whole
egg beaten slightly with 1 tablespoon of ice water, or use thick cream
instead.

## BOTTOM CRUST AND SOLID TOP

Double the recipe for All-purpose Pie Crust for One Pie (page 201).
Divide the dough in half. Roll the bottom half thin and follow directions
for placing it in pan. Roll the dough for top crust. Fold it in half and
then in half again. Cut off the tip end and slash each of its edges,
making short gashes 1 inch apart. Place over filling in pie, putting hole
as near the center as possible. Unfold the dough gently. Press around
the edge once more with a fork dipped in flour. Trim the edges with a
dull knife. Brush the surface with 1 whole egg beaten lightly with 1
tablespoon of ice water. Bake according to directions.

## VARIATION OF PIE CRUST FLAVORS

If you are making an orange or lemon pie, try using the grated peel
(yellow part only) of one orange or one lemon to each cup of flour.
Mix the rest of the ingredients according to the recipe given and, if
desired, substitute fruit juice for water. If a sweet crust is liked, add ¼
cup sifted powdered sugar or 2 rounded tablespoons of granulated sugar
for each cup of flour. One teaspoon vanilla is also good in a crust where
a Vanilla Custard, Chess Pie or Transparent Pie is to be made. For
Cottage Cheese, Buttermilk, or Sour Cream Pie as well as Apple Pie,
use powdered cinnamon in the crust allowing 1 teaspoon for each cup of

flour used. Some people like grated Cheddar cheese crust with apple pie. To make this, add ½ cup of the grated cheese to each cup of flour used for the dough.

## PIE CRUST SHAPES FOR SPECIAL OCCASIONS

Instead of putting strips or solid tops on holiday pies, roll the crust thin, prick it and cut it out with the cookie cutter, using Christmas bells, stars or trees for mincemeat pie or eggnog pie or any pie you would serve for the Christmas holidays. For George Washington's Birthday, you would, of course, make a cherry pie, and the cookie design would be a hatchet. For the Thanksgiving pumpkin pie make crescents, or pumpkins (use a toothpick to make extra lines). A special birthday pie could be a candlestick. Put the raw cut-out pie-crust shapes on the filling before baking just as you would any other top crust.

## OTHER USES FOR PIE CRUST

The uses of pie crust are legion. Here are a few tried and true recipes, using the pie crust base. These are wonderful emergency dishes, but should be used the day they are baked; they do not keep too well. Store cooked leftovers in a tin box and reheat before serving again.

### CHEESE STRAWS          *(Quickie!)*
#### *(From pie crust dough)*

Make up the pie crust recipe for a single pie (page 201). Add ½ cup grated Cheddar cheese to the dough. Roll out very thin according to directions given for regular pie crust—⅛ to ¼ inch. Cut in ½-inch-wide strips and twist before placing on ungreased cookie tin. Also cut out some rings of dough with the doughnut cutter. Bake the rings and twists in a hot oven (450°) until golden-brown, 8 to 12 minutes. Remove from stove and serve with soup or salad. They make an attractive tidbit when several sticks are placed through a cheese ring on the plate on which they are passed. One-half teaspoon of paprika added to the dough will give it a very pretty pinkish cast.

### COCKTAIL SEED-SNACKS          *(Quickie!)*
#### *(From pie crust dough)*

Roll pie crust ¼ inch thick and cut into fancy shapes with a pastry wheel or small cookie cutters. Brush the tops with cream, or beaten egg mixed with 1 tablespoon of water. The yolk or white may be used as well as the whole egg. Sprinkle with poppy, sesame, or caraway seeds and bake until brown in a hot oven (450°).

## EMERGENCY COOKIES            *(Quickie!)*
### *(From pie crust dough)*

Roll pie crust ¼ inch thick. Cut into cookie shapes or make into strips 1 inch wide by 2 to 2½ inches long. Transfer to an ungreased cookie tin, brush the surface with an egg white or yolk and sprinkle with:

| | |
|---|---|
| 2 T granulated sugar (rounded) | 1 t cinnamon<br>2 T chopped almonds or pecans |

Bake in a hot oven (450°) from 10 to 12 minutes, or until cookies are done throughout. Remove from pan when cool. Nice for tea.

## INDIVIDUAL JELLY AND NUT ROLLS
## OR CIGARETTES            *(Quickie!)*
### *(From pie crust dough)*

Roll out pie crust as thin as possible and cut into rounds with the doughnut cutter, center cutter removed; or use the top of a glass tumbler, as you want a cookie with a 3- or 4-inch diameter. Spread the center with stiff jelly—grape, plum, raspberry and currant or whatever you wish, using ½ to 1 teaspoonful in each—leaving a circle ½ inch wide around the edge. Dust cinnamon over the jelly, then add a sprinkling of blanched, toasted, chopped almonds, or chopped pecans, or English walnuts. Roll up like a cigarette, pinching the edges together and turning the seam side down on the pan. The cigarettes are cooked on an ungreased pan or cookie tin. Bake in a hot oven (450°) for 12 to 15 minutes or until they are golden-brown. When cool, roll in powdered sugar and serve for tea or with wassail, eggnog, mulled wine or grape juice.

## JAM OR MARMALADE TURNOVERS
### *(From pie crust dough)*            *(Quickie!)*

Roll out pie crust to ¼-inch thickness and cut into rounds, edging a tea saucer with a dull knife (the rounds should be about 4 inches in diameter). Spread each turnover with a scant tablespoon of marmalade or jam or thick jelly—peach marmalade or apricot, peach and orange marmalade, raspberry and rhubarb jam, damson preserves are only a few of the many that make good fillings.

Spread evenly, leaving a circle of dough about ½ inch wide, around the edge. Fold the tarts or turnovers in half, pressing the edges together with a fork and turning the edges up so that no filling escapes. Transfer to an ungreased pie pan or cookie tin. Prick the top surface of the turnover 3 times with a fork (but do not stick through to the bottom). Bake in a hot oven (450°) until top is brown and turnovers are done, 12 to 18 minutes should be long enough. Dust with powdered sugar or sprinkle with sugar and run under the flame a moment until sugar melts slightly and turnovers are glazed on the surface. Serve hot with coffee for a winter dessert.

## JAM ROLL *(Quickie!)*
### *(From pie crust dough)*

Roll pie crust as thin as possible on a floured board. I like best to roll the crust about 4 to 5 inches wide and 10 inches long, or in that neighborhood. Use the pie crust recipe for one crust (page 201). Spread with thick jam or marmalade—I usually bake two rolls, one of jam, another of marmalade. Do not spread too thick or the mixture will seep out when cooking. Roll up like a jelly roll, pinching edges together, and transfer to a greased biscuit pan, placing the seam edge down on the pan. Brush the surface with beaten egg white mixed with a little water, or use the whole egg if you prefer. Bake in a hot oven (450°) until golden-brown. This takes about 30 minutes. Remove from stove and, when cool, dust with powdered sugar. Cut into inch slices and place them side by side on a cake plate. Wonderful with tea, or served warm for dessert with a good lemon or brandy sauce. Some people prick the surface of the roll when baking; others do not.

## MOLLY WALSH'S CREAM CHEESE CRUST
## FOR PIES AND TARTS *(Quickie!)*

| | |
|---|---|
| 1 C flour (¼ lb.) | 2 T powdered sugar (optional) |
| ½ C butter or margarine | ⅛ t baking powder |
| ½ C cream cheese | ½ t vanilla (optional) |

Soften butter and cheese to room temperature but do not melt. Cream together with sugar. Add to sifted dry ingredients and crumble with the fingers as for pie crust. Blend well and roll into a ball. Wrap in wax paper or foil and set in icebox overnight. Next morning roll out. Use a floured board or marble-top table or pastry cloth and a floured rolling pin, adding as little extra flour as possible to roll dough thin. Use for pie crust for jam tarts or turnovers (page 204). A wonderful crust for cheese or buttermilk pie. Prick the crust all over, then bake until done but not brown before adding filling. This crust must be rolled very thin, as it has baking powder in it. This can also be rolled into small loaves, wrapped in wax paper and kept in the icebox until needed. It makes a very good icebox cookie. When ready to make the cookies, remove the small loaf from the icebox and with a sharp knife cut into as thin slices as possible. Place on an ungreased cookie tin and bake in a hot oven (450°) until cookies are done throughout and are slightly tan in color. Remove from stove and let cool in pans. Dust with powdered sugar and remove cookies from pan with a spatula or pancake turner.

## Miscellaneous Pastries

### LITTLE COLONEL'S CHRISTMAS CRULLERS
### (Raggedy Britches)
#### (6½ dozen crullers)

This is the recipe of the original *Little Colonel*—Hattie Cochran (Mrs. Albert Dick). It is with her permission that I give it here, and I must add that it makes the most delicious crullers I've ever eaten. In my opinion they are the perfect accompaniment for eggnog; and are equally good with hot chocolate or coffee for Sunday brunch or afternoon tea. These crullers keep fresh for a long time, too, if put in a sealed tin box—but who could keep them!

1 C butter softened but not melted
2 C granulated sugar
6 egg yolks
6 C flour, measured after sifting

6 egg whites
2 whole nutmegs, grated
Grated rind of 2 lemons (yellow part only) or 1 t vanilla, if you prefer that flavor
Powdered sugar for dusting

Cream butter and sugar. Add slowly the egg yolks, grated nutmegs, grated lemon rind (or vanilla if preferred). Stir the butter-egg mixture into the flour. Fold in the well-beaten whites. The dough is soft but can be handled. If too soft, put in a covered bowl in the icebox for several hours before using. Roll small amounts at a time, although more flour may have to be added. The cruller dough should be rolled thin—about ¼ inch thick. Cut into strips 1 inch wide by 6 inches long. Use a knife, or a pastry wheel if you own one. Fold these strips in half and twist together. Fry until golden-brown in deep hot melted lard or vegetable shortening (375°). As soon as the crullers are golden-brown, lift out of the fat with a skimmer and drain on absorbent paper, and dust heavily with powdered sugar.

Another way to shape the crullers is to cut them into 1½-inch squares. Make 3 gashes in the center and pinch each end gash with the center one. This will make 2 slits to help fry the centers evenly. Cook as above.

## CARRIE TODD'S DERBY CAKE
## OR SCOTCH SHORTBREAD

Carrie Todd is one of Kentucky's best and most famous cooks. She sent me this recipe for Scotch shortbread and said that she bakes it in a large pie pan and cuts and serves it in wedges to be eaten with tea or wine. In many old American cookery books these cakes were called Derby cakes, and so I am using the name again.

½ lb. of flour (about 2 C)          ¼ lb. butter (about ½ C)
¼ lb. sugar (about ½ C)

Rub ingredients together and blend with the fingers. The dough is too short to roll. Press it into two 9-inch pie or square pans and flatten with the palms of the hands, so that dough is about ⅓ or ½ an inch thick. Prick the surface with a fork and bake in a hot oven (450°) like pie crust for 10 to 15 minutes, or until golden-brown. Mark into wedges or squares at once and leave in the pan until cold. Dust with powdered sugar and remove sections to a platter, using a pancake turner. These cakes can be topped with fresh strawberries and cream for dessert.

## INDIVIDUAL SHORTCAKES FOR BERRIES,
## SLICED PEACHES, OR OTHER FRUIT
### *(4 servings)*

| | |
|---|---|
| 1 C flour | 2 T sugar |
| 1½ t baking powder | 1 egg |
| 2 rounded T butter or margarine | 1 to 3 T cream or milk (if necessary) |
| ⅛ t salt | ½ t vanilla (optional) |

Sift flour, baking powder, salt and sugar. Add the butter or margarine and crumble with the fingers until the mixture resembles corn meal. Add egg, slightly beaten, and mix again, and if the dough is too stiff to roll, add cream or milk to make a dough that is semi-soft but not too soft to roll. Add vanilla extract if you like the flavor. Toss dough on a floured board and roll ¼ inch thick. Cut out with a large round cookie cutter or a glass tumbler. Brush surfaces with melted butter or margarine and put 2 buttered sides together. Place shortcakes on a greased cookie tin or biscuit pan and bake in a hot oven (450°) 10 to 15 minutes, or until golden-brown. Remove from stove. Split shortcakes and spread with sweetened fruit, allowing ½ cup sugar to each pint of berries, sliced peaches or other fruit. Put more fruit on top layer and crown the whole with a tablespoon of sweetened whipped cream, flavored with vanilla.

VARIATION: Some prefer a crisp, wafer-like shortcake. If so, do not put the two pieces of uncooked dough together, but bake separately and then place layers of sweetened fruit between the two crisp rounds, and on the tops. The whipped cream garnishing is used also.

## LARGE SHORTCAKE
### *(6 to 8 servings)*

Double the recipe for individual shortcakes. Divide dough in half. Roll one half about ½ inch thick, keeping the mixture round. Place in the bottom of a greased 9-inch pie pan. Brush surface with butter or margarine. Top with the other half of dough rolled ½ inch thick. Brush again with butter or margarine. Bake 20 minutes to ½ hour in a hot oven (450°). When the shortcake is golden-brown, remove from the stove. Split, butter and spread with a layer of sweetened fruit. Pour more sweetened fruit over the top and pass the sweetened, flavored whipped cream with the cake. Cut in pie-shaped wedges to serve.

## SNOWBALLS OR SNOWFLAKES

These delicious pastries do not require any irons at all—only a good right arm to roll the dough thin enough. This is my great-grandmother's recipe and I recommend it most heartily for eggnog or mulled wine, for the snowflakes are only slightly sweet and are light and fragile. They are at home on a tea table also or to accompany a cup of hot chocolate. Great-grandmother's snowflakes were round and large, but I found it impractical to cut the dough in rounds because the scraps could not be rerolled (at least by me). So I now roll the dough as thin as possible and cut it into strips 1 inch wide by 3 or 4 inches long. I use a pastry wheel to make my strips, but a dull knife will do. Make 2 to 4 little slashes about ½ inch apart down the center of each strip. Pinch little gashes together to make holes larger. This allows the fat to cook the center of the strip and makes it crisp. Here is my revised recipe based on the old family formula:

1 C plus 2 T all-purpose flour after sifting once
1 T sugar
⅛ t salt
1 T softened sweet butter (no substitutes)

1 whole egg and
1 egg yolk
1 t white wine, brandy, lemon juice or vanilla
Melted grease—bland lard or vegetable shortening

Measure the flour after sifting, then sift again into a bowl, with sugar and salt. Work into this the softened sweet butter just as you would for a pie crust. Now add the whole egg and the extra yolk and the white wine, brandy, lemon juice or vanilla. I use brandy, but any of the other flavorings will do. If the lemon juice is used, add the grated rind of ½ lemon (yellow part only). This dough resembles noodle dough. Make it into 2 round balls, wrap them in a clean towel and set in the icebox for 20 minutes, to chill. I find it necessary to roll the dough on a floured pastry cloth or kitchen towel in order to get it thin enough. At any rate, flour the rolling pin as well as the towel, using as little extra flour as possible. Turn the dough frequently and when it is as thin as gauze, as they said in the ante-bellum cook books, it is ready to be cut into shapes. Cut with a pastry wheel or dull knife, as directed at the beginning of the recipe.

To fry, have a skillet ½ full of melted grease. My great-grandmother used her own home-churned butter, but I have had very satisfactory results with bland lard. Vegetable shortening will also work perfectly well. When the fat registers 370°, or when it browns a cube of bread in 45 seconds, drop the snowflakes into the fat, 2 or 3 at a time. Do not try to cook too many at once—they take only a few seconds to cook. As soon as they are light-brown on one side, turn and brown on the other. When that is also brown, remove with a perforated spoon or skimmer to a sheet of absorbent paper to drain. Sprinkle at once with powdered sugar or a mixture of ½ teaspoon cinnamon to every 2 tablespoons of powdered sugar. Stack log-cabin-wise on a plate and serve. These snow-flakes should be made an hour or two before using. They will not stay crisp overnight.

# Miscellaneous Fillings for Pies

### (Unless otherwise noted all these fillings are for 9-inch pies)

## BROWNED BUTTER AND BOURBON PIE

| | |
|---|---|
| 3 eggs | 1 C milk, or ½ C milk and ½ |
| 1 C medium or dark-brown | C cream |
| sugar | 2 T flour, browned * |
| 2 T bourbon whiskey | 2 T butter, browned |
| | F. G. salt |

* To brown flour, see note under General Directions for Baking Cakes (page 231).

Beat yolks of 2 eggs with 1 whole egg. Add sugar and blend. Add butter, which has been melted and browned, and the flour mixed to a paste in milk and cream. Put mixture in double boiler and stir until thickened. Add bourbon. Pour into an 8-inch pie crust after pastry is baked. Beat 2 egg whites with 2 tablespoons sugar for meringue. Put on top of custard and brown in oven. One teaspoon of vanilla may be substituted for the 2 tablespoons of bourbon, if preferred.

## BUTTERMILK PIE
### (6 servings)

This is a Kentucky specialty, but most of the recipes for it used too much flour and buttermilk. Finally I hit upon these proportions and we think the pie delicious, even better than a cottage cheese pie, of which it is certainly a first cousin.

Make up your favorite pie crust and place in a 9-inch pie pan. Prick the surface to keep from blistering and bake the pie for 10 minutes in a hot oven (450°). It should be done through but not brown.

### The Filling

| | |
|---|---|
| 3 eggs | ¾ t vanilla |
| ¾ C sugar | 3 T lemon juice |
| 3 T flour | Grated rind 1 lemon (yellow part only) |
| 3 T melted butter (no substitutes) | Cinnamon to dust top |
| 1½ C churned buttermilk | |

To make the filling, beat the eggs with the sugar. When light and lemon-colored, add the flour. Beat again, then pour into this the churned buttermilk with fat particles still intact. Add vanilla, lemon juice, grated rind and butter. Pour the filling into the baked pie crust and dust the surface with cinnamon. Return to a moderate oven (375°) and bake until filling just sets. Do not cook too long, for it is a custard and, like the other members of the tribe, will become tough if it stays in the stove too long—20 to 30 minutes should do the trick. Remove from the oven and allow to cool slightly before serving. Bake in individual pie pans if desired.

## BUTTERMILK BOURBON PIE

Follow the recipe for Buttermilk Pie, substituting bourbon whiskey for lemon juice. Omit the lemon rind and vanilla and use nutmeg on top instead of cinnamon. If desired, ½ cup currants may be added to the filling before baking.

## CHESS PIE, Huntsville

This recipe came from Huntsville, Alabama, where it was such a specialty of a certain inn that people went to Huntsville from miles around, just to taste this particular confection. Someone in Montgomery got the recipe, finally, and passed it on to me.

| | |
|---|---|
| ½ C butter (no substitutes) | 2 eggs, separated |
| 1 C sugar | 2 T double cream |
| 1½ t white Southern corn meal | ½ t vanilla (optional) |
| (Use pearl or finely ground meal for this) | F. G. salt if sweet butter is used |

Cream butter and sugar. Add egg yolks and beat well. Add corn meal mixed to a paste with cream. Fold in the well-beaten whites and a little salt. Add vanilla if you like the flavor—the original recipe did not call for it, but I like it. Pour into a pie crust previously baked 10 minutes or until done but not brown. Set in a moderately hot oven (400°) for 5 minutes, then reduce heat to 375° and cook 20 to 25 minutes or until filling just sets—take out while the center is just off the runny side. Do not overcook, or the pie will be grainy and leathery. If the filling begins to get too brown before it has finished cooking, place a piece of heavy brown paper over it.

## DOROTHY CLARK'S CHOCOLATE FUDGE PIE
### *(The best chocolate pie I've ever tasted)*

| | |
|---|---|
| 4 sqs. (¼ lb.) bitter chocolate | 4 egg yolks |
| ½ C cream | 2 C sugar, mixed with 1 T |
| ½ C milk | flour |
| ½ C pure butter | 2 t vanilla |

Melt chocolate in double boiler with the cream, milk and butter. When thick and well blended set aside to cool slightly. Beat the egg yolks. Slowly pour the chocolate mixture into these. Add the sugar mixed with the flour and return to the stove until the mixture cooks quite thick— 20 to 30 minutes. Add vanilla extract to this and pour into a 9-inch pastry shell previously baked until done but not brown in a hot oven (450°). (Ten to 12 minutes should be sufficient.)

## The Meringue

| | |
|---|---|
| 4 egg whites, well beaten with | 4 T sugar |
| ⅛ t salt | ½ t vanilla |

Make a meringue of the egg whites well beaten with the salt. Add sugar and vanilla. Place over chocolate mixture and roughen the top with a fork or spoon. Return to a moderate oven (375°) and cook until meringue browns—20 minutes. Serve warm or cold. Do not put in refrigerator but keep at room temperature if all of pie is not used the day it is made.

VARIATION: I make half this recipe and find it quite enough for 5 individual pies, provided 3 egg whites and 3 tablespoons of sugar are used in meringue to cover the chocolate. I do not cook my filling quite as much as the original recipe calls for. I make it the consistency of a thick custard instead of a paste. Take your choice.

## CONFEDERATE PIE

| | |
|---|---|
| ½ C butter | 3 egg yolks |
| ⅔ C sugar | ½ C cream |
| 2 T (heaping) tart jelly (about ¼ C) | 3 egg whites, 6 T sugar and ½ C chopped pecans for meringue |
| 1 T flour (heaping) | |

Cream butter and sugar and add jelly (grape jelly is delicious in this filling). Beat to a froth—I use an electric beater. Add egg yolks and beat again. Add cream mixed to a smooth paste with flour. Beat once more. Pour into a precooked pie crust and set in a moderate oven (375°), cooking 25 to 30 minutes or until custard sets. Do not overcook. Make a meringue of the 3 egg whites and 6 tablespoons of sugar and put on top of custard. Dust with chopped pecans and run under the flame to brown slightly; have the grill cold when the pie is put in and keep the door open while it cooks, as it burns easily.

## COTTAGE CHEESE PIE

| | |
|---|---|
| 1 C cottage cheese, whipped free of lumps | 1 T flour |
| ⅛ t salt | 1 T melted butter or margarine |
| ½ C sugar | ½ C thick cream, sweet or sour |
| 2 well-beaten eggs | ½ t cinnamon |
| ½ t vanilla | Grated rind of ½ lemon |
| | 1 T lemon juice |

Beat eggs well with flour and sugar. When thick and lemon-colored, add cheese, cream, and all other ingredients except cinnamon. Pour into a 9-inch pie pan lined with slightly baked pie crust. Sprinkle with cinnamon on top and set in a moderately hot oven (450°) for 15 minutes.

Reduce heat to 375° and cook until filling sets—15 to 20 minutes longer. If sour cream is used, the lemon juice and rind may be omitted.

## EGGNOG PIE

3 egg yolks
1 egg white
½ t nutmeg
F. G. salt
2 egg whites for meringue

⅔ C sugar
¼ C butter
2 T whiskey (bourbon) or rum
1 T whiskey and 2 T sugar, to
flavor meringue

Cream butter and sugar. Add well-beaten egg yolks and white. Add nutmeg and whiskey or rum. Pour into unbaked pastry shell in an 8-inch pie pan. Bake 5 minutes in a hot oven (425°), and 10 minutes in a moderate oven (375°) until custard sets. Do not let it get too firm. Top with a meringue made by beating 2 egg whites and a pinch of salt until stiff. Add 1 tablespoon of whiskey and 2 tablespoons of sugar and beat again. Spread on filling and return to oven until meringue browns. A nice winter dessert.

## MAPLE PECAN PIE WITH MAPLE MERINGUE

Into a baked 9-inch pie crust pour the following filling:

2 T butter
¼ C flour
1 C maple syrup
3 egg yolks

1 t vanilla
F. G. salt
½ C water
¾ C coarsely chopped pecans

Beat yolks until light and spongy. Add the flour, alternating with water. Add syrup, salt and vanilla and pour into a double boiler. Add the butter, set the pan over flame on top of stove and *stir* and *stir* and *stir* until custard is smooth and thick. Fold in the nuts and pour into baked pie crust. Top with:

### Maple Meringue

3 egg whites
3 T maple syrup

F. G. salt

Add salt to whites and beat until very stiff. Add syrup slowly. Spread over maple filling and roughen the surface. Put in a moderate oven (375°) and bake until meringue browns—15 to 20 minutes. Serve warm or cold. This is really a delectable pie of the butterscotch variety.

## LORRAINE BELL'S NUT AND RAISIN CHESS PIES
### (8 individual pies)

½ C butter
1 C brown sugar
4 eggs
3 T granulated sugar

½ C English walnuts (chopped coarsely)
½ C seedless raisins or chopped seeded raisins
F. G. salt

Cream butter and brown sugar. Add 1 whole egg and 3 egg yolks, well beaten. Mix well, then fold in nuts and raisins. This filling is poured into 8 slightly-baked pastry shells and placed in a hot oven (400°). The pies are allowed to remain for 5 minutes, when the temperature is reduced to 375°, then they are left to cook until the mixture sets, which should take from 20 to 30 minutes, depending on their size. Should the edges of the filling begin to brown too much before the centers have cooked, reduce the heat to 350° and place clean pieces of brown paper over the tops. When the filling sets, the crusts should be brown and the pies done. (This can be baked as one 9-inch pie if preferred, in which case it might have to cook a little longer.) When done, remove from oven and top with meringue made by beating the 3 egg whites very stiff with the salt and granulated sugar. Return to oven and allow to brown. Serve warm or cold but never hot. These are nice pies to take on picnics as they keep well and are not as fragile as most chess pies.

## PECAN PIE
### (As served at Ashbourne Inn)

For note about the Inn see Chicken Cacciatore (page 99).

3 eggs
½ C sugar
¼ t salt
1 C light corn syrup

½ t vanilla
1 C coarsely chopped or broken pecans

Beat eggs slightly. Add all other ingredients and mix well. Line pie pan with plain pastry (the recipe doesn't call for it but I prick the raw pie crust and bake it 10 minutes in a hot oven (450°), before adding filling). Pour filling into crust, then return to the oven and bake 40 to 50 minutes in a slow oven (325°), or until filling just sets. Do not overcook. Chill and serve.

## PECAN BOURBON PIE

Omit vanilla in above recipe and add 3 tablespoons of bourbon whiskey instead of vanilla, using dark instead of light corn syrup.

## JENNIE SELLIGMAN'S CREAM CHEESE CAKE-PIE
### *(16 to 18 servings)*

Mrs. Selligman is noted in Louisville for her elegant food. Once, when she was living at one of the local hotels, she had given her cheese pie recipe to the chef and asked him to prepare it for some guests. While he was mixing it, a representative from a cheese concern came into the hotel kitchen. He noticed that the pie was being made with cottage cheese and thought how delicious it would be made of cream cheese— so much smoother and richer. He asked Mrs. Selligman's permission to take her recipe back to his laboratories and have the expert cooks work out a cheese cake-pie with his brand of cheese. She consented and this is the result. She was generous enough to give me the recipe.

### Crust

| | |
|---|---|
| 1 box zwieback, ground (24 slices of the sweet toast, making about 2 C of crumbs) | ¾ C butter, melted, or yellow margarine |
| 1½ C sugar | Save out 2 T crumbs to sprinkle over the top of filling |
| 1 rounded t cinnamon | |

Grind the zwieback. Add to this the sugar, cinnamon, and melted butter or yellow margarine. Mix well with the fingers and save out about 2 tablespoons of crumbs to sprinkle over the top of the filling. Use an 11- or 12-inch spring form. Pour the mixed crust into this and press with the fingers and palms, spreading the mixture over the bottom and sides of the pan, being careful that there are no cracks or breaks where the filling can seep out onto the pan. Some people use the back of a tablespoon to spread the zwieback mixture evenly, then press it into place with the fingers or palms.

### Filling

| | |
|---|---|
| 1 lb. of any preferred brand cream cheese | 1 t vanilla |
| | Juice and rind of 1 lemon |
| 1¼ C granulated sugar | 1 qt. sour cream |
| ¼ C flour (sifted with sugar) | 8 egg whites beaten with a little salt |
| 8 egg yolks | |

Cream the cheese with sugar and flour. Beat well. Add the egg yolks, one at a time, vanilla, juice and rind of lemon, or add a little more lemon juice to taste, if necessary. Add the sour cream and fold in the egg whites well beaten with the salt. Sprinkle surface with the zwieback crumbs and powdered cinnamon. Bake 5 minutes at 375°, then reduce heat to 300° and bake 1 hour, or until filling sets.

## PRESIDENT TYLER'S PUDDIN' PIE
### *(A 9-inch pie)*

This recipe was given to me by Priscilla Stevenson, great grand-daughter of President Tyler, tenth President of the United States. She says the pie was often served at the White House during the administration of her ancestor. It is truly a culinary masterpiece, undoubtedly related to the chess-pie clan. As far as we are concerned, it is the President of them all.

| | |
|---|---|
| ¾ C white sugar | 2 eggs |
| ¾ C brown sugar | ½ t vanilla |
| ½ C cream | ¼ t nutmeg grated over pie |
| ½ C butter | |

Cream butter and sugar. Add eggs, cream and vanilla. Have ready a pie shell baked in a hot oven until crust is done but not brown, 10 minutes. Add filling, and dust the top with the grated nutmeg. Put pie back in a slow oven (350°) and remove when pie is golden-brown and filling is firm and slightly shaky in middle. If cooked too long, the filling will be granular or candied. It should be like a firm, transparent jelly when properly baked.

If individual pies are to be baked, the recipe will make 12 small ones. Cook 15 to 20 minutes after filling has been put in the precooked crusts. As soon as filling no longer shakes all over, take from the stove. Dust with powdered sugar and cool slightly before removing from pans. These are delicious for out-of-door barbecues or backyard picnics, as they can be picked up and eaten with the fingers.

## FLEXNER SPECIAL PUMPKIN PIE

| | |
|---|---|
| 1½ C steamed, strained pumpkin pulp (frozen or canned will do) | ¼ t allspice |
| | ¼ t cloves |
| | ¼ t mace |
| 2 T melted butter | ¼ t nutmeg |
| 1 t cinnamon | 2 or 3 T brandy or bourbon whiskey |
| ½ t ginger | |
| 1 T lemon juice | 2 T flour |
| 2 eggs | F. G. salt |
| ½ C dark brown sugar | 1 C rich milk, or half milk, half cream |
| ½ C white sugar | |

To the pumpkin pulp add the melted butter, cinnamon, ginger, allspice, cloves, mace, nutmeg, lemon juice and brandy or whiskey (the latter must be to taste). Beat eggs until light and lemon-colored. Add flour and when well blended add dark and white sugar, salt and milk. Combine the two mixtures. Pour into a 9-inch pie pan lined with uncooked, all-purpose pie crust. Bake 15 minutes in a hot oven (450°), then reduce heat to 375° and cook ½ hour longer, or until the custard sets. To test, run a knife into the center of the filling and if the knife comes out clean the pie is done. Serve plain or with thick cream. If you like whipped cream with this, try flavoring a cup with ¼ cup of diced crystallized ginger.

## BELLE CHRISTY'S STACK PIE OR CHESS CAKE-PIE
### (12 servings)

This recipe dates from colonial days when the all-day picnic was a major holiday and each family made some contribution to the feast. Because it was difficult to pack so many pies in a hamper, someone conceived the idea of stacking them, then holding them together with an icing. These chess cakes or stack pies became very popular at the "infairs" of the plantation Southern hostess in pre-Civil War days. Four, five or six shallow pies were baked and put together. The pie fillings usually followed a recipe similar to the Transparent Pie or Sugar Pie given in this chapter, but there was this difference—the filling was very shallow, and it was cooked a little stiffer than the average chess-pie filling, though it was not leathery. Here's a recipe for a stack pie or chess cake of five layers. It was given me by Mrs. Belle Christy, a practical nurse near Louisville who was with us many years ago. Mrs. Christy said her old mother, who was then in her eighties, had such a chess cake for her wedding cake. It is cut into thin, pie-shaped wedges, for it is very rich. Here's Mrs. Christy's recipe:

### Crust

| | |
|---|---|
| 4 C flour | ½ t soda |
| 1 generous C lard | 1 t cream of tartar |
| 1 t salt | 8 to 10 T water (ice water) |

Sift dry ingredients. Add lard and crumble with the fingers until mixture resembles corn meal. Add water and mix to make a stiff dough but one that will hold together. Cut into 5 portions and roll on a floured board or cloth or marble-top table using floured rolling pin and rolling out only one pie at a time. The layers should be very thin—¼ inch or less —⅛ inch is better. Prick the crusts all over and bake them in a hot oven (450°) until done but not brown—8 to 10 minutes should be enough. I use 9-inch pans. The pie that is put on the bottom is regulation height, the others are cut short, just the height of the baked shallow filling. Trim off the excess crust while the pies are still hot—the minute they are taken from the oven. If they cool, the dough will be too brittle to cut evenly. To make the filling for the five pies, use:

2 C sugar  
1 C butter (no substitutes)  
12 egg yolks

1 t lemon juice, or a little more to taste

Cream butter and sugar. The butter should be softened to room temperature but not melted. When light and spongy, add the egg yolks one at a time. I use an electric mixer to beat this filling properly but it can be blended by hand if you have a strong right arm. Add the lemon juice. Mrs. Christy used only 1 teaspoon of the juice, but I like the flavor of lemon and so use a whole one and the grated peel—yellow part only—but this is a matter of taste. Divide the filling into five parts and place in 5 crust-lined pans. Smooth the filling evenly with a dull knife. Bake in a moderate oven (350°) until filling just sets and no longer shakes in the middle when pie is moved. I bake only two pies at a time. Do not cook too long. Let filling cool in pans. To remove baked pies from pans run a spatula around them and gently remove them with a pancake turner, placing the bottom pie on the serving plate and stacking the others in layers on top of that, filling side up.

### Frosting for Stack Pie

Mrs. Christy said they frosted their stack pie with a boiled white icing, flavored with lemon juice. See recipe for frosting used with Mary Todd's White Cake (page 237) or use this recipe Cissy Gregg recommends for Stack Pie:

### Brown Sugar Frosting for Stack Pie

2 C brown sugar                    1 C heavy cream

Combine the two in a saucepan and cook until the mixture reaches the hard soft-ball stage. By that, Cissy means that when a teaspoon of this mixture is dropped into a cup of ice water it will form a ball that is easily picked up with the fingers and will hold its shape. Let mixture stand a few minutes, then beat until creamy and spread over top and sides of pie. Do not wait too long to spread this on the pie, for when it begins to harden it sugars quickly. If it gets too hard to handle, add a little cream and beat and heat again in a pan over boiling water until the frosting reaches the proper consistency to spread. This also makes a nice icing for old-fashioned white, spice or jam cake.

## MINN-ELL MANDEVILLE'S TRANSPARENT PIE
### *(6 servings)*

One of the favorite Louisville anecdotes concerns the local judge whose cook was celebrated far and wide for her delicious transparent pies. The judge refused to part with the recipe, and when the cook was approached, she insisted, "Ah ain't got no receipt. Ah jest mixes up whut come into my mind at de time."

A charming Lexington bride and her new husband were visiting the judge, and the bride asked for the transparent pie recipe. The judge's answer was a decided "No," but not wanting to seem inhospitable, he assured her that whenever she wanted to serve the pies for dessert he would send them to her. Not long afterwards she wrote him, reminding him of his promise. He replied that he would keep his word, she had only to name the day. She did, and thought no more about dessert for her dinner until her guests were seated and her own servant whispered that nothing had arrived from Louisville. As the meal progressed she became more uneasy, but just as the salad plates were cleared away, in bounced the judge's cook, clad in her best starched uniform, bib apron, and red bandanna, a crested silver platter of the treasured confections in her hands.

Minn-Ell Mandeville, one of the best cooks Kentucky ever produced, shared with me her heirloom recipe for transparent pie many years ago, before her untimely death. Here it is:

### The Dough

Make up your favorite rich pie crust dough—enough for a 9-inch pie pan or 6 individual pans. Prick it with a fork to keep it from blistering, and put it in a hot oven (450°) for 10 or 12 minutes or until crust is done but not browned. Then remove it from the oven.

### The Filling

| | |
|---|---|
| 8-oz. glass tart jelly | 3 eggs, well beaten |
| 1 C butter, softened but not melted | F. G. salt, if sweet butter is used |
| | 1 C sifted white sugar |

Empty the jelly into the bottom of the pie pan onto the crust, or divide into 6 parts, and place in the bottom of individual pans. Spread the jelly evenly over the bottom of the crust or crusts with a knife. We prefer raspberry and currant jelly, but plum, grape, blackberry or any good homemade jelly will do, and damson plum preserves are also acceptable.

Now, cream the butter with the sifted white sugar. If you own an electric beater by all means use it. Add to this the eggs and continue to beat the mixture until it is light and spongy. This filling, which in old English cookery books was called a *cheese*, is probably the ancestor of all Southern chess pies, the word *chess* being a corruption of *cheese*. At any rate, the mixture is poured over the jelly and this too is spread evenly. Put the pie or small tarts into the oven set at 450° and leave 5 minutes. Then reduce the heat to 375° and let remain until the top mixture sets. This takes from 20 to 25 minutes. I test my pie by slightly shaking the pan. When the center of the filling is almost firm, remove pan or pans from the stove. Be careful not to overcook. Serve warm or cold but never hot. These pies are very rich, and demand a large cup of strong, aromatic, steaming black coffee.

## MY OWN VARIATIONS OF
## MINN-ELL MANDEVILLE'S TRANSPARENT PIE

### Bob Andy Pie

This is a Frankfort, Kentucky recipe and the original is so rich and so sweet that I hesitate to give it here. I have made a very palatable substitute by adding ⅔ cup of cream to the Transparent Pie recipe given above and omitting the jelly. Some versions of Bob Andy Pie require a meringue to top the filling. It should be made as follows:

| | |
|---|---|
| 3 egg whites | 3 T sugar (rounded) |
| F. G. salt | ½ t vanilla |

Beat the salted whites until stiff. Add the sugar and beat again. Add vanilla. The meringue should stand in peaks when ready, or should stay in the bowl when the bowl is turned upside down. Spoon this over the transparent filling and run under the flame until meringue becomes a golden-brown. Watch to see that it does not burn.

### Sugar Pie

As far as I can judge, Sugar Pie is made in the same way as the Bob Andy Pie with the meringue, except for the addition of 1 teaspoon of vanilla to the filling.

# Fruit Fillings

## APPLE CHARLOTTE OR SOUTHERN SKILLET PIE
### The Dough

| | |
|---|---|
| 2 C flour | ⅛ t salt |
| ¼ t baking powder | ½ C shortening (half lard, half |
| 1 T sugar | butter if possible) |
| 1 egg | Cold water |

Sift together flour, baking powder, sugar and salt. Add shortening and crumble with the fingers, or cut the shortening into the dry ingredients with a pastry fork. Add the egg and enough cold water to make a dough the consistency of pie crust. Roll thin—about ¼ inch—and put into a well-greased 8-inch iron skillet. Do not trim the edges of the crust.

### The Filling

| | |
|---|---|
| 3 large apples | Juice of ½ lemon |
| ½ t cinnamon | Grated rind 1 lemon |
| ¼ C coarsely chopped pecans | 1 glass white wine (about 4 T) |
| or almonds | 2 T butter or margarine |
| ¼ C raisins or currants | |

Dice apples or slice in thin rings. Add cinnamon, chopped nuts, raisins or currants, lemon juice and rind, and white wine. Put in crust-lined skillet. Dot apples with the butter or margarine. Fold crust over the top so that it overlaps. Pinch edges together and brush with melted butter or margarine, beaten egg, or thick cream, to glaze the surface. Bake in hot oven (450°) for 15 minutes, then reduce heat to 375° and cook 30 minutes longer or until crust is brown. Serve from the skillet in which the pie was baked or turn upside down on a platter with 2- or 3-inch sides, or in a shallow bowl. Cut Charlotte in pie-shaped wedges. Top each slice with hard sauce, vanilla ice cream or whipped cream sweetened and flavored with vanilla.

## GRANDMOTHER FLEXNER'S APPLE CUSTARD PIE
### (For winter apples)

| | |
|---|---|
| 6 large, firm apples | 1 C sugar |
| ¼ C water | 2 T butter |
| 1 t cinnamon | ¼ t nutmeg |

Peel and core apples and cut into eighths. Boil water and sugar. Add apples and cook 10 to 15 minutes or until they can be easily pierced with a toothpick or straw. Then place them in the bottom of a partially baked crust (the All-Purpose Pie Crust) side by side in rows. Pour the syrup over them if any is left. Dust with spices, dot with butter. Cook 5 minutes in a hot oven (450°), then reduce the heat to 375° and let remain 15 minutes. Pour over the apples the following custard mixture:

1 egg                                        1 T flour
⅔ C cream

Beat egg and flour, adding cream slowly until the mixture is smooth. Pour over apples without moving pie pan from oven. Close oven door and let pie continue cooking until custard sets. This takes about 8 to 10 minutes. Serve warm or cool. *Do not make this recipe with anything but winter apples*—the early June apples will cook to pieces and not hold their shape.

## LEONTINE'S CHERRY PIE
### *(With sour red cherries)*

We once had a cook named Leontine who made delicious sour red cherry pies with an old-fashioned flavor. I think the secret ingredient was the brown sugar. Here is her recipe:

1 qt. sour cherries, measured be-       2 T butter
    fore stoning                        ¼ C brown sugar, firmly
1 C white sugar                             packed
2 T flour

Line a 9-inch pie pan with All-Purpose Crust and sprinkle the brown sugar over it. Mix the stoned cherries with the sifted white sugar and flour. Add melted butter and stir well, leaving a few minutes for cherries to draw their own juice. Pour into pie shell and place strips of crust over the top. Set in a hot oven (450°) and leave for 15 minutes, then reduce heat to 375° and leave 30 minutes longer, or until top strips brown. Remove from stove and cool slightly before serving. This pie is one of the best to serve à la mode—a scoop of vanilla ice cream on each slice of warm pie.

## DAMSON PLUM PIE

This is one of the most delicious of all fruit pies, yet until I came to Kentucky I had never tasted it. But we now have a damson plum tree in our yard to assure ourselves that we will have enough damson pie. The fruit freezes well, too, and we put up enough to tide us over the winter.

3 C stoned damson plums (measured after stoning). About 1 qt. beforehand

1 C white sugar or more to taste

1 T flour
2 T butter
½ t cinnamon
¼ C brown sugar
½ C water

Mix damson plums, ⅓ cup of water and sugar and boil 5 minutes. Add butter and flour mixed to a paste with the remainder of the water and cook until sauce has thickened, stirring constantly. Pour into partially baked pie crust cooked about 10 minutes in a hot oven (450°). The crust should be done but not brown. Dust filling with cinnamon. Place strips over the top. Return to a hot oven (450°) and cook 10 minutes. Reduce the heat to 375° and cook 15 to 20 minutes longer, or until top strips brown. Dust with powdered sugar and serve warm but not hot. A scoop of vanilla ice cream for each serving makes a delicious company dessert.

## GREEN TOMATO PIE

This is another Kentucky specialty. Select firm green tomatoes. Be sure there is no red about them, and if tomato is red inside when cut, discard it for a tomato that is firm and green throughout. The tomatoes should weigh ½ pound each after trimming off stem ends. Three such tomatoes should produce 1 quart of sliced tomatoes. I cut them in rings about ¼ inch thick and then in halves. Add more slices if needed to make a full quart.

1 qt. sliced green tomatoes
½ C water
½ C seedless raisins
¾ t cinnamon
½ t ginger
Grated rind 1 lemon
1 C sugar

2 T flour
¼ t nutmeg
2 T butter
1 wineglass brandy or whiskey (4 T, or a little more to taste)
1½ T lemon juice

Pour water over tomatoes and let simmer 5 minutes or until tomatoes have absorbed most of the water and seem tender. Add the raisins and cook a little longer. Drain off any remaining liquor, saving the juice, and dump the tomatoes and raisins into a 9-inch pie pan lined with uncooked pie dough. Sprinkle with the sugar and flour mixed, and the spices. Dot the surface with the butter. Add the grated rind and lemon juice. Now pour over the whole a "spilling wineglass" (as they say in Kentucky) of brandy or whiskey. If the pie will hold it, add a few tablespoons of the tomato liquor, or enough to moisten the tomatoes well. Top with a slashed solid crust or use strips across the top as you prefer. Set the pan in a hot oven (450°) for 15 minutes. Reduce the heat to 375° and leave ½ hour longer, or until crust is brown.

NOTE: At the end of summer, just before frost, the markets are filled with green tomatoes. They are delicious fried, made into pickles, or into the above pie.

## CAMILLE GLENN'S MINCEMEAT TARTLETS FLAMBE

Urged by those friends whom she had helped with parties as a guest, Camille Glenn began to cater professionally about a year ago, much to Louisville's good fortune. This is one of her outstanding recipes.

To make the crust for the tartlets, use tiny French tartlet pans, but if you don't own any, use medium-sized muffin tins. Make up the All-Purpose Pie Crust recipe given in this chapter; cover the backs of the tartlet pans or muffin tins with the crust, pricking it all over, and trimming the edges evenly. Bake these until golden-brown—12 to 15 minutes—in a hot oven (450°). Let them cool and remove them gently from the pans with a dull knife. Place them on a platter or dish on the table beside a chafing dish. When ready to serve the tartlets, flame the mincemeat in brandy in the chafing dish and fill the individual tartlets with the hot mixture. A teaspoon of sweetened whipped cream flavored with brandy tops each tartlet. Here's how to make the mincemeat filling:

### Mincemeat for Tartlets Flambé *(Quick method)*

| | |
|---|---|
| 1 C chopped apples | 1 C sugar |
| ½ C raisins, chopped | Pinch of mace |
| ¼ C butter | Pinch of grated nutmeg |
| 1 T molasses | 1 t cinnamon |
| 1 t salt | Pinch of cloves |
| 1 C minced cooked beef with stock to moisten | ¼ C brandy, or more to taste |

Mix ingredients, except meat and brandy, and simmer until well blended in a double boiler. Then add meat. Simmer 15 minutes longer. Add brandy. Be sure the mixture is hot when the brandy is added, or it will not burn. Put mincemeat in chafing dish and light with a match. Tilt the dish back and forth until the flame dies. Serve at once.

### ORANGE PUDDIN'-PIE
#### *(A traditional Kentucky recipe)*

| | |
|---|---|
| ¼ C butter | 1½ T white corn meal (or flour) |
| ½ C sugar | ½ t cornstarch |
| 3 egg yolks | ½ C orange juice |
| F. G. salt, if sweet butter is used | Grated peel of 1 orange |

Cream butter with sugar. Add egg yolks, corn meal or flour, and corn-starch dissolved in the orange juice. Add the grated orange peel, and salt, if sweet butter is used. Put in top of double boiler and set over the flame on top of stove. *Stir* and *stir* and *stir* until the custard is thick. Set aside to cool. Pour the cool custard into a baked pie shell—one that has been cooked 10 minutes in a hot oven (450°) but not allowed to brown. Top with the following meringue:

**3 egg whites beaten with F. G.**  **1 T orange juice**
    **salt**      **Grated rind of ½ orange**
**3 rounded T sugar**

Beat the whites of the eggs with the salt. When very stiff add the sugar, orange juice and grated orange rind. Spoon meringue over the orange custard, being careful not to mix the two. Smooth with a knife and make any pattern you wish on the meringue. I usually make peaks by placing the fork on top of the smooth meringue and lifting it slightly. Serve warm or cold, never hot.

## TRANSPARENT STRAWBERRY PIE

Place 2 cups of fresh strawberries, washed, drained, capped, cut in half and mixed with ¼ cup of sugar, in the bottom of the unbaked pastry shell. Allow berries to stand 10 minutes to draw juice before using in crust. Cover with the topping used for the Damson Plum Preserve Kuchen (page 227). Spread evenly over the strawberries. Set the pie in a preheated oven (450°) and leave for 15 minutes, then reduce the heat to 375° and cook 30 minutes longer, or until strawberries seem done. Serve warm but not hot—an oh-so-delectable pie!

# Kuchens

## MOTHER F'S KUCHENS WITH FRUIT FILLINGS

If I had to name our most successful and distinctive family dessert, this one would lead the list. We serve it on all occasions, especially in the summer when we can get fresh fruit. Somehow kuchens are not the same prepared with canned or frozen fruit. We like peaches best, but we do not turn up our noses at black or red raspberry kuchen, or apple kuchen, especially when made with our own backyard early June apples. The kuchen dough, when properly made, is too soft to roll and has to be pressed into the pan as graham cracker crust is pressed. Once you get the knack of fitting this dough into the pan, all the rest is easy. We always make up two crusts at a time, lining two pans with the kuchen dough and keeping one in the icebox until ready to bake. The dough seems to improve that way and will keep for over a week. I use square 9- by 9-inch pans and cut the kuchens into 6 squares or rectangles when serving. These kuchens taste more like a piece of French pastry than a pie and you can serve them whenever pastry would be indicated.

## KUCHEN DOUGH
### *(Enough for one 9-inch-square pan with sides 1½ inches high)*

1¼ C flour                    ¼ C butter or margarine
¼ C sugar                     1 to 2 T cream if necessary
¼ t salt                      1 egg
¼ t baking powder

Measure flour after sifting and sift again with dry ingredients. Add butter or margarine and mix with the fingers as for pie crust. Add egg and if the dough holds together the cream will not be necessary. Use as little cream as possible. Make the dough into a ball. Flour your hands and pat the dough with the flour just enough to keep it from sticking to your hands and the pan. Dump into the pan and, with the fingers and palms, spread dough all over bottom of pan. Continue to flour the hands. I put a scoop of flour on a plate and press the palms of my hands into that every once in a while when I am making this dough. Now, with the fingers press bits of dough against the sides of pan. The dough should "scoot up." Don't worry if there are holes on the bottom, you can smooth those later with your palms. Just get the dough to cover the sides. I do this by pressing a mass of dough with my fingers and letting it come to the top of the pan of its own accord. Then I smooth it against the side of the pan. Now spread more dough over the bottom and up the sides. This sounds much more difficult than it is. Be sure there is not too much dough in the corners and around the bottom edges where the sides begin. Remember, this dough, unlike pie crust, has baking powder in it. It should be as even as your palms can press it. A good way to do the corners is to use your floured thumb, pressing it against the dough and forcing the dough up the side of the pan. You'll work out your own technique after the first time. Try to make a shell of dough into which you can pour your filling.

The kuchen crust is not baked before the filling is poured into it. Both filling and crust are cooked at the same time. Here are some of our favorites:

# VARIATIONS OF MOTHER F'S FRUIT KUCHENS

## Apple Kuchen
### *(For a 9-inch-square pan)*

| | |
|---|---|
| 4 to 6 apples, according to size | ¼ C sugar |
| Grated rind and juice of ½ lemon | 2 T butter |

Peel apples and cut in quarters or eighths, depending on size. Place in rows on bottom of prepared kuchen dough, setting them spoon-fashion side by side. See recipe for Peach Kuchen (page 228). Dribble the lemon juice with rind over the apples, and sprinkle them with sugar, getting it as even as possible. Dot with the butter, then sprinkle over all the following crumbs:

| | |
|---|---|
| ¼ C sugar | 2 T ground almonds or bread |
| ½ t cinnamon | crumbs |

Put this mixture in a skillet and stir until it becomes crumbly, but not gummy or caramelized. Sprinkle over prepared apples in kuchen dough. Bake in a hot oven (450°) for 15 minutes. Reduce the heat to 375° and bake 30 minutes longer, or until apples are done. If early June apples are used, they will bake in half an hour or so instead of the 45 minutes which winter apples will require.

## Black or Red Raspberry Kuchen

Follow the recipe for Peach Kuchen (page 228) substituting 2 cups of washed drained berries for the peaches. The berries are placed in the kuchen dough and spread all over the bottom evenly, then the topping added as directed for peaches.

## Cheese Kuchen

In making the dough for this kuchen, follow the recipe for Mother F's Kuchen Dough (page 225) adding ½ teaspoon of vanilla. After the dough has been pressed into the pan, fill with the mixture given for Cottage Cheese Pie (page 212).

## Damson Plum Preserve Kuchen

This is truly delectable, a Kentucky recipe of note. Prepare the raw kuchen crust according to directions for Mother F's Kuchen Dough. Fill with 1 cup damson preserves. Cover with the following topping:

½ C softened but not melted
   butter
¼ C sugar
1 egg

1 T thick cream or enough to
   make a mixture easy to
   spread but not runny

I use an electric beater for this. Cream butter and sugar, add egg and
beat until light and spongy. Add cream and beat again. This makes a
thick mixture. Spread over preserves. Cook 10 minutes at 450° and
20 to 30 minutes at 375° or until topping sets. Do not cook too long.

## Peach Kuchen
### *(For a 9-inch-square pan)*

We make this kuchen often, using only freestone peaches; Hale or
Elberta are our favorites. You will need 1½ to 2 pounds of peaches for
each kuchen. Peel the peaches and cut into quarters or eighths, depending on the size of the fruit. If gigantic peaches are used, it may even be
necessary to cut them into sixteenths. Lay them in straight rows, fitting
them into one another spoon-fashion. Do not put more than one layer
over the bottom of the uncooked crust. If there are gaps in the rows put
an extra slice to cover, as the whole bottom should be solid with the
peach rows. Sprinkle with the following:

1 T flour
½ C sugar
2 T butter to dot over surface

¾ t cinnamon
1 T lemon juice if peaches are
   sweet and dead-ripe

Sprinkle the cinnamon over the peaches. Mix the flour with the sugar
and sprinkle that on top of the fruit, getting it as even as possible. Then
add a few drops of lemon juice if the peaches seem dead-ripe. Now dot
with the butter. Set the pan in a preheated hot oven (450°), and leave
15 minutes. Reduce heat to 375° and cook for 30 minutes longer, or
until peaches seem done. Serve warm or cold. For special occasions, top
with vanilla ice cream. A wonderful dessert for supper, or a pastry to be
heated over for Sunday morning brunch.

# *Cakes*

❋❋❋❋❋❋❋❋❋❋❋❋❋❋❋❋❋❋❋❋❋❋❋❋❋❋❋❋❋❋❋❋❋❋❋❋❋❋❋❋❋❋❋❋❋❋❋

## GENERAL HINTS ON CAKE MAKING

Unless otherwise stated, all flour used in cakes should be sifted once before measuring and as many times afterwards as indicated in the recipe.

\* \* \*

If a recipe calls for cake flour and you want to use all-purpose flour instead, use 2 tablespoons less flour to every cup.

\* \* \*

With sweet milk all recipes in this book require cream of tartar baking power (Royal). If buttermilk, sour milk or sour cream is called for, use phosphate-and-calcium-base baking powder (Calumet).

\* \* \*

All recipes in this chapter calling for sour cream require commercially soured cream, not sweet cream that, after being kept a long time, goes sour and tastes bitter.

\* \* \*

The oven for baking cakes should be preheated unless otherwise indicated in the recipe.

\* \* \*

If salty butter is used in making cakes, do not add extra salt. If sweet butter is used, add ⅛ teaspoon of salt to the average 2 cups of cake flour.

\* \* \*

Store all leftover cakes in tin boxes with tight-fitting lids. Cakes frosted with meringue or whipped cream should be kept in the icebox.

\* \* \*

If a recipe calls for half an egg consult standard weights and measurements table in front of this book.

To distribute cake batter evenly, put the same number of spoonfuls of batter in each layer to be baked. Otherwise one layer will be higher than the other.

\*     \*     \*

Do not use butter or margarine for greasing cake pans as the salt in the butter might cause the batter to stick. Using a pastry brush, grease the pans very lightly with salad oil; then put a little flour in the pan and tilt the pan back and forth, covering the bottom surface and sides with the flour. Turn the pan upside down over a paper and tap the bottom and sides with a dull knife to remove excess flour. If this method is used (except for fruit cakes) the pans will not have to be lined with greased waxed paper. I use this method for all my cakes, even for sponge and angel food cakes. Cissy Gregg says she greases her angel food or sponge cake pans as I do but spreads granulated sugar instead of flour over the bottom and sides of the pan.

\*     \*     \*

For a smaller cake, cut cake recipe in half, and if it is a two-layer cake, bake only one layer. Then when putting it together, cut that layer in half with a saw-tooth knife, and divide the frosting recipe in half also. Put the two half-layers together with frosting and you will have half a cake. Frost over the top and cut side also to make the cake keep fresh longer. If the cake is a solid or loaf cake, use a smaller pan—the batter should only half fill it.

\*     \*     \*

If sugar is lumpy, sift before using. Several siftings make lighter cakes, especially in sponge and angel food cakes.

\*     \*     \*

To find out if cake is done, insert a cake wire, a clean broom straw or a wooden toothpick into the cake batter before removing the cake from the stove. If the wire, straw or toothpick comes out clean with no batter clinging to it, the cake is done. Some people press the surface of the cake with the finger, making a little indentation. If the indentation remains, the cake is not ready to be taken out of the stove; if the cake springs back into shape, it is done. Neither of these methods is foolproof and sometimes, as in a fruit cake, a crumb will adhere to the straw even when the cake has been sufficiently cooked. But on the whole I find the wire or straw test the most reliable.

\*     \*     \*

Be sure to place the cake pan in the center of the oven while the cake is baking. To help prevent uneven baking, be sure that two pans do not touch each other.

## TO BROWN FLOUR FOR CAKES AND OTHER DISHES

METHOD No. 1. Place a metal skillet over a flame on top of the stove, add a cup of flour, and stir constantly, scraping the flour away from the bottom and sides of the pan to avoid scorching or sticking. When all the flour is an even tan color, it is ready to use. It darkens when water or other liquid is added to it. If it gets too brown it is apt to have a bitter taste. Store in covered jars.

METHOD No. 2. This does not have to be watched as carefully as Method No. 1. The flour is put in the skillet and placed in a moderately hot oven (375°). Scrape bottom and sides of skillet from time to time to keep flour from sticking and burning.

METHOD No. 3. The skillet can also be put under the flame in the broiler if you are in a great hurry, but this method is more risky than the other two, for the flour is apt to get too dark or burned. The safest method is No. 2. Make up 2 cups of this flour at a time and keep to use for sauces, black cake, etc. It gives gravies a much richer flavor than plain flour, although it is not quite as good a thickening agent. Use a little more of the browned flour than the plain, or combine the two.

# *Butter Cakes*

## HICKORY NUT OR BLACK WALNUT CAKE

This is a Southern favorite. I bake this cake in an old-fashioned, fluted tin or copper pan and dust it with powdered sugar. It doesn't need an icing, according to my taste. But in all honesty I must tell you the original recipe called for a boiled white frosting. Here is the cake recipe:

½ C butter or margarine, softened but not melted
1 C sugar
3 egg yolks
1½ C all-purpose flour (measured after sifting, then sifted 3 times)

1½ t baking powder
1 t vanilla
3 egg whites, well beaten
1 C finely-chopped hickory nuts or black walnuts
1 C milk

Cream the butter with the sugar. Add slowly the egg yolks and beat well. Add the milk. Add this to the flour that has been measured after sifting, then sifted 3 times with the baking powder. Add vanilla and fold in the well-beaten egg whites. Now fold in the chopped nuts. Pour the batter into a greased, floured tube pan and bake until the cake tests done, in a moderate oven (375°). This takes about 1 hour to bake; test after 50 minutes, however. Do not overcook, as then the cakes will be dry.

There's nothing to prevent your baking the cake in 2 layers and putting them together with whipped cream sweetened to taste and seasoned with a little whiskey, then topping the cake with more of the same. This makes a nice dessert, cut into pie-shaped wedges. Or it can be put together with white icing. Bake the layers only 25 to 30 minutes or until cake tests done. A butterscotch icing is preferred by some—use the same icing as for Raspberry Jam Cake (page 236) or if you prefer an old-fashioned caramel frosting, see recipe for Mary Todd's White Cake (page 237).

## THE HUNDRED-DOLLAR
## CHOCOLATE CAKE AND VARIATION

This is one of the most delicious cakes I ever ate. It is rumored that a certain Louisville matron, having tasted it in a New York restaurant, wrote back and asked for the recipe. She foolishly added—in writing— that she'd be glad to pay for the information. She did, and through the nose, for accompanying the restaurateur's reply was a bill for $100.00. The lady is said to have taken the matter up with her lawyer, but when he pointed out that legally she didn't have a case, she sent the check. She wisely gave the recipe to her church circle and they are said to have made quite a bit, too, by selling it to their friends. Finally the secret leaked out, as all secrets do, and so I pass it on to you. I use cake flour with it, for the ingredients seem so perfectly blended I didn't want to make any substitutions. But some of my friends have been using 1¾ cups of all-purpose flour instead of the 2 cups of cake flour and they report good results.

| | |
|---|---|
| ½ C real butter, or half butter, half margarine | 2 egg yolks, well beaten |
| | 1 t vanilla |
| 2 C sifted sugar | ¼ lb. bitter chocolate (4 sqs.) |
| 2 C cake flour (or 1¾ C all purpose flour) | 2 t baking powder |
| | 2 egg whites, well beaten |
| 1½ C sweet milk | |

Cream butter and sifted sugar. Add the melted bitter chocolate. Fold into this the yolks of eggs and vanilla. Sift flour (measured after sifting once) with baking powder—I use cream-of-tartar baking powder—and sift twice more. If butter is sweet, salt will be necessary (¼ t should be enough). Do not add salt if salty butter or margarine is used. Combine the two mixtures, alternating with the sweet milk. Lastly, fold in the well-beaten egg whites. Pour batter into 2 greased and floured 9-inch cake tins. Bake in a moderate oven (350° to 375°) for 30 to 35 minutes or until cake tests done. Remove from oven and cool before icing. I turn cakes out on wire cake racks after about 5 minutes, first loosening the sides of the cake from the tins.

The original recipe called for 1 cup chopped pecans to be folded into the cake batter, but we prefer to add them to the frosting. You can take your choice. I ice this cake with the same frosting used for Carrie Byck's Double Fudge Cake (page 242) and add 1 cup of chopped pecans to it. I also like this cake with the pink peppermint frosting given below.

### Pink Peppermint Frosting
#### *(For the Hundred-Dollar Cake)*

| | |
|---|---|
| 2 unbeaten egg whites | 5 T water |
| F. G. salt | 1½ t white corn syrup |
| 1½ C sifted sugar | 2 or 3 drops oil of peppermint |
| Crushed peppermint-stick candy | 1 or 2 drops pink vegetable col- |
| Chocolate shot or grated sweet | oring |
| chocolate | |

In the top of a double boiler place the egg whites, salt, sugar and water mixed with the white corn syrup. Use a rotary egg beater and cook the mixture 7 minutes by the clock, beating all the while. An electric beater is better, but the rotary beater is a good substitute if your arm is strong enough. Have the water boiling when you begin to make the icing. When done it should stand in peaks. Add the oil of peppermint (buy this from your druggist) and taste the frosting to get the right amount. Color a delicate pink with vegetable coloring. After you put the frosting on the cake and while it is still soft, decorate the top of the cake with alternating rows of crushed peppermint-stick candy and chocolate shot or grated sweet chocolate. If, after you make the frosting, it is too soft, frost the cake and run it in the oven for a few minutes until icing sets. Do not leave in long or it will dry out.

### CHOCOLATE WHIPPED CREAM MUFFINS
#### (Weary Willies)

Make the Hundred-Dollar Chocolate Cake batter and pour into greased, floured muffin pans; fill ⅔ full. Bake according to directions for the large cake, removing the muffins from the stove when they test done— 20 to 25 minutes should be enough. Cool. Hollow out each muffin with an apple corer or grapefruit knife and frost with the Double Fudge Icing (uncooked) used for Carrie Byck's Double Fudge Cake. Fill the frosted muffins with whipped cream sweetened and flavored with vanilla, stuffing the cream into the cake hollow and piling half a teaspoonful on top of each muffin. These are not only very pretty but taste delicious. This makes a large batch of muffins. Cut the recipe in half and cook the muffins in small pans if only a plateful will be needed. These can also be baked in Mary Ann pans (those little muffin pans with the central indentations) and filled with icing or whipped cream topped with Hot Fudge Sauce. Or this same batter can be baked in individual ring molds and treated the same way.

## ISLE OF SPICE CAKE

¾ C butter or margarine

1¾ C flour, sifted before meas-
    uring

1½ C sugar

½ t soda

1 t vanilla

3 eggs

⅛ t salt

½ t baking powder

1 t cinnamon

2 T cocoa

¾ C thick sour cream

1 t nutmeg (or ½ t nutmeg, ½
    t mace)

Soften butter or margarine to room temperature and cream with the sugar. Add the well-beaten egg yolks. Sift the dry ingredients twice and combine the two mixtures, alternating with sour cream. Add vanilla and fold in the whites, well beaten with salt. Pour batter into two 9-inch cake pans, greased and floured. Bake in a moderate oven (375°) from 25 to 30 minutes or until cake tests done. Turn out on a cake rack and let cool. Put the layers together and frost the outside of the cake with the spice icing recipe given below.

To make muffin cakes of this batter, pour it into greased floured muffin pans—it should make about 12. Fill each cup only ⅔ full. Bake in a moderate oven (375°) from 20 to 25 minutes, or until the muffins are done. Remove the pan from the stove, loosen the edges of the cakes from the pan, and cool. Turn out, and dust with powdered sugar or frost with Coffee Sea Foam Frosting (page 240) or with Spice Icing.

### Spice Icing (uncooked)
#### (For Spice Cake or for Spice Muffins)

3 C powdered sugar

2 t cinnamon

1 t nutmeg

1 t vanilla

6 T melted margarine or
    butter

4 to 6 T strong coffee or cream

6 t cocoa

Sift powdered sugar with cinnamon, nutmeg and cocoa. Add vanilla, melted margarine or butter, and the strong coffee or cream—enough to make a smooth paste. Beat and beat and beat. When mixture is creamy, spread between. layers and on outside of cake. If put on while cake is warm the icing will form a glaze. If put on when cool it will remain fluffy and thick. (Use half this recipe for muffins as only the tops are frosted.)

## MAPLE LOAF CAKE WITH MAPLE FOAM ICING

⅓ C butter or margarine
½ C white sugar
1 t vanilla
1½ t baking powder
F. G. salt
¼ C maple syrup

1½ C flour (sifted once before measuring and twice afterwards)
½ C milk
1 egg

Cream butter and sugar. Add egg yolk well beaten, then vanilla and syrup. Add flour, alternating with the milk. Add baking powder and, last of all, fold in the egg white, stiffly beaten with a few grains of salt. Pour into a greased, buttered loaf pan (about 5 by 9 inches) and bake in a moderate oven (375°) from 45 minutes to 1 hour, or until cake tests done. Let it stand a few moments before removing from the pan. Stand on a wire cake rack or towel placed over a board, until cake is cold. Frost with:

### Maple Foam Icing

1 C maple or brown sugar
½ C maple syrup
F. G. salt

2 T water
1 egg white
½ t vanilla

Boil sugar, syrup and water for 5 or 6 minutes until mixture is very thick and will spin a thread or make a hard ball in cold water. Meanwhile beat the egg white very stiff with a little salt. When the syrup is done, pour a tablespoonful into the egg, beating vigorously all the while. Two pairs of hands will be found helpful, as time is an important factor in making this icing. Add another tablespoonful and another until 4 have been blended with the egg, then quickly pour the rest of the syrup into the egg mixture, beating constantly. If an electric beater is handy, by all means use it. Add the vanilla and when icing is firm enough to stand in peaks, spread it over top and sides of cake. If beaten too long it is apt to become granular, and if not beaten enough it will not harden. Practice alone will tell when the moment is right for spreading this icing on the cake. However, it is delicious whether hard or soft or medium.

## RASPBERRY JAM CAKE WITH
## BUTTERSCOTCH ICING

I used this in a story for Gourmet once and it is almost my favorite cake. I make it in two layers at Christmas and during the holidays and ice it with the butterscotch frosting. It isn't as rich as fruit cake, yet serves the same purpose. In summer we have it for backyard picnics. Then I bake it in a large biscuit pan, frost it in the pan, and when the frosting is cool, cut it into small squares. It made 42, the last time I counted the squares. I think it one of Kentucky's finest confections and when I serve it I do not have any other dessert, though many people like it with plain ice cream or caramel ice cream. The jam used in this cake is the old-fashioned sort with seeds. Bought jam works as well as homemade.

### The Cake Batter

⅔ C butter (no substitutes)
⅔ C sour cream
½ C white sugar
½ C brown sugar
1 t cinnamon
1 T vanilla
1 C dark seedless raisins

2½ C flour (sifted before measuring)
1 t soda
3 eggs
2 T cocoa
½ t grated nutmeg
1 C black or red raspberry jam
1 C coarsely chopped pecans

Cream butter and sugar. Add egg yolks. Sift flour twice, the third time with spices and soda. Combine the 2 mixtures, alternating with sour cream. Add jam, nuts and raisins, folding in until well blended. Add vanilla and, last of all, fold in the well-beaten whites. Bake in two 9-inch-square pans—why square instead of round I don't know, but these cakes are usually baked that way. I grease and flour the pans and cook the cake in a preheated oven set at 375°. Cook until the cake tests done—35 to 40 minutes. If the cake is baked in the large biscuit pan it may take a little longer. Turn the layers out on a wire cake rack after 5 minutes. Let stand until cool and, if necessary, loosen edges with a dull knife or spatula, being careful not to break the cake when removing it from the pan. Frost with the following:

### Butterscotch Icing

3 C medium brown sugar (or half dark-brown, half light-brown)
⅔ C heavy cream (sweet)

1 T butter
1 t white corn syrup (optional)
F. G. salt

Mix cream and sugar. Add butter and salt and corn syrup, if you are using it, and let simmer over a flame in a saucepan until syrup forms a hard-soft ball in ice water—one that holds its shape and can be picked up with the fingers. It reaches 246° on my candy thermometer. Remove from the stove and set aside to cool. Beat until creamy, using the electric beater if you own one. Spread between layers and over outside of cake. This frosting is like soft fudge—it never gets hard but is never sticky or runny. If the old-fashioned caramel-fudge type of icing is liked, omit the white corn syrup.

## MARY TODD'S WHITE CAKE

President Lincoln is said to have remarked that Mary Todd's White Cake was the best he had ever eaten. This confection was originated by Monsieur Giron, a Lexington caterer, on the occasion of Lafayette's visit to that city in 1825. The Todds got the recipe from him and treasured it ever after. Here it is:

| | |
|---|---|
| 1 C butter | 1 C finely chopped blanched almonds |
| 2 C sugar | |
| 3 C flour (sifted before measuring) | 3 t baking powder |
| | Whites of 6 eggs |
| 1 C milk | 1 t vanilla (or any other preferred flavoring) |

Cream butter and sugar, sift flour and baking powder together 3 times, and add to butter and sugar, alternating with the milk. Stir in the nutmeats and beat well. Then fold in the stiffly-beaten whites and the flavorings. Pour into a well-greased and floured pan. The old-fashioned, fluted copper pan with a center funnel was probably used originally. Bake 1 hour in a moderate oven, or cook until the cake tests done. Turn out on a wire rack and cool. This makes a large cake. The batter can be cut in half and baked in two 9-inch layers if desired. For a good basic white cake, omit almonds. Frost this cake with the following old-fashioned boiled white icing:

### Frosting for Mary Todd's White Cake

| | |
|---|---|
| 2 C sugar | 1 t vanilla or ½ t vanilla, ½ t almond extract |
| 2 egg whites, beaten stiff with F. G. salt | ½ C crystallized cherries, cut in halves |
| ½ C diced candied pineapple | |
| 1 C water | |

Boil sugar and water until syrup spins a 5-inch thread. Fold in slowly to the well-beaten whites adding a tablespoon at a time until 4 have been used. I use an electric beater for making this frosting. Now add the remaining syrup slowly, pouring it in a thin stream. Beat hard until all is used and the mixture stands in peaks when dropped from a spoon. Just before spreading between layers and over cake add flavoring and fold in pineapple and cherries. If desired, the almonds can be omitted from the cake batter and added to the frosting or sprinkled over the top and sides while icing is still soft. If used in this way, brown them slightly in the oven before sprinkling over cake.

The pineapple and cherries can be omitted from the above recipe and the plain frosting put between the layers and on the outside of the cake. Sprinkle freely with freshly grated cocoanut; it will take two average-sized cocoanuts to yield enough for this large cake. This was a pre-Civil War favorite known as Merry Christmas Cake.

## VARIATIONS OF MARY TODD'S WHITE CAKE

Omit almonds from cake batter and ice with this delicious

### Old-Fashioned Caramel Frosting

| | |
|---|---|
| 3 C  sugar (white) | 1 t vanilla |
| 1 C milk | F. G. salt |
| 2 T butter (no substitutes) | |

This is the genuine caramel frosting made with white sugar that has been caramelized according to the directions given for French Caramel Sauce (page 199). It is enough to put between two 9-inch layers and to frost the outside of the cake.

To make it, put 2 cups of white sugar and the milk into a large saucepan and let boil hard. Meanwhile, caramelize another cup of sugar in a heavy iron or metal skillet. When all lumps disappear and the mixture is brown and clear, add butter and stir for a moment, then pour the caramelized sugar mixture into the other mixture, beating with a wooden spoon. It is best to turn off the fire for a moment as the mixture is apt to sputter and pop when the hot brown sugar is first added. Turn on the fire again and when the mixture boils, let it cook 3 minutes by the clock or until a spoonful dropped in cold water forms a ball that holds its shape and can be picked up with the fingers. Then take off the stove and add the vanilla and salt. Let stand until cool. Beat the frosting until it resembles a thick fudge, then spread between layers and on top of cake.

Or bake the cake in a large biscuit pan, pour the frosting onto this, and cut into 1½-inch squares when frosting hardens. This frosting is a marvelous confection, but it is apt to break when cut. I prefer to prepare it in a single sheet rather than in layers, but that is a matter of choice.

# UNION CAKE
### (A Civil War cake)

Kentucky was a border State during the Civil War and its sons fought on both sides. So, since we are including in this chapter a recipe for General Robert E. Lee Cake, it seems only right to give details for baking Union Cake. But you can enjoy it whether your sympathies are with the North or the South, for it is a truly delicious cake. It originally consisted of 4 layers, the bottom a fruit-studded spice one, then a white layer, then a dark, then a white, but I have reduced the gigantic proportions to make just enough for a 2-layer cake, a dark layer and a light one. The old recipe must have been enough for a regiment! I've added an original frosting of my own also, instead of the boiled sugar frosting used in the Civil War days. Mine is a Coffee Sea Foam of which I am quite fond, and I trim it with chocolate shavings to give a more party-ish appearance. This is one of the few unusual cakes I've tasted in a long time. I hope you like it as much as I do.

### Dark Cake Batter

⅓ C butter (no substitutes)
6 T of sugar
2 egg yolks or 1 egg, well beaten
⅓ C buttermilk or coffee
⅓ C New Orleans molasses
⅓ t soda
½ t cinnamon
1 C sifted flour

⅛ t mace
⅛ t nutmeg
⅛ t cloves
¼ C raisins (seeded and cut in pieces)
3 T diced citron
¼ t allspice

Cream butter and sugar. Add molasses and buttermilk or coffee, and well-beaten egg. Set aside. Sift flour 2 more times. Put 2 tablespoons aside. Sift remaining flour once more with the spices and the soda. Combine the liquid and dry mixtures. Beat to make a smooth batter. Mix the 2 tablespoons of flour with the citron and raisins, which have been cut in half. Fold into the cake batter. Put the batter in a greased and floured 9-inch cake pan. Bake in a preheated oven set at 375° from 25 to 35 minutes or until cake tests done. Cool and turn out on a wire rack.

### Light Cake Batter

⅓ C butter (no substitutes)
⅔ C sugar
2 egg whites
1 C flour (measure after sifting)

1 t baking powder
F. G. salt
⅓ C milk
⅓ t vanilla

Cream butter and sugar. Sift the flour once. Sift twice more, the third time adding the baking powder. Combine the 2 mixtures, adding the milk, beating slowly and folding to make a smooth batter. Add the vanilla and, last of all, fold in the whites, well beaten with salt. Pour into a greased, floured 9-inch cake pan and bake 25 minutes in a moderate oven (375°) or until cake tests done. Remove from the stove and cool. Then turn out on a wire cake rack. When putting the two layers together, the dark one goes on the bottom, the light one on top. Spread Coffee Sea Foam Frosting between the layers and over the top and sides of the cake. Sprinkle freely with grated sweet chocolate or chocolate shot for decoration. This cake keeps unusually well if stored in a tin box with a tight-fitting lid.

### Coffee Sea Foam Frosting
#### (For Spice or Union Cake)
#### (An icing with that old-timey, spicy flavor)

2 egg whites
1 C dark brown sugar
½ C white sugar
½ t vanilla
F. G. salt
2 oz. of semi-sweet chocolate
    shavings or chocolate shot
    for decorating frosting

5 T double-strength coffee made by adding an extra t of instant coffee to the 5 T of plain coffee, drip or percolated

Do not beat the whites but dump them with the rest of the ingredients into the top of a double boiler. The water beneath them should be boiling and should continue to boil while the icing cooks. Beat with the electric mixer for 7 minutes while frosting cooks, or use a Dover egg beater if your right arm is strong. When done, the frosting should stand up in peaks. Put between layers and over top of cake. If frosting doesn't harden sufficiently, put frosted cake in a moderate oven for a minute. Do not leave too long or it will dry too much. If you wish, sprinkle with shaved semi-sweet chocolate or chocolate shot while frosting is still soft.

# Butterless Cakes

An angel food cake pan with a tube center and sides that slip out, or a spring form where the sides are held by a pin and can be loosened when the butterless cake is done, greatly simplifies removing angel food or sponge cakes from their pans. Otherwise, as soon as they are taken from the oven they should be placed upside down on a cake rack and allowed to stand until they drop out of their pans of their own accord. When cold, if they still remain obstinate, loosen the edges with a spatula or dull knife and assist the cake from the pan onto the plate on which it is to be served. Old-fashioned tube cake pans or copper tube pans known as Turk's Heads were the accepted cooking vessels for these cakes until comparatively recent times.

Directions for greasing pans for butterless cakes will be found under General Hints, at the beginning of this chapter.

## PAULINE PARK WILSON'S
## CHOCOLATE ANGEL FOOD CAKE

Pauline Park Wilson has many talents. She is, at present, Dean of Women and Professor of Home Economics at the University of Georgia. She is also a superior cook. Here is a noteworthy recipe she once gave me:

| | |
|---|---|
| ¾ C twice-sifted all-purpose flour | 1¼ C granulated sugar |
| | 1 C egg whites |
| ½ C cocoa | F. G. salt |
| 1 t cream of tartar | 1½ t vanilla extract |

Measure the flour after sifting twice. Add cocoa and sift 4 more times, the last time adding the cream of tartar. Sift sugar 4 times. Beat egg whites with the salt until stiff but not dry. Gradually fold in the sugar and flour-cocoa mixture. Add vanilla extract. Pour into a greased, floured or sugared angel food cake pan and smooth the dough with a knife. A 9-inch pan is large enough for this amount of batter. Bake 15 minutes in an oven set at 350°. Reduce heat to 300° and cook 45 minutes longer, or until cake tests done with a straw or wire. Invert the pan on a wire rack and leave until cake cools—1½ to 2 hours. Remove side pieces and insert a knife under the cake to loosen it from the pan. Put on a cake plate and ice with

### Chocolate Mocha Frosting

| | |
|---|---|
| 1½ C powdered sugar | 2 to 3 T hot strong coffee |
| ½ C cocoa | (enough to make a smooth, |
| 1 t vanilla | thick icing) |
| 4 T margarine or butter, melted | |

Sift the powdered sugar with the cocoa. Add vanilla, margarine or butter, melted, and the hot strong coffee. Beat until mixture is free from lumps. Spread over the surface of cake and set aside to harden.

Cut this cake with a cake knife or saw-tooth knife, or tear apart with 2 forks. Do not cut with a plain knife, as it will mash and become tough. The cake keeps fresh a remarkably long time if put in an airtight tin container, and is an excellent way to use leftover egg whites.

This cake is also delicious iced with a plain Mocha Frosting (page 253).

## CARRIE BYCK'S DOUBLE FUDGE CAKE

This is one of the most delicious chocolate cakes I have ever tasted, and while the icing calls for butter, the cake does not. It keeps well, too, if stored in a tin box. The original recipe came from Georgia and was given me by our devoted family friend, Carrie Byck, 25 years ago when I first came to Louisville.

| | |
|---|---|
| 4 sq. bitter chocolate (¼ lb.) | 1 t vanilla |
| 1 C milk | 4 egg yolks |
| 1 C flour | 2 C sugar |
| 1 t baking powder | 4 egg whites |

Dissolve the chocolate and milk in a double boiler. Beat to a paste. Cool slightly. Measure the flour after sifting and sift 3 times more, the last time with the baking powder. Beat the egg yolks light, add sugar and vanilla. Add the cooled chocolate mixture to this and fold into the flour and baking powder. Mix well. Fold in the well-beaten egg whites. Grease and flour two 9-inch square or round cake pans (page 230). Divide the batter equally between pans. Bake in a moderate oven (375°) until the dough tests done with a cake wire or straw or with the fingers—the cooking time is from 25 to 30 minutes. Do not cook too long or the cake will dry out. Loosen edges of cake and turn onto a wire cake rack. Leave until cake falls from pan, or when it is cool, gently remove it. Put layers together and ice with the following:

### Double Fudge Frosting (uncooked)

| | |
|---|---|
| 4 sq. bitter chocolate (¼ lb.) | 2 to 3 T cream, or enough to |
| 4 T butter | make the frosting the proper |
| 1 lb. sifted powdered sugar | consistency to spread |
| 1 t vanilla | |

In a double boiler melt chocolate and butter. Remove from stove and add the powdered sugar, vanilla and cream (enough to make a semi-stiff paste thick enough to spread but not runny). It is better to add a little cream at a time. This is the best uncooked fudge frosting I've ever tasted and I use it for nearly all cakes calling for uncooked chocolate icing.

## VARIATIONS OF CARRIE BYCK'S
## DOUBLE FUDGE CAKE

### Chocolate Torte

Follow the recipe for Carrie Byck's Double Fudge Cake. Add 1 cup of chopped pecans or walnuts, if desired, although I like this better without nuts. Bake in a greased, floured spring form instead of 2 layer pans, in a slow oven (350°) from 40 minutes to 1 hour or until cake tests done. It should be a little more moist than the cake baked in 2 layers, although not so moist that it will fall. When it tests done, remove from stove and cool before removing sides of pan. Frost with sweetened whipped cream flavored with vanilla. Decorate with pecan, walnut or almond halves, and maraschino or crystallized cherries. Strips of angelica are good, too, if you can find them.

### Chocolate Squares or Butterless Brownies

Bake the Double Fudge Cake batter in a rectangular, greased, floured biscuit pan in a moderate oven (375°) until cake tests done—15 to 20 minutes. Do not overcook. Cut into squares, dust with powdered sugar and serve. One cup of coarsely chopped pecans may be added to the batter if desired, and the cake frosted with the Old-Fashioned Chocolate Fudge Icing given below. Cut into squares as soon as the icing hardens.

### Old-Fashioned Chocolate Fudge Frosting

| | |
|---|---|
| 2 C sugar | ½ C cream |
| 2 sq. bitter chocolate (⅛ lb.) | 1 T butter |
| 1 t vanilla | F. G. salt |
| ½ C milk | |

Place all ingredients, except vanilla, in a saucepan and boil until a little of the mixture makes a soft ball when dropped in cold water. The ball must hold its shape, however, when picked up with the fingers (236° on your candy thermometer). Add vanilla and set pan aside to cool. Then beat until fudge is creamy. Pour at once over top surface of cake and spread evenly. Cut into squares as directed above.

Camille Glenn says that if 1 teaspoon of white corn syrup is added to the frosting ingredients when they are put on the stove to cook, the fudge icing will remain soft and will not crack and break when cut.

## MARY CLEGG'S YELLOW ANGEL FOOD CAKE OR
## COLD WATER SPONGE CAKE

| | |
|---|---|
| 6 egg yolks | ¼ t salt |
| ½ C cold water | 6 egg whites |
| 1½ C sugar, sifted once | ¾ t cream of tartar |
| 1 t lemon juice | ¼ t salt |
| 1 t vanilla or almond extract | ½ C cold water |
| 1½ C cake flour | |

Take eggs out of icebox 1 hour before using. Measure flour before sifting
and sift 6 times afterwards. Separate eggs. Beat yolks well, adding sugar.
When light and spongy, add a little cold water at a time until the half
cup has been used. Fold in the sifted flour gradually as you continue
beating, but do this by hand. Add lemon juice and almond or vanilla
flavoring. Beat the egg whites with the salt until they stand in peaks, but
do not beat them dry. Add the cream of tartar and mix well but do not
beat hard, folding this into the whites. Then pour the yellow mixture
into the beaten whites, folding and cutting until the batter is smoothly
blended. Pour into an ungreased spring form with a tube center and
bake in a moderate oven (350°) until cake tests done; cooking time will be
from 1 hour to 1 hour and 10 minutes. Turn upside down and leave until
cold. Then remove from the pan if cake has not come out of its own accord. Dust with powdered sugar and serve plain, or frost with an uncooked
lemon frosting or with the same frosting used for the Robert E. Lee
Cake (page 251). Although the original recipe says not to grease the pan,
I prepare my pans according to the directions given in the General
Hints on Cake Making. This recipe makes a tall cake.

# Sheet Cakes

## DR. ALICE PICKETT'S BISHOP'S BREAD OR
## BUTTERMILK COFFEE CAKE

Dr. Alice Pickett, a distinguished Kentucky obstetrician, contributed
this recipe to the Query Club (a small, select Louisville literary group)
when they once published a tiny pamphlet of members' recipes.

According to Dr. Pickett, circuit-riding bishops and other church dignitaries would often drop in on a farmhouse in some rural Kentucky
community for early Sunday morning breakfast. On one occasion a re-
sourceful housewife concocted this delightful coffee cake, dubbing it

Bishop's Bread, after her distinguished guest. Its fame traveled throughout the South, from Kentucky to Virginia and the Carolinas. Here in Kentucky, it is still known as Bishop's Bread.

| | |
|---|---|
| **2 C flour, measured after sifting** | **½ C chopped pecans or** |
| **1½ C brown sugar** | **almonds** |
| **½ t soda** | **⅔ C buttermilk** |
| **1 egg, well beaten** | **1 t cinnamon** |
| **½ C butter or margarine** | **½ C currants or raisins** |

Make crumbs of the flour, brown sugar, and butter or margarine. Add the nuts and mix again. Set aside ½ cup for the topping. To the remaining crumb mixture add the soda dissolved in the buttermilk, the egg, cinnamon, and currants. Stir to make a smooth batter. Pour into a greased, floured biscuit pan and sprinkle the sugar-butter crumbs on top, scattering them evenly over the surface of the raw batter. Set the pan in a preheated oven set at 425° and leave for 10 minutes. Reduce the heat to 375° and cook 25 to 30 minutes longer or until cake tests done. If you are particularly fond of cinnamon flavor, an extra ½ teaspoon can be sprinkled over the crumb topping before baking the cake.

## CHESS CAKES OR CARAMEL SQUARES

Our family is partial to these delightful squares which resemble a brown sugar chess pie. They have a cookie crust and a transparent filling that literally melts in the mouth. We serve them with our picnic fried chicken, or grilled steak sandwiches, and no other dessert is necessary.

| | |
|---|---|
| **¾ C butter or margarine** | **2¼ C dark brown sugar** |
| **1½ C sifted flour** | **3 egg yolks** |
| **3 T granulated sugar** | **1 C pecans, coarsely chopped** |
| **½ t vanilla** | **3 egg whites** |

Cream butter or margarine (but do use butter if you can get it). Add slowly the sifted flour and granulated sugar. Pat into a long rectangular biscuit pan with 1½-inch sides. Bake 20 to 30 minutes in a moderate oven (375°), or cook until the crust is golden-brown. Meanwhile make the filling by mixing the dark brown sugar with the beaten egg yolks. When thick and spongy, add the pecans. Add vanilla and fold in the stiffly-beaten whites. Spread filling evenly over the crust. Return pan to oven and cook 25 to 30 minutes longer, or until the filling sets. Do not cook too long, as the filling should be transparent and semi-soft, never hard or chewy. Dust with powdered sugar and when cool cut into 1½-squares.

## CHOCOLATE ROLL
### (9 to 10 slices)

5 eggs, separated       1 t vanilla
1 C powdered sugar    F. G. salt
4 T cocoa

Beat yolks with sugar until light and lemon-colored. Add vanilla. Beat whites with salt until firm enough to stand in peaks, but not until dry. Sift cocoa and add slowly to yolks, alternating with whites. Pour into a greased rectangular cookie sheet or biscuit pan, 10 by 15 inches approximately, well lined with wax paper or greased stiff brown paper. Bake roll in a moderate oven (350°) for 20 to 25 minutes or until cake tests done. Turn out on a cloth or brown paper well sprinkled with powdered sugar. Cover at once with a damp but not wet cloth, and let cake cool. It cannot be spread with the filling until it cools. Transfer cake to the platter on which it is to be served, remove brown paper carefully, spread with the filling, roll and frost according to directions given below. Slice into 1- or 1½-inch pieces at the table, using sharp saw-tooth knife.

### Filling for Chocolate Roll

1 C double cream      1 T chocolate frosting, recipe
½ t vanilla          below (optional)
2 T powdered sugar, or more
   to taste

Beat cream, add sugar, vanilla and the tablespoon of chocolate frosting. Spread on chocolate sponge sheet cake. Roll up and frost with the following:

### Frosting for Chocolate Roll

2 C powdered sugar    4 T strong coffee or enough to
3 T cocoa          make a frosting stiff enough
1 t vanilla        to spread easily

Mix all above ingredients, saving out 1 tablespoon to add to whipped cream mixture above. Frost the surface of the cooled Chocolate Roll, ends included. Serve at once or keep in the icebox until ready to serve.

## VARIATIONS OF CHOCOLATE ROLL

### Chocolate Mocha Roll

Follow the recipe for Chocolate Roll, substituting 1 teaspoon of instant coffee in the whipped cream filling for the tablespoon of chocolate frosting.

## Chocolate Peppermint Roll

Make the Chocolate Roll according to directions given above. Fill with the following:

1 C double cream, whipped          ¼ C crushed peppermint-stick
                                                candy or peppermint balls

Mix and spread on baked cooled chocolate sheet cake. Roll up at once. Slice into 1- to 1½-inch rounds and dust with powdered sugar. Serve plain, or top with Hot Fudge Sauce (page 198).

## Chocolate Whipped Cream Roll with Hot Fudge Sauce

Make the Chocolate Roll according to directions given above.

Fill with the whipped cream as directed. Frost the outside of the filled roll with another cup of the whipped cream sweetened and flavored according to the same directions given for the filling. Cut into 1- or 1½-inch slices at the table and douse with Hot Fudge Sauce.

## DIXIE TEA CAKE OR
## GRANDMOTHER'S QUICK KUCHEN

This is a wonderful pre-Civil War tea cake or plain cake to be served with simple desserts such as custards, zabaglione and stewed or fresh fruits. And, as its name implies, it can be made at a moment's notice.

1 C sugar                              3 eggs, well beaten
½ C butter or margarine    1 t vanilla
2 C flour                              2 t baking powder
½ C milk

Cream sugar and butter or margarine. Use an electric beater if you have one. Add to this the flour measured before sifting and sifted twice afterward, the last time with the baking powder, alternating flour with the milk, and last of all, folding in the well-beaten eggs and vanilla. Pour into a long, greased, rectangular biscuit pan with 1½-inch sides. Sprinkle the top with the following mixture:

1 T cinnamon                      ¼ C chopped almonds
¼ C sugar                            or pecans

Bake in a moderate oven (375°) 15 to 20 minutes. Cut into 1½-inch squares when cool. This is also nice for brunch or Sunday morning breakfast, with coffee or hot chocolate. Half the recipe will fill a pan 9 by 9 inches. When the recipe is halved, use 1 whole egg and an extra white or yolk.

## VARIATIONS OF DIXIE TEA CAKE

### Tea Cake with Baked Icing

Dixie Tea Cake or Quick Kuchen makes a fine basic cake to be varied by the use of different icings. One of the most delicious is the following:
    Instead of using the topping given in the original recipe, substitute one made of

| | |
|---|---|
| 2 egg whites, well beaten | ½ t vanilla |
| 1 C dark brown sugar, firmly packed | 1 C chopped pecans or walnuts |

Add sugar, vanilla and nuts to egg whites, well beaten. Mix well and spread on raw cake batter. Bake as directed in the above recipe.

### Tea Cake with Praline Frosting

| | |
|---|---|
| 1 C brown sugar firmly packed | ½ t vanilla |
| 2 T flour | 1 C coarsely chopped pecans or walnuts or any preferred nuts |
| ½ C melted butter or margarine | |
| 2 T water | |

Mix the brown sugar with the flour, butter or margarine, water, vanilla and nuts. Spread evenly over the Dixie Tea Cake just as it is taken from the oven. Run cake under flame of broiler immediately. Let it remain until icing bubbles and browns to form a glazed surface. When cake is cool, cut into 1½-inch squares. This makes a most unusual and delightful topping.


# *Dessert Cakes*


When I was young we frequently served a dessert cake—a nut or plain torte or filled layer cake, or a hollowed-out cake shell into which custard, blanc mange or some fruit mixture had been poured and allowed to stiffen. Sometimes these cakes were topped with meringue or flavored sweetened whipped cream, again they would boast a more exotic frosting, but oftener they would just be given a decorative sprinkling of powdered sugar and sent to the table.
    Unlike their plain cousins, dessert cakes are cut into sizable wedges, and one cake will usually serve a dozen to a dozen-and-a-half people comfortably. These cakes are especially indicated following a meal where

a thick soup and a salad have been featured, or a single casserole dish is the pièce de résistance; or at a buffet luncheon or dinner.

In looking over my family recipes, I was delighted to find so many dessert cakes made without butter; and even where this costly item is called for, margarine may very often be substituted without detection. But where a cake calls for butter, as in the Alabama Lane Cake, and where *no substitute* is written beside it, by all means use the butter to insure perfect results.

## CORRIE HILL HURT'S
## ALABAMA LANE CAKE AND VARIATION

I haven't been able to find out much about the origin of this distinctively different cake. Some claim that it originated in Eufaula, Alabama. They take it for granted down there that the cake was honored by being given the same name as the family who introduced it in that town, but I haven't been able to prove that. Mrs. Will Hill, who came from Pineapple, Alabama to Montgomery to live many years ago, says the recipe was made all over the State. Her mother and grandmother served it and she was of the opinion it may have come from England. Her daughter, Corrie Hill Hurt, gave me the family recipe. This cake is served in Alabama at Christmas for those who do not care particularly for traditional fruit cake. But it is delicious at any season.

### The Cake

| | |
|---|---|
| 7 egg whites | 3 C flour, sifted before measuring |
| 2 C sugar | ing |
| ⅔ C butter (no substitutes) | ½ C milk |
| 1 t vanilla | 2 t baking powder |

Sift flour once before measuring, then sift 4 more times, the last with the baking powder. Set aside. Meanwhile, cream butter and sugar until light and lemon-colored. Add the butter mixture to the flour, alternating with the milk. Add vanilla and, last of all, fold in the well-beaten whites. The batter is baked in 2 or 3 lightly greased and floured 9-inch pans in a moderate oven (375°) until the layers test done. This will take from 25 to 35 minutes, depending on whether you used 2 or 3 pans, and the thickness of the batter in each. (Mrs. Hurt bakes her cake in two layers.) When done, remove the layers from the stove and allow to remain in the pan a little while before loosening the edges and turning pans upside down on wire cake racks. When cool, put together with this filling:

## The Filling

| | |
|---|---|
| 7 egg yolks | 1 C freshly grated cocoanut |
| 1 C sugar | 1 C whiskey (bourbon) or |
| ½ C butter (no substitutes) | brandy (8 oz.) |
| 1 C seeded raisins, cut fine | ½ t vanilla |
| 1 C coarsely chopped pecans | |

Beat egg yolks light. Add sugar gradually and beat until light and lemon-colored. Add the whiskey or brandy. Meanwhile melt the butter in the top of a double boiler. Add the egg-whiskey mixture and stir and stir until mixture is very thick—this takes 15 to 20 minutes of constant stirring; I use a wooden spoon for this. Remove from stove, and add all other ingredients. Cool, and spread between layers of cake. Frost with Boiled White Icing, using the same recipe as given for Mary Todd's White Cake (page 237), but omitting pineapple and cherries.

## LANE CAKE MUFFINS
### (A variation of Alabama Lane Cake)

Bake the Alabama Lane Cake in muffin tins and when the muffins are cool, hollow out the centers with an apple corer, or grapefruit knife. Frost with the same Boiled White Icing as suggested for the Lane Cake and, when cool, fill the centers with the Lane filling, piling it up on top of the cake. This is a delicious small cake for weddings or receptions or formal occasions and was first introduced to me by Leila Dowe at her inestimable Blue Moon restaurant on the outskirts of Montgomery, Alabama.

## ALMOND RUM TORTE
### (12 servings)

| | |
|---|---|
| 6 eggs, separated | ⅓ C freshly ground dry bread |
| 1 C sifted granulated sugar | crumbs |
| Grated rind (yellow part only) | ½ lb. finely ground blanched |
| and juice of ½ lemon | almonds |
| 1 C raspberry jam mixed with | 1 T rum for flavoring cake |
| 1 or 2 T rum | batter |
| 1 t baking powder | Sweetened whipped cream fla- |
| | vored with rum |

Separate the eggs. To the yolks add the sugar. Beat and beat, using an electric beater if you own one, as the lightness of this cake depends on the amount of beating the eggs are given. Add the grated rind and juice of ½ lemon, baking powder, bread crumbs, and blanched almonds which have been thoroughly dried before grinding. Fold in the stiffly-beaten whites of eggs and add the 1 tablespoon of rum. Bake in two floured 9-inch layer pans in a moderate oven (350°) for 25 to 30 minutes or until the cake tests done. Turn out and cool. Put together with the raspberry jam mixed with the 1 or 2 tablespoons of rum (amount depending on the stiffness of the jam). Ice with sweetened whipped cream also flavored with rum.

## GENERAL ROBERT E. LEE CAKE

This is said to have been the favorite cake of the South's most beloved General. It is simply a 4-layer sponge cake put together with a lemon jelly filling—or a lemon cheese filling, as they call it in Old England, where it undoubtedly originated—then frosted with an orange-lemon icing. It is one of the most beautiful and delicious of all the homemade cakes, and will serve 16 to 18 persons. No other dessert is needed when a slice of this rich cake is served.

In the old days, the frosting alone was often put between the layers, and the jelly omitted. But this is not nearly so unusual or tasty as when the cake is made by the recipe I have worked out after trying numerous "receipts," each claiming to be "the original Robert E. Lee Cake."

This cake can be cut in half to make a delectable 2-layer cake. Remember to cut the filling and frosting recipes in half also, if you bake the smaller size.

| | |
|---|---|
| 8 eggs, separated | 2 C flour, sifted twice before |
| 2 C sugar | measuring |
| 1 lemon, juice and grated peel | 1½ t baking powder |
| (yellow part only) | ½ t cream of tartar |
| | F. G. salt |

Measure sugar and sift 6 times. Sift measured flour 6 times, the last time adding the cream of tartar and baking powder. Beat egg yolks light —I use an electric beater—adding the sugar slowly and letting the eggs and sugar beat until they form a light-yellow sponge. Add the lemon juice and rind. In another bowl add a few grains of salt to the egg whites and beat until they stand in peaks and have a moist, glazed look; but do not beat until dry. I beat the egg whites by hand, not with an electric mixer. Fold the egg yolk mixture into the flour mixture, alternating with the beaten whites. Use a folding, not a beating motion, and blend this batter also by hand. Grease and flour four 9-inch pans. Divide the cake batter evenly among the 4 pans, smoothing the surface of each panful with the back of a spoon or a dull knife. Put the pans in a preheated oven (325°) and leave from 20 to 25 minutes, or until cake tests just done. Loosen cakes from sides of pans at once and invert over wire racks, or over a biscuit board covered with cellophane paper and dusted with powdered sugar to keep cake from sticking. Cool before spreading with the filling, which is divided among the 3 bottom layers. The top layer has no filling but is frosted according to directions given below.

### Lemon Jelly Filling for Robert E. Lee Cake

| | |
|---|---|
| 6 egg yolks | Juice 4 lemons |
| Grated rind 2 lemons | ½ C melted butter |
| 2 C sugar | |

Beat the egg yolks with the sugar. Add grated lemon rind and lemon juice. It is much less acid after cooking. Stir mixture until sugar dissolves. Put in top of double boiler with the melted butter. Stir until thick. There is no flour or cornstarch, so it will thicken more when cool. Cook 20 minutes or until mixture is quite thick. Set in icebox to chill sufficiently. Spread between layers of cooled cake.

(This same filling is often given as a Christmas gift in England. Put into little jars or pots with tight-fitting lids, it can be kept in the icebox to use as a filling for lemon pies topped with a meringue, to put on soda crackers for a tea-time sweet, or to be used for the cake filling as above.)

The filled cake is frosted with this icing, which should be quite thick on top and sides of cake:

### Lemon-Orange Frosting

| | |
|---|---|
| 1 lb. sifted powdered or confectioners' sugar | 3 to 4 T orange juice (enough to make frosting easy to spread) |
| Grated rind 1 lemon (yellow part only) | ¼ C butter, softened but not melted |
| 2 T lemon juice | 1 egg yolk |
| Grated rind 2 medium-sized oranges | |

Cream butter and sugar, add a little of the fruit juice, add egg and more fruit juice, if needed. Last of all, add peel. Spread all of frosting on top and sides of cake. Roughen slightly with spoon or fork.

## MOCHA CRÊME CAKE
### *(6 to 8 servings)*

| | |
|---|---|
| 4 eggs, beaten separately | ⅓ C flour, measured before sifting |
| 1 C powdered sugar | |
| ½ t vanilla | ⅓ t baking powder |
| 1 T regular strength coffee | ½ t cinnamon |
| ¼ t cloves | ¼ t allspice |
| 1 t instant coffee | F. G. salt |

Separate the eggs. To the yolks add the powdered sugar, vanilla, and coffee mixed with instant coffee (I find that the instant coffee added to the regular gives extra zest). Measure the flour before sifting, then sift twice more. Sift again with the baking powder and spices. Combine the two mixtures and fold in the well-beaten egg whites with a few grains of salt. Line the bottom of an 8-inch-square pan with greased paper. Add batter and smooth with a knife. Bake in moderate oven (350°) until cake tests done—about 40 minutes. Remove from stove and let stand 10 minutes. Turn out of pan and gently remove paper. Cool, then carefully split in two. A saw-edged bread or cake knife is excellent for this. Spread the bottom layer with Mocha Crême and put top layer on this. Ice with Mocha Frosting.

### Mocha Crême Filling

2 egg yolks
1 T flour
¼ C sugar
½ C extra strong coffee (page 197)

½ C cream
¼ C ground blanched almonds (optional)

Beat egg yolks. Add flour, sugar, coffee (our choice is ½ cup of regular coffee mixed with 1 teaspoon of instant coffee) and the cream. Pour in top of double boiler and set over a flame. Stir until custard is thick. If desired, add the ground blanched almonds.

### Mocha Frosting

1½ C powdered sugar
2 T softened but not melted margarine

2 to 3 T strong coffee
¼ C blanched, chopped, toasted almonds

Sift the powdered sugar. Add the softened margarine and enough strong coffee to make a paste just stiff enough to spread without running. Spread on cake and, while icing is still soft, sprinkle top with the almonds.

## RUM CAKE
### (From Miss Jennie Benedict via Cissy Gregg)

Today in Louisville the catering firm and restaurant of Miss Jennie Benedict is no more, but her recipes are still served with a certain nostalgia by her many admirers of a quarter of a century ago. The most famous of all her cakes was perhaps her Rum Cake, which she did not include in her delightful Blue Ribbon Cook Book. However, Cissy Gregg, the clever and able Food Consultant of the Louisville Courier-Journal, gave me her

permission to print her version of Miss Jennie's masterpiece. We serve it
alone, slicing it into pie-shaped wedges, but Mrs. Gregg says Miss Jennie
served it as an accompaniment to vanilla ice cream—gilding the lily,
according to my notion.

| | |
|---|---|
| 1 C butter | 1 C milk, not too cold |
| 2 C granulated sugar | 8 egg whites, beaten stiff but |
| 3½ C cake flour (sifted once | not dry |
| before measuring) | 1 t vanilla |
| 3½ t baking powder | 1 pinch of salt |

Cream butter and sugar until the two are blended, then beat hard. The
mixture should be light and fluffy and lemon-colored when ready to put
in the cake batter. Use an electric mixer for this if you own one; if not,
use your hands. Sift the flour three more times, the third time sifting
with the baking powder. Add the salt to the egg whites and beat until
stiff but not dry. Add the butter-sugar mixture to the flour mixture,
alternating with milk and well-beaten eggs, folding them together slowly
a little at a time until all ingredients have been used. Do not beat this
batter with the electric mixer. Add vanilla. Pour into two greased and
floured 9-inch cake pans. Divide the batter evenly between the two pans
and set in a moderate oven (375°). Bake until cake layers test done—
20 to 25 minutes should be enough. Turn out on wire cake racks or onto
a piece of wax paper dusted lightly with powdered sugar, and cool before
adding the filling.

## Filling for Rum Cake

| | |
|---|---|
| 2½ C powdered sugar | ⅔ C soft, creamed butter |
| 4 oz. Jamaica rum (½ C) | |

Take the powdered sugar and butter and blend, beating until soft and
smooth. Sifting the powdered sugar makes the blending lighter work, too.
Add the rum. Mix well again. Put in the icebox until firm enough to
spread. The filling should be ½ to ¾ inch thick. After the filling is
spread between the layers, put the cake into the refrigerator until filling
no longer runs and the top frosting is ready to cover all.

## Frosting for the Rum Cake

| | |
|---|---|
| 2 C granulated sugar | 12 to 15 marshmallows |
| Water to moisten | 1 or 2 T rum |
| 2 egg whites, beaten | |

Moisten the sugar well with water. Boil together until the syrup will
spin a thread when poured from a spoon. Pour slowly in a fine stream
over the well-beaten egg whites. Just keep on beating. An electric mixer

comes in handy at this stage for the soft-in-arm-muscle people—it takes beating and the outcome is worth the effort. While the mixture is hot and the beating is going on, add the marshmallows, a few at a time. Add the rum. When mixture is stiff enough to spread without running, pile high on top of the cake and spread over the sides.

## ROSE FRANKEL'S SPICE CAKE WITH SHERRIED DATE FILLING
### (12 servings)

This is one of the best winter desserts I have in my files. The filling can be made of fresh or dried dates.

1 C sugar  
2 T margarine or butter, softened but not melted  
1 egg  
1 t soda  
1½ C sifted flour  

1 t cinnamon  
½ t cloves  
1 t cocoa  
1 C rich buttermilk or sour cream  

Cream the sugar with the margarine or butter, previously softened but not melted. Add the egg and beat again. I use an electric beater for this. Measure the flour after sifting once, then sift twice more, the last time adding the spices and cocoa. Mix the soda with the rich buttermilk or sour cream. Add the flour to the butter mixture, alternating with the buttermilk or cream mixture. Beat to make a smooth batter. Pour into two 9-inch cake pans, previously greased lightly and floured. Bake in a moderate oven (375°) from 20 to 25 minutes or until cake tests done. Turn out on a wire cake rack and cool. Put the 2 layers together with the following:

### Sherried Date Filling and Whipped Cream Frosting

1 lb. dates, seeded  
1 C water  
2 to 3 T sherry, or more to taste  

1½ C double cream, whipped stiff and mixed with 1 to 2 T sherry  
4 T powdered sugar  

Put the seeded dates in a saucepan with the water. Set over a flame and let cook slowly until dates become mushy—this takes 10 to 15 minutes. Keep stirring to prevent scorching. If dates cook dry before they are done, add a little more water. Put through the strainer or food mill. Add 2 to 3 tablespoons of sherry, or more to taste. Spread on one layer of the cake. Top with the other and ice with the double cream whipped stiff and mixed with powdered sugar and 1 to 2 tablespoons of sherry.

# Fruit Cakes

NOTE: Fruit cakes lose weight in baking. Five lbs. of batter will weigh 4½ lbs. when cooked.

## Preparing the Pans

The pans should be of heavy metal—the best being the old-fashioned copper Turk's Head or tube pan, silver- or tin-lined. Enamel pans are good too, or very heavy iron or aluminum ones. These should be washed, and greased lightly with salad oil, then lined with unglazed paper—the sort that grocery paper bags are made of. If your pan is thin, use 2 or 3 thicknesses of paper. The paper too should be well greased.

These cakes can also be cooked in loaf pans. Line them with heavy greased brown paper also.

In fitting the paper to the pans remember that it must be smooth—no wrinkles or creases or the baked cake will have wrinkles and creases. The best thing I have found for greasing cake pans is pure olive oil. Salad oil is apt to taste, and most melted butter has some salt particles in it, which might cause the cake to stick to the paper. Peanut oil is the next best substitute.

Add the batter by tablespoonfuls, evening it as you go along to keep out any air holes. The pans should never be more than ⅔ full. After baking, let cakes stand in the pans until cold. Brush with brandy or whiskey. If tops of cakes brown too much before the cake tests done, cut a circle of brown paper and place it over the whole cake until time to remove the cake from the oven.

## Note on Storing Fruit Cake, Black Cake, Pecan Bourbon Cake or any Cake of the Fruit Cake Clan

Brush the baked cold cake with whiskey, brandy, sherry or any preferred liquor. Wrap in wax paper or, better still, in aluminum foil—it can now be bought in a roll at any grocery. If the foil is used, no further wrapping will be necessary. If wax paper is used, put another wrapping around the cake—this time a napkin saturated with whiskey, and wrung out until it is damp but not wet. Store the cake in an airtight tin box until needed; if no tin box is available a large pressure cooker, roasting pan or Dutch oven will do. Some people also put a cut apple in the box to keep the cake from drying out. If properly sealed, these cakes should keep a year —provided they are never allowed to dry out. Look at them from time to time, change the apple and occasionally brush with brandy, then re-wrap if they are to be kept a long time.

## KENTUCKY BLACK CAKE
### *(A 3-pound cake)*

I had never heard of this cake before I moved to Kentucky, but it is very tasty and is a member of the fruit cake clan. Most recipes give the ingredients in gigantic proportions, but here is one to fill a bread loaf or a 3-pound fluted tube pan.

| | |
|---|---|
| 2 C flour | 1 C butter |
| ½ C seeded raisins | 1 C brown sugar, packed firm |
| ½ C chopped dates | 2 well-beaten eggs |
| ½ C chopped figs | ⅓ C sour cream |
| 2 T whiskey | 1 t cinnamon |
| ½ t soda | ¼ t allspice |
| ¼ t cloves | ½ t nutmeg |
| ½ C raspberry or blackberry jam | ½ C chopped nuts—pecans, almonds or English walnuts |

Brown the flour in the oven until it becomes golden-brown. Stir from time to time to prevent sticking.* Set aside and cool. Sift. Mix the seeded raisins, chopped dates and chopped figs. Pour the whiskey over the fruit and mix well. Let stand 2 hours or until all the liquor has been absorbed. Cream butter with sugar. Add the beaten eggs and sour cream. Sift the flour once more with the soda and spices. Pour the liquid ingredients into the dry, stirring constantly to keep from lumping. Add the jam and chopped nuts and the whiskey-soaked fruit. Pour into a greased and floured tube pan or a loaf pan and bake in a moderate oven (375°) from 1½ to 2 hours, or until cake tests done. Remove from oven and let cake cool in pan before turning out.

## PEGGY GAINES'S KENTUCKY PECAN BOURBON CAKE
### *(This recipe makes one 3-pound cake)*

While we are on the subject of cakes, let's discuss Kentucky's most glamorous candidate for the culinary sweepstakes. Surely her Pecan Bourbon Cake is known from coast to coast. In trying to trace the genealogy of this lusty confection, I unearthed a bit of scandal which in all honesty I must report. This cake isn't a native Kentuckian at all, and Dame Rumor asserts with authority that a certain Frankfort matron (about 25 years ago) coaxed a famous New York maître d'hôtel to give her the recipe by crossing his palm with a lot of silver. But if it wasn't born here, it has become a Kentuckian by adoption and certainly

---

* For details on browning flour see note under General Hints at the beginning of this chapter.

deserves a place in any collection of the State's most delicious dishes. Peggy Gaines's recipe is the best I've found, and no wonder—she's made this cake professionally for years!

| | |
|---|---|
| 1 lb. shelled pecans | 2 t freshly grated nutmeg |
| ½ C butter | ½ C (4 oz.) bottled-in-bond |
| 3 eggs, separated | Kentucky bourbon whiskey |
| 1½ C flour | Jumbo pecan halves and can- |
| 1 t baking powder | died cherries for decorating |
| 1 C plus 2 T sugar | top of cake |
| ½ lb. seeded raisins | |

Break the pecans in pieces with the fingers or chop very coarsely; cut the raisins in half; set aside. Measure the flour after sifting once, then sift twice more. Take ½ cup of this flour and mix with the nuts and raisins. To the rest of the flour add the baking powder and sift again. Cream butter and sugar. Add yolks of eggs one at a time, beating until mixture is smooth and lemon-colored.

An electric beater is excellent for this, if you own one. Soak the nutmeg in the whiskey for at least 10 minutes, then add to the butter mixture, alternating with the flour, and beating as the batter is being blended. When it is finished it looks and tastes a great deal like eggnog. Slowly fold the raisins and nuts into the batter, using a heavy wooden or large metal spoon. Last of all, fold in the egg whites, stiffly beaten with a few grains of salt. Grease a metal tube pan—one large enough to hold 3 pounds of batter. Line it with brown paper, previously greased on both sides. Fill the pan with the batter—and here's a secret: Let it stand for 10 minutes, allowing the mixture to settle into the pan. Meantime, decorate the top of the cake with the candied cherries and jumbo pecan halves. Now put the pan into a warm but not hot oven—325° is about right. Let the cake remain 1¼ hours, but if the top seems to brown too quickly put a piece of heavy wrapping paper over the surface. Test the cake by pressing the surface of the dough with the fingers. If it seems firm and the indentation does not show, the cake is ready to remove from the stove. It should always be slightly moist and when the straw or wire test is made, a few crumbs may adhere even though the cake is ready to take out of the oven; but I let it remain the full 1¼ hours before testing it at all. Let the cake stand in the pan for 30 minutes before trying to remove it. Then place a plate a little larger than the pan over the surface and quickly turn the pan upside down. Then gingerly turn the cake right side up on another plate, being careful not to disturb the decorations on top of the cake. It makes a beautiful and delicious Christmas gift. Cut the slices with a saw-edged knife, as it crumbles easily. Save crumbs and turn into Fruit Cake Crumb Ice Cream (page 184).

## HORTENSE DREYFUS'S UNCOOKED FRUIT CAKE

A 1-lb. box graham crackers
1½ C cream
½ lb. candied pineapple
1 lb. candied cherries
½ lb. dried figs
1 lb. pitted dates (2 pkgs.)
   (fresh dates will do if you
   can't get others)

1 lb. shelled pecans
½ lb. white seeded raisins
   (dark raisins will do if you
   cannot get white)
1 t cinnamon
¾ C whiskey

Roll crackers until they are like powder. Cut dates in halves, lengthwise. Cut figs in 4 strips each. Cut pineapple in chunks. Leave nuts and cherries whole. Mix ingredients, adding cream and whiskey last. Do not whip cream. Add slowly and stir lots. Pack in graham cracker box which is lined with wax paper and tie very closely with string. Wrap in yellow paper and tie again. Leave in icebox for 10 days or 2 weeks before using. Keep wrapped up this way on ice until used up. Keeps indefinitely.

## MARGUERITE T. FINNEGAN'S WHITE FRUIT CAKE

Marguerite T. Finnegan is recognized as one of Louisville's most experienced cooks and gourmets. She has her own food column in the Louisville *Times* and her recipes not only turn out well but she has the knack of writing directions clearly and accurately. Once she told me her "boss" walked into the office when she was baking a White Fruit Cake. "Is that thing really going to be as good as it looks?" he asked, and went on to explain that his wife wanted to make some Christmas fruit cakes but had never found a recipe that pleased her. "I'll let you taste a piece of the cake when it's cooked," Mrs. Finnegan told him, "then you two can judge whether or not you want the recipe." Well, to make a long story short, they "et of it," as the Kentucky mountain woman remarked; they asked for the recipe; and they have never bothered to try any other White Fruit Cake recipe since, for they are satisfied that this one is perfect.

3 C sifted flour
1 t baking powder
¼ t salt
1½ t cinnamon
1 t allspice
1 t cloves
1 t nutmeg
1 lb. white raisins
1½ C diced candied pineapple
1 C butter (no substitutes)

2 C sugar
6 eggs, well beaten
½ C good strong sherry
2 C almonds, blanched
   (halved)
1½ C pecans, coarsely broken
½ C walnuts, coarsely broken
1½ C diced citron
½ C chopped candied orange
   peel

Sift flour, baking powder, salt and spices 3 times. Cream butter and sugar until light and fluffy. Add the 6 well-beaten eggs, one at a time, to the butter and sugar mixture and let the machine do the actual beating. Remove the bowl from the electric beater if you have used one, and scrape the bowl clean, then add the sherry, almonds and other nuts, and the candied fruit—a most unorthodox method according to the fruit cake recipes I've read, but knowing Marguerite Finnegan I'm following her directions to the letter. Now stir in the flour mixture. Fold this into the rest until all has been used and the batter seems smooth. Spoon the batter into greased, paper-lined loaf pans or tube pans, smoothing with the back of a spoon to even batter and prevent air holes from forming. Put in a preheated oven set at 325° and bake until cake tests done—it will take about one hour in a loaf pan, two in a tube pan. Remove paper and cool cake on rack, brush with brandy or whiskey, then store in covered containers.

For those who do not own electric mixers, a Dover egg beater and a strong right arm are adequate substitutes.

## *Cookies*

### ANISE SEED DROP COOKIES

A Christmas cookie that tastes exactly like those German ones called springerles, but is much easier to prepare; a "must" for holiday food boxes.

| | |
|---|---|
| 1 egg | ⅔ C flour |
| ½ C sugar | 1 t anise seed |
| ¼ t grated lemon rind | F. G. salt |
| 2 drops oil of anise * | |

Beat egg light. Add sugar, salt and flour sifted together. Beat well. Add all other ingredients. Beat again. Drop a coffeespoonful at a time on well-greased tin cookie sheets. Let stand overnight or for 12 hours at room temperature. The dough will form into two layers, the top one resembling frosting. Bake in a very slow oven (300°) until dough is set and tops begin to turn brown. These cookies keep indefinitely in a tin box with a tight-fitting lid.

* Get this from your druggist.

## BITTER CHOCOLATE COOKIES

This was the recipe of my husband's mother—and very good it is, too! The cookies have no baking powder in them and are a soft, not a crisp, cookie, closely related to fudge cake. They have body, too, and keep well in a covered tin box.

½ C butter (no substitutes)
1 C sugar
1 egg, well beaten
¼ lb. Baker's bitter chocolate
(4 squares)

1 t vanilla
1½ C flour, or more if needed
F. G. salt (if sweet butter is used)

Stir butter to a cream with sugar and add salt if sweet butter has been used. Add egg and beat well, using an electric mixer if you own one. (I know my mother-in-law did not, but she did not seem to need one.) Put chocolate in top of a double boiler. When melted, add to creamed butter-and-egg mixture. Add vanilla and just enough flour to enable you to roll the dough. Use 1½ cups to begin with and add more if necessary. If dough is too soft, put in the icebox for an hour or so to stiffen. Roll small pieces of dough at a time on a floured board, using a floured rolling pin. Roll dough ¼ inch thick and cut with a small round biscuit cutter or fluted cookie cutter. Place cookies side by side on a greased tin or biscuit pan and bake in a hot oven (450°) until cookies are done but not hard—5 to 8 minutes should cook them (test one to see when they are done). Watch carefully when baking, as they burn easily.

## BRAZIL NUT, HAZELNUT, OR PECAN MACAROONS
### *(About 4 dozen cookies)*

½ lb. dark brown sugar
½ lb. light yellow sugar
2 C Brazil nuts, hazelnuts or pecans (heaping cups)

1 t vanilla or ½ t vanilla and
½ t almond extract
⅛ t salt
2 egg whites

Beat egg whites very stiff with the salt. Add sugar gradually, beating until the mixture resembles icing or meringue batter. Add coarsely chopped nuts and flavoring. Drop heaping teaspoonfuls on a greased cookie tin covered with waxed paper. Bake 10 minutes in a moderate oven (375°). As soon as outsides of macaroons seem to hold together, they are done. Do not leave too long in the oven, as the inside of the cookies should always be moist. Set aside to cool before lifting from the wax paper. These do not keep very well, but are delicious the first few days. For that reason, we bake only a few at a time.

Another method of mixing these macaroons is to grind the nuts and sugar together. Then fold the beaten egg whites into this and add flavoring. Somehow the dough gets stiffer than when the first method is used. Measure a teaspoonful of this dough at a time and roll the size of marbles. Place 3 inches apart on a greased cookie tin. Flatten the top of each with the bottom of a water glass or goblet dipped in flour each time; do not mash too thin—cookies should be about ½ inch thick. You can also use the palms of your hands (dip them in flour to keep the cookie balls from sticking to them). Bake in a moderate oven (350°) until macaroons hold together. Be careful not to cook too long or they will be hard; they should be soft and chewy.

## BRITTLE BROWN SUGAR COOKIES
### *(An old-fashioned cookie with a true butterscotch flavor)*

| | |
|---|---|
| ½ lb. butter | 3 eggs |
| 2 C granulated sugar | 1 C brown sugar |
| 6 C sifted flour | 1 t soda dissolved in 1 T water |
| 1 t baking powder | Juice ½ lemon |
| 2 T cinnamon | 1 C ground pecans |

Cream butter and sugar. Add eggs, blend, and beat until light. Add flour sifted with baking powder, soda dissolved in water, and all other ingredients. Set on ice 2 hours before rolling thin and cutting into shapes. Bake in a hot oven (400°). Dough can be rolled into 2 loaves, wrapped in wax paper or foil, and kept on ice for days without spoiling; and cookies can be sliced very thin and baked when needed.

## MINA COLE'S BROOMSTICK CRUNCH WAFERS
### *(2 dozen wafers)*

Mrs. Lewis Cole, who gave me this recipe, called it Brandy Snaps, but since there is no brandy or liquor of any kind in it, and since the cookies themselves are rolled over the handle of a broom, I rechristened it. The cookies resemble old-fashioned Scotch cakes and when filled with ice cream become a delicate, candied casing, brittle, fragile and delightful to eat. Serve 2 filled wafers to each person.

| | |
|---|---|
| ¼ lb. butter (½ C) | 1 C flour, sifted before measuring |
| 1 C dark Karo syrup (or corn syrup) | Pinch of salt |
| ½ C light brown sugar | ½ t ginger |

Melt together the butter, syrup and sugar. Cool slightly. Stir this into other ingredients, which have been previously sifted into a bowl. Drop from a teaspoon onto a greased cookie tin. Do not cook more than 2 cakes at a time. They spread, so space must be left all around them. The oven should be set at 325° and the cookies will take about 15 minutes to cook. Remove at once with a pancake turner and shape into cylinders over a broomstick. If allowed to cool before rolling, the cookies will be too brittle to shape.

## ROSA FLEXNER'S BUTTER COOKIES

Every collection of cookie recipes should include a delectable plain cookie, and I consider this one of my mother-in-law's outstanding. The dough is so easy to handle it can be cut into any desired shape, and it can be varied by garnishings of nuts, fruits, etc. It stays fresh a long time, too.

| | |
|---|---|
| 1 C butter | Juice of 1 lemon |
| 1 C sugar | 1 lb. flour (about 4 C) |
| 1 whole egg | Extra egg white for brushing |
| 1 extra egg yolk | tops of cookies, plus 1 T |
| 1 t vanilla | water |

Sift flour once before measuring and 3 times afterwards. Set aside. Cream butter and sugar. Add the whole egg and extra yolk, vanilla and lemon juice. Add flour, just enough to enable you to roll the dough thin—about 4 cups.

Pinch off small amounts of dough and roll as thin as possible on a floured board with a floured rolling pin. Cut out with fancy cookie cutter or make into squares or rectangles with a pastry wheel. Place side by side on greased cookie tins or biscuit pan. Brush surface of each cookie with the extra egg white beaten slightly with a tablespoonful of water. Leave plain, or sprinkle with the following topping:

| | |
|---|---|
| 2 T sugar | 2 T chopped almonds or pecans |
| 1 t cinnamon | (optional) |

To bake, place cookie tins in a preheated moderate oven (375°) and watch to see that they do not burn. Cook until golden-brown. These cookies are crisp and crunchy and keep indefinitely in a proper container.

## VARIATIONS OF
## ROSA FLEXNER'S BUTTER COOKIES

### Filled Cookies

Roll Rosa Flexner's cookie dough thin and cut out with a biscuit cutter about 2 inches in diameter, or use the top of a glass tumbler. Spread half of each round with a little of the mixture given below, not letting it come to the edge. Fold the other half over and press the edges together with a fork, being careful that the filling is sealed in. Brush with the egg white and bake according to directions for the plain cookies. These may take a few minutes longer to bake.

### Filling for Above Cookies

| | |
|---|---|
| 1 T flour | 1 T lemon juice |
| ¼ C water | Grated rind of ½ lemon |
| 4 T sugar | 4 T chopped nuts |
| ½ C chopped dates or raisins | |

Mix the flour with the water and beat until it becomes a smooth paste. Add sugar and chopped dates or raisins and the lemon juice. Cook until thick in a saucepan. Add the grated rind and chopped nuts.

### Mincemeat Cookies

Mincemeat laced with brandy (page 224) also makes a good winter cookie filling. Substitute it for the one given above if you wish.

## CHEROKEE DATE ROCKS
### (Nice for the Christmas cookie basket or box)

| | |
|---|---|
| ½ lb. dates, seeded and chopped | 1 t allspice |
| 2 C English walnuts or pecans, chopped coarsely | 1 T cinnamon |
| 4 C sifted flour | 3 eggs, separated |
| 1 t soda dissolved in 2 T water | 1½ C butter |
| | 1½ C brown sugar |

Sift flour with allspice and cinnamon. Cream butter and sugar and add egg yolks, and soda dissolved in water. Combine flour mixture with butter-egg-yolk mixture. Fold in the stiffly-beaten egg whites and, last of all, the dates and pecans or walnuts. Drop by teaspoonfuls onto a well-greased cookie tin or sheet, leaving about 3 inches between each "rock." Bake 15 to 18 minutes in a moderate oven (375°) until cookies are done in the center. Do not cook too long, as they will be as hard as their name implies. Remove from pan with a spatula or pancake turner and dust with powdered sugar. These cookies keep well if wrapped when cold in wax paper and stored in a tin box with a tight-fitting lid. If you wish, frost with Vanilla Glaze (page 76) while rocks are still hot.

## GRANDMOTHER K'S
## CHOCOLATE ALMOND COOKIES

This is a crisp cookie of unusual merit, a "must" in all our Christmas gift cookie boxes. The icing is put on before the cookies are baked and they are both pretty to look at and delightful to eat.

| | |
|---|---|
| 3 egg whites | ½ lb. grated chocolate |
| 6 egg yolks | (sweet or semi-sweet) |
| ½ lb. ground almonds | 1 t cinnamon |
| Grated rind ½ lemon | ½ t cloves |
| 1 t lemon juice | ½ t allspice |
| Pinch of salt | Flour enough to roll |
| ½ lb. sugar | |

Beat yolks light with sugar. Add salt to whites and beat stiff but not dry. Add grated chocolate, ground almonds, spice, and lemon peel and juice. Add flour to make a stiff paste. Press into pan or roll out thin. Cover with the following icing:

| | |
|---|---|
| 3 egg whites, beaten stiff | 2 C powdered sugar |
| 1 t lemon juice | F. G. salt |

Mix all the above ingredients and beat well. Spread over cookie dough in pan. Bake in a moderate oven (375°) until icing becomes a light tan color. Remove from the oven and cut in squares while still hot. When squares are cool, lift them from pan, using a spatula or pancake turner.

## CHOCOLATE BOURBON OR RUM BALLS
### *(Uncooked whiskey or rum cookies)*

This is a wonderful way to utilize leftover and slightly dried-out pound, white, cup or gold cake. Grind or crumble enough of the cake to make a cup of crumbs, or if cake is very hard or stale, put a few pieces on the bread board and roll with the rolling pin. Do not use fresh cake, as it is too moist. Bought vanilla wafers or pound cake may also be used. To this add:

| | |
|---|---|
| 1 C ground nuts (pecans, almonds or walnuts) | Powdered sugar, or a mixture composed of 1 t cocoa and |
| 2 T cocoa | ½ t cinnamon to every |
| 2 T white corn syrup | rounded T sifted powdered |
| ¼ C good bourbon whiskey, or Jamaica rum or a combination of both | sugar |

Mix cake crumbs with ground nuts, then add cocoa, white corn syrup and whiskey. Knead well. Take a teaspoonful of the dough at a time and mold into balls. Roll in plain powdered sugar or the mixture of cocoa, cinnamon and sifted powdered sugar. Place balls on a tin cookie sheet for 2 to 3 hours to dry. Roll once more in plain powdered sugar or the cocoa-cinnamon-sugar mixture. Wrap each separately in wax paper and store in a box with a tight-fitting lid. This recipe makes 18 to 20 balls. These balls are delicious, reminding me of some very fancy "patisserie" I had in Paris before the last war. Don't let the fact that they are made of stale cake discourage you; they are well worth including in your nicest gift box collection.

## AUNT ROSE'S CINNAMON STICKS

| | |
|---|---|
| 3 egg whites | 1 t cinnamon |
| ¾ lb. powdered sugar | ¾ lb. ground almonds |

Beat egg whites stiff. (Take out 2 tablespoons of this for frosting later.) Sift sugar and add to eggs. Add cinnamon and almonds. Mold into sticks 3 inches long by ½ inch wide. Place in buttered pans and spread tops with egg white reserved for frosting. Bake in moderate oven (350°) until set. Do not bake too hard; ten minutes should be enough. I like a little more frosting on my Cinnamon Sticks than this recipe calls for. Make up a little more by adding ½ to ¾ C sifted powdered sugar to 1 well-beaten egg white. If too stiff, add a little cream or milk; if too runny, add more sugar.

## MARY LEE WARREN'S PECAN LACE COOKIES

| | |
|---|---|
| 2 eggs, well beaten | ½ lb. pecans, broken |
| ½ lb. medium brown sugar | ⅓ t baking powder |
| 4 T sifted flour, heaping (about ½ cup) | F. G. salt |

Mix all ingredients together. Drop ½ inch apart on buttered pans and bake in a moderate oven (375°) for 10 minutes. These will not keep long, but are wonderful when first baked.

## ELIZABETH COLGAN'S PECAN MARBLES

| | |
|---|---|
| 1 C butter | 2 C ground pecans |
| ½ C sugar | 1 t vanilla |
| 2 C flour | Ice water, if needed (about 2 t) |

Cream sugar and butter. Add flour, nuts and vanilla and mix with the fingers until thoroughly blended. If dough is too stiff to hold together, add a bit of ice water. Mold into balls the size of marbles and bake in a hot oven (400°) until cookies are done throughout. As soon as the centers are done remove them from the stove. (Break open a cookie to see if it has baked thoroughly.) Roll in powdered sugar while still hot.

## PEPPERNUTS (Pfeffernuesse)
### *(A traditional Christmas spice cookie)*

| | |
|---|---|
| 3 eggs | 1 lb. seedless raisins, ground |
| 2 C sifted flour | ½ t black pepper, freshly |
| 1 C nuts | ground |
| 1 t cloves | 2 t cinnamon |
| ½ t soda | ½ t baking powder |
| ¼ t salt | 1 oz. citron, ground |
| 2 C brown sugar | |

Beat whites and yolks separately, then fold together. Add sugar and spices sifted with soda, then add raisins, nuts and citron, and flour to make a stiff dough. Roll into balls. Place on greased pan and bake in moderate oven (375°) until cookies will hold their shape. Do not bake hard; cookies should be moist inside, as they dry out as they are kept. Dust with powdered sugar.

## VELMA'S RUM RINGS

Once when we were baking Christmas cookies, Velma, my neighbor's German cook, came over and showed me how to prepare Rum Rings, which she said were made at her home in the "Old Country" every holiday season.

| | |
|---|---|
| 1 C powdered sugar | Grated rind of 1 lemon (yellow |
| 1 C butter, softened but not | part only) |
| melted | 4 T Jamaica rum |
| 3 hard-boiled egg yolks | 2 to 3 C sifted flour, or enough |
| mashed to a paste | to make a dough stiff enough |
| | to handle |

Cream butter and sugar. Add lemon rind, rum, and egg yolks mashed to a paste with a fork. Add flour, previously sifted—the less used the richer the cookie will be. Set dough in the icebox in a covered bowl, about 20 minutes before molding, to become firm.

Break off small pieces of dough—about a teaspoonful—and roll with the palms to resemble a small pencil. Then press the two ends together to make a wreath. Place about an inch apart on a greased cookie tin. Brush with the white of raw egg mixed with a tablespoon of water and slightly beaten. Sprinkle with colored sugar, or sugar and cinnamon mixed in these proportions: 2 teaspoons of cinnamon to every ¼ cup of sugar. Or, if you are energetic, decorate with tiny red candies and bits of angelica to make holly wreaths. Bake in a moderate oven (375°) until cookies are done throughout—8 to 10 minutes should be sufficient. Remove from pan at once and cool before storing.

## TOFFEE SQUARES
### (An Alabama cookie with a delightfully "different" flavor)

| | |
|---|---|
| 1 C butter | 1 T ground cinnamon |
| 1 C sugar | 1½ C pecans, chopped very fine |
| 1 egg, separated | F. G. salt |
| 2 C sifted flour | |

Cream butter and sugar. Add egg yolk unbeaten, salt, cinnamon and flour. Mix well, as for pie crust. Place in a long cookie tin, previously floured. With fingers or spatula work dough into place. It should be evenly distributed over bottom of pan and the dough should be not more than ¼ inch thick. Over the surface of the dough pour the slightly-beaten egg white and with a brush smooth the whole surface. Now cover the dough with the nuts. Bake 20 to 25 minutes. Use a moderate oven (375°) for 5 minutes, and 400° for the rest of the time. Remove from oven, and while dough is still hot cut into 2-inch squares, but do not try to remove from pan until cookies are cold. Place cookies in a tin box. They will keep fresh for two weeks and make nice additions to Christmas gift boxes.

## ZIMSTERNE OR CINNAMON STARS
### (About 4½ dozen cookies)

Every Christmas collection of cookies should contain a few of these delicious cinnamon-almond stars.

| | |
|---|---|
| 6 egg whites | 1 lb. almonds (not blanched) |
| 2 C sugar, sifted | 2 T cinnamon |
| Grated rind 1 lemon | 2 T sifted flour (scant) |
| (yellow part only) | ¼ t salt |

Beat egg whites stiff with salt. Add sugar, cinnamon and grated lemon rind. An electric beater is a great help here. This makes a meringue that will stand in peaks or stay in the bowl when turned upside down. The original recipe required the egg mixture to be beaten 15 minutes, but that was before the days of electric beaters. Take out ¾ of a cup of this mixture and set aside; it is to be the frosting. To the rest of the egg mixture add the grated or ground almonds, which have been mixed with the flour. Stir well. Roll small amounts at a time on a floured board, flouring the surface but adding just as little flour as possible. Roll thin— about ¼ to ⅓ inch—and cut out with a star cookie cutter. Place on greased cookie tin and frost the top of each lightly with a bit of the egg mixture you set aside. Bake 20 minutes to half an hour in a slow oven (300°). The cookies should be a delicate tan color on top, and the insides should be done. They will get crisp when cold. After cookies have cooled slightly, remove from the pan with a spatula or pancake turner and set aside to cool.

A quicker way to make these cookies (although they will not be in star shape) is to drop them from the end of a teaspoon, making little mounds on a greased cookie tin. Put a dab of the frosting on top of each and cook as above. The mound cookies, being thick, should not be allowed to get hard or done as the thin cookies were. As soon as they are done enough to hold together and the top frosting is slightly brown, remove from the oven. They taste like a cinnamon macaroon. Cool slightly before attempting to remove from pans. Let get cold before wrapping and storing in boxes.

# *Fruit Butters, Conserves, Jams, Jellies, Preserves*

## WAYS TO TEST JELLY

If you do not own a kitchen thermometer, here are two old-wives' tests for telling whether or not your jelly has cooked sufficiently.

1. Take some jelly in a cooking tablespoon and hold the spoon high over the kettle, letting the jelly fall into it. If it falls in thick flakes rather than a quick stream, it is ready to pour into glasses.
2. Test the jelly by putting a teaspoonful into a shallow saucer and letting it cool in the refrigerator for 5 minutes. If the jelly thickens by that time, it is ready to pour into glasses.

## BAR-LE-DUC

***(Wonderful with cream cheese and English muffins)***

**3 qts. currants (red)**
**3 lbs. sugar**
**½ C white honey, strained**

Remove stems from currants and wash well. Drain. Place in an iron skillet or preserving kettle and boil 2 minutes. Add sugar and boil 5 minutes. Next add honey and boil 3 minutes. Remove scum. Pour into jelly glasses or small jars. When cool, top with paraffin before putting on lids. If a small amount is cooked at a time, the currants will not fall to pieces and the color remains vivid.

## HARRODS CREEK FALL FRUIT CONSERVE
### *(To serve with game or roasts or to use as a sauce for ice cream)*

5 lbs. firm pears, peeled and cut in slivers

1 grapefruit, sliced thin, seeds removed, but not peeling

1 orange, sliced thin, seeds removed, but not peeling

3 lemons, sliced thin, seeds removed, but not peeling

5 lbs. sugar

1 lb. seedless raisins (dark)

1 lb. shelled pecans

Put the pears, grapefruit, orange and lemons through the meat grinder, saving juices. Combine the juices with the fruit. Add sugar and mix well. Let stand in a covered bowl overnight. Next morning put the fruit and sugar in a preserving kettle on the stove. Let come to a hard boil, then reduce the heat and cook ¾ hour over a very slow fire, stirring occasionally to prevent sticking. Add the raisins and cook ¾ hour longer. Add the pecans and cook 1 minute longer. Remove from fire and pour into sterile glasses or jars. When cold, top with paraffin and seal.

This conserve is delicious used as a topping for ice cream, if a little brandy, whiskey or rum, or a combination of two of them is added before serving. To a cup of this conserve add 2 or 3 tablespoons of liquor, or more to taste.

## MARRONS (Preserved Chestnuts)
### *(3 pints)*

6 C peeled, boiled chestnuts whole or in pieces

3 C sugar

3 C water

1 T vanilla, or more to taste

F. G. salt

Boil about 3 quarts of chestnuts in their hulls for about 30 minutes. Peel and skin. Make a syrup of the sugar, salt and water and boil 5 minutes before adding the peeled chestnuts. Add chestnuts and simmer for 35 minutes. Remove pan from stove and add vanilla. If chestnuts look dry, add extra syrup made by boiling 1 cup of water and 1 cup of sugar for 5 minutes and flavoring with 1 teaspoon of vanilla. Cover chestnuts and set aside until next day. Boil chestnuts again for 5 minutes or until they look transparent. They may cook up very thick, but no matter; there are many ways to use them. Remove from stove and put in sterile pint jars. They will keep for about 4 months this way. If ½ cup of French brandy or Jamaica rum is added, they will keep longer and the flavor will be greatly improved. We put the liquor in each jar—about 3 tablespoons to a pint jar. Kentucky bourbon may be substituted for the brandy or rum. Stir the liquor into the marrons before sealing jars.

## OLD-FASHIONED PEACH PRESERVES
### *(3 pints)*

4 lbs. ripe peaches          Juice of 2 lemons
3 lbs. sugar

Peel and cut peaches in eighths. Add sugar and lemon juice. Simmer very slowly and cook until syrup becomes thick. This will take from 40 to 50 minutes. Stir occasionally with a wooden spoon to keep from sticking. Skim when necessary. Pour into jars, and when cool cover with paraffin. If the peaches are acid, omit lemon.

## OLD-FASHIONED SPICED PEACH PRESERVES

My mother-in-law used these preserves in puff paste or to make turnovers, spreading the preserves on unbaked rounds of pie crust, folding in half and pinching the edges together, brushing with cream or beaten egg, and baking in a hot oven until brown. The turnovers were then served very hot, dusted with powdered sugar. An excellent and quick winter dessert.

Follow the recipe for Old-Fashioned Peach Preserves, adding a cheese-cloth bag containing the following spices:

2 sticks cinnamon            8 cloves
2 t coriander seeds          1 blade of mace
6 allspice

NOTE: Tie string around top of bag, leaving plenty of room for the spices to expand. Discard bag after peaches are cooked.

### To Prevent Peaches Turning Black

If a great many peaches are to be peeled at the same time, put the peeled pieces in the following solution and leave until ready to use

1 gal. water, mixed with      2 T salt
  2 T vinegar

## PLUM BUTTER, SPICED

Plums (wild plums are best, or    1 lb. of sugar to every lb. of
  use tart yellow or red jelly      plum pulp made according
  plums)                            to directions given below
¼ C water to every lb. of fruit   Spices (see below)

Wash fruit and make 3 gashes in each plum with a knife. Place in a preserving kettle with ¼ cup water for each pound of fruit. Boil 30 minutes, stirring constantly to prevent sticking. Press through a sieve. Measure fruit pulp. To every pound allow 1 pound of sugar and the following spices:

| | |
|---|---|
| 1 t cinnamon | ¼ t cloves |
| ¼ t nutmeg | ½ t allspice |

Place sugar, spices and plum pulp in a heavy skillet or saucepan (do not cook more than 2 pounds of plum pulp at a time). Stir constantly to prevent sticking, and let mixture cook slowly for 20 minutes or until quite thick. Skim. Pour into jelly glasses or small jars and, when cool, top with melted paraffin. Cover, and store until needed. This is fine with venison or any game.

## RASPBERRY JELLY (Black or Red)
### *(With apple juice)*

| | |
|---|---|
| 2 qts. early June apples | 2 C water |
| 5 pts. raspberries | Sugar in equal measurement with juice |

Wash apples, measured after coring, removing spots and quartering but not peeling. Put in a kettle with just enough water to keep the apples from sticking. Cook until apples begin to get mushy. Drain off juice and set aside to use later. (Make applesauce out of the pulp by putting it through strainer or food mill. Sweeten and flavor with ground spices to taste. If too thick, add orange juice until sauce becomes the proper consistency, or use bottled apple juice if you prefer.)

Crush 5 pints of raspberries with the potato masher. Place in a saucepan with the apple juice. Cook ½ hour from the time mixture begins to boil. Pour while hot into a dripping-bag and allow to drip overnight. Do not squeeze the bag. Next morning, measure juice. Add an equal measure of sugar. Mix and set over a low flame on the stove. When this comes to a hard boil, cook 10 minutes longer, or until jelly drops from a spoon in large flakes. Pour into glasses and let cool without covering. Pour melted paraffin over the top and seal. This makes a beautiful clear jelly, with a strong raspberry flavor. The apple taste is not noticeable.

## RASPBERRY PRESERVES (Red or Black Raspberries)

Pick over berries and wash. Then measure 2 cups of berries. Put in a saucepan and add 2 cups of sugar. Boil 8 to 10 minutes over a very low flame being very careful not to burn. Never boil more than 2 cups of berries and sugar at a time. Fill jelly glasses or pint jars, cover with a clean cloth, and let stand overnight. Next morning cover with paraffin. Do not stir while boiling—just shake the saucepan or lift the berries gently with a kitchen fork. We cook our raspberry preserves in a heavy 12-inch iron skillet.

## RASPBERRY AND RHUBARB CONSERVE

2 qts. red raspberries        5 lbs. sugar
1 lb. young red rhubarb stalks

Wash raspberries. Slice rhubarb into inch pieces. Add sugar to fruit and cook until quite thick (20 to 30 minutes). This recipe makes 5 pints. Seal in jars and cover with paraffin, or cellophane rounds.

## SEEDLESS RASPBERRY JAM (Red or Black Raspberries)

4 qts. raspberries (black or red)
Sugar in equal proportion to
raspberry purée (see directions below)

Wash fruit. Force through a fine wire sieve or strainer. If a food mill is handy, by all means use that. If too many seeds come through, it may be necessary to strain again through the fine wire strainer, forcing the juice and pulp through with a wooden potato masher. A few seeds will remain, but this does not matter. Now weigh the purée. Add an equal amount of sugar, by weight. Stir the sugar and fruit purée well. Put on the stove over a low flame and when the mixture begins to boil, time it. Eight to 10 minutes should cook it, but if it is not as thick as jelly, cook a little longer. It is advisable to cook the jam in small amounts—I never cook more than a pound of purée and a pound of sugar at a time, and use an old-fashioned iron skillet. This makes the color and flavor better. Skim when necessary. Pour into pint jars or jelly glasses and when cool cover with paraffin.

## RASPBERRY AND CURRANT JAM

Follow the recipe for Seedless Raspberry Jam, using 2 quarts of red raspberries to each 2 quarts of currants, instead of all raspberries.

## STRAWBERRY PRESERVES
### *(A foolproof family recipe)*
### *(1 pint)*

1 qt. strawberries        1 T lemon juice, if berries are
1 lb. granulated sugar        dead-ripe

Wash and cap berries, removing bad spots but leaving as whole as possible. Combine strawberries and sugar, mixing with two forks to avoid crushing berries. Put on the stove in a saucepan and allow to come to a hard boil, then cook 10 to 15 minutes or until syrup drops from the end of a tablespoon in flakes just as it does for jelly. Skim and pour into pint jars, well washed and drained, and cover with a clean cloth until berries are cold. Then top with paraffin and seal. A quart of berries should make 1 pint of preserves, and the best results are obtained by cooking only a pound of sugar and a quart of berries at a time. Berries cooked in small amounts retain their color for a long time, although all strawberry preserves will darken after a few months. Use firm red berries, but mix in a few that are not dead-ripe, in order to give a slightly acid taste. If berries are too ripe, the syrup will not jell. In this case, add lemon juice a few minutes before removing from the stove—1 tablespoon for each quart is the right amount. Store jam in a cool, dark place.

## JEAN RUSSELL'S WILD CHERRY JELLY FOR GAME, FOWL, ROASTS, ETC.

> 1 qt. ripe wild cherries (some-
> times called bird cherries or
> seed cherries)
> 1 C water

Pick over the cherries, wash in a strainer under running cold water and remove stems. Add water and boil 10 minutes. Drip through a muslin or cheesecloth bag, without squeezing. Measure juice—there should be about 3 cups. This jelly will have to be made with commercial pectin; if you use a bottle of the liquid pectin, measure your juice and sugar and add the pectin according to the directions on the bottle. Jean Russell uses a box of "Sure Jell" with hers and this is how she does it.

> 3 C wild cherry juice, prepared     1 box commercial pectin
> and dripped as above                  (Sure Jell brand)
> 4 C sugar

Stir all ingredients together and let come to a boil, then cook 1 minute by the clock. Pour into jelly glasses and allow to become cool and firm. Pour boiling paraffin on the tops and seal.

# Catsup, Chutney, Pickles, Relishes

✛✛✛✛✛✛✛✛✛✛✛✛✛✛✛✛✛✛✛✛✛✛✛✛✛✛✛✛✛✛✛✛✛✛✛✛✛✛✛✛✛✛✛✛✛✛✛✛✛✛✛✛✛

## LENA TACHAU'S BEET AND HORSERADISH RELISH
### (For game, poultry, cold fowl, ham)

On "Pop" Tachau's birthday (he was 82 last fall) his friends all congregate at his house, "Three Acres," to wish him well. Year after year old and young gather at the charming Tachau residence on Lightfoot Road to celebrate. Always the menu is the same: Turkey and Country Ham with Beet and Horseradish Relish, Creamed Cottage Cheese, Rolls and Butter, Spaghetti; Shrimp and Vegetable Aspic, Fruit Aspic and Homemade Mayonnaise; Cheese and Crackers, and Schnecken (Cinnamon Snails) with hot coffee for dessert. Here is Mrs. Tachau's recipe for her Relish:

12 medium-sized beets, cooked
4 T prepared horseradish
1 T brown sugar, or more to taste
1 T white sugar, or more to taste
3 T apple cider vinegar
Salt to taste

Grind beets, mix all ingredients together and let stand at least 2 hours in the refrigerator before serving. (I use canned beets.)

## NELL WOLFE'S BREAD-AND-BUTTER PICKLES
### (For sandwiches or cold meats)

5 qts. large unpeeled cucumbers, sliced thin
5 large onions, peeled and sliced into thin rounds
1 C salt
1 gal. water
1 qt. apple cider vinegar
4 T turmeric
½ t powdered alum
4 C sugar
2 T celery seed
2 T mustard seed
4 hot red peppers, cut in thirds
2 t dry mustard
2 t salt

276

Pour the brine, made of 1 cup of salt and 1 gallon of water, over cucumbers and onions. Set aside for 4 hours. Drain vegetables and pat dry on a bath towel.

Meantime, in a kettle place the vinegar, sugar, 2 teaspoons of salt, celery seed, mustard seed, peppers, dry mustard, turmeric and alum. Add the cucumbers and onions. Place on the stove over a low flame and when mixture comes to a hard boil, remove kettle from the stove.

Fill quart jars with the pickles and seal immediately, while hot. Do not use for 3 or 4 days. Chill before serving.

## IRENE BOHMER'S CHILI SAUCE
### (6 pints)

24 tomatoes (firm, very ripe, large)
8 medium-sized onions, peeled and chopped
6 large sweet green peppers, seeded and chopped
1 hot red pepper, cut in quarters or ½ t powdered hot red pepper
2 t powdered cinnamon
2 t nutmeg, freshly grated
2 t powdered allspice
2 t celery seed
2 C apple cider vinegar
2 pods garlic minced fine
1 t powdered cloves
¼ C salt
1 C sugar

Peel and quarter tomatoes. Place all ingredients in a large preserving kettle. Put over a low flame and let boil, stirring occasionally to prevent sticking. Cover and let cook 3 to 4 hours or until mixture is quite thick and no longer watery. Pour into sterile pint jars and seal while very hot. Serve with meats and fish; as a sauce for meat loaf or omelets; as an accompaniment to fried eggplant, fried green tomatoes, or to any foods where Chili Sauce is the specified condiment.

## MARY LOUISE McNAIR'S CHUTNEY

I was at a luncheon not long ago and when I remarked that I was trying to get recipes that were typical of Kentucky, everyone said in unison, "Get Mary Louise McNair's chutney. It's marvelous with lamb or curries." So she wrote it out for me and here it is. She says the basic fruit can be peaches, pears or apples, depending on the time of year you decide to make the chutney. She prefers the peach chutney, however.

4 lbs. peeled, seeded peaches, pears or apples
1 C crystallized ginger
1 T salt
1 T chili powder
1½ lbs. sugar
½ C onions
½ lb. raisins
2 T mustard seed
3 C cider vinegar

Cut fruit and onions into slivers. Add all other ingredients. Put in a preserving kettle and set over a flame on top of the stove. Have flame high until the mixture begins to boil, then reduce the heat and let simmer 2 to 3 hours, or until fruit cooks done and mixture is thick; it should have a little syrup, however, and not cook to a mush or paste. Pour into jars and seal while hot.

## CONFEDERATE RELISH OR GREEN TOMATO SOY

I came across the recipe for this delicious and distinctively flavored pickle quite by accident. We had gathered some slightly frostbitten green tomatoes and I hated to throw them away. I decided to make a ground-tomato relish like that I had tasted when I was a child in Alabama. Looking over the really old Southern cook books, I found this recipe which I could adapt to my needs. The proportions called for were Gargantuan, so I reduced them and combined several other vegetables with my tomatoes, but I added the same spices and flavorings. Use this relish in salad dressings, with game and cold meats, or as a flavoring for dressed eggs, and you will be pleased with the results.

| | |
|---|---|
| 12 green tomatoes, stem ends removed | 2 large green peppers |
| | ¾ C salt |
| 12 medium-sized onions | 4 C brown sugar, tightly packed |
| 2 cucumbers | ½ C prepared horseradish |
| 1 qt. cider vinegar | |

Wash the green tomatoes and remove the stem ends. Cut up and grind. Peel the onions and grind also. Peel the cucumbers and put them through the food grinder. Remove seeds from the green peppers and grind also. Drain off excess juices and put ground vegetables in a crockery bowl. Add salt. Stir. Cover bowl and allow the vegetables to remain overnight. Next morning squeeze out excess moisture—I put the ground vegetables in a bath towel and squeeze them dry. Set aside.

Boil the vinegar, brown sugar and prepared horseradish in a preserving kettle. Mix the following spices in a bowl:

| | |
|---|---|
| 2½ T dry mustard | 2 t ground cloves |
| 1 T freshly ground black pepper | 1 t ground mace |
| 1 T ground allspice | 1 T ground ginger |
| 1 t grated nutmeg | |

Pour some of the hot vinegar over the spices and stir to make a smooth paste. Then add the spices to the vinegar and sugar boiling on the stove. Drop the drained vegetables into this mixture and stir. Let mixture come to a quick boil. Turn the heat low, cover the kettle and simmer slowly until the relish is the consistency of marmalade.

VARIATION: Some of the old recipes called for 1 tablespoon of turmeric also. But when I mixed the vinegar and spices I liked the flavor so much I hesitated to add another ingredient. Next time I make it I will try it this way but I did not want to gild an already flawless lily.

### QUEENIE WILLIAMS'S PICKLING SYRUP
*(Enough for a peck of fruit)*

Queenie and Bert Williams live near Louisville in Anchorage and they are famous for their brand of gracious hospitality and their unusual dishes. An invitation to their Stone Gates Farm is a treat indeed. This recipe came from Bert's mother. It can be made up at the beginning of summer, put in a 2-quart jar and kept in the icebox to use as needed. Or make it up whenever you wish. It is simple and so delicious—one of the recipes I'm glad I heard about.

| | |
|---|---|
| 1 qt. cider or white vinegar | Spice bag containing: 2 doz. cloves (whole), 1 T coriander seed, 1 T whole mace (or 1 t ground mace), 4 or 5 sticks cinnamon bark, 2 T mustard seed (or 2 t powdered mustard), 8 whole allspice |
| 6 C sugar | |
| 1 C white corn syrup | |

Mix all ingredients together in a preserving kettle. Add bag of spices. Cook 20 minutes from time syrup begins to boil. Cool. Remove spice bag, pour syrup into jar and keep in icebox until needed, or use at once if desired. If you prefer, spices may be cooked in syrup without spice bag, and the syrup may then be cooled and strained before pouring into jars.

### PICKLED FRUITS WITH
### QUEENIE WILLIAMS'S PICKLING SYRUP
*(Use with crabapples, cherries, peaches, pears, plums, nectarines, etc.)*

Peel fruit if necessary (do not peel cherries, crabapples, plums or nectarines; peaches are always peeled). Drop into boiling syrup and cook until fruit sticks tender or can be pierced easily with a cake wire or a broomstraw. Cooking time will depend on the size and ripeness of the fruit. For instance, peaches may take 10 to 20 minutes, plums 5 to 8 minutes, cherries 10 to 15 minutes. As soon as the fruit is tender and soft, remove from the stove. With a perforated spoon lift fruit from boiling syrup and put in well-washed jars. Fill to the tops and shake slightly to pack fruit, but do not press with spoon. Let the pickling syrup come to a hard boil. Pour the boiling syrup over the fruit and fill to the tops of the jars. Seal while fruit and syrup are still hot. Store in a cool dark place.

## JOSEPHINE COX'S MIXED PICKLE
### *(12 quarts)*

This is a famous Louisville recipe which Mrs. Cox inherited from her mother's family, and one you will want to put up year after year. It makes a dozen quarts in its present form and I always cut it in half. It's fine for Christmas gift baskets, however, and you may want to put up the full amount.

| | |
|---|---|
| 2 doz. large cucumbers | 1 doz. medium onions |
| 2 medium heads of firm cabbage | 1 doz. medium green peppers |

Shred cabbage, chop peppers (removing seeds and discarding them), peel cucumbers and cut in strips 1 inch long, slice onions ¼ inch thick. Sprinkle vegetables with 1 cup of salt and let stand overnight. Next day, squeeze vegetables well. (I put them in a towel after they have been drained, and squeeze out all the moisture.) Put the squeezed vegetables in a kettle and pour over them the following:

| | |
|---|---|
| 2½ lbs. brown sugar (dark) | Enough cider vinegar to barely |
| 2 oz. celery seed | cover vegetables (just so you |
| 2 oz. mustard seed | can see the vinegar—it does |
| 1 oz. turmeric | not completely cover vege- |
| ½ lb. dry mustard mixed to a paste with a little vinegar | tables) |

Let this come to a boil, then simmer slowly 30 minutes. Just before removing from stove, add:

| | |
|---|---|
| 1 large onion, ground (juice and pulp) | 6 small pods of garlic, ground (juice and pulp) |

Let boil once more and put in jars. Seal while hot. Do not use for several weeks.

## MY PRIZE DILL PICKLES
### (For winter use)
### (This recipe won first prize in a pickle contest in the Louisville Courier-Journal)

This is a recipe evolved after many years of experimenting, and makes a crisp, crunchy dill pickle that will keep all winter. We prefer to make it with tiny gherkins about 3 inches long, but it does perfectly well with firm large cucumbers, too. Select those of straight shape, not too ripe or too large. Put up a peck of cucumbers at a time. Scrub them and pack them side by side in 2-quart jars for the large ones, quart jars for the smaller ones. For every quart jar allow the following ingredients:

1 pod garlic, cut in half
1 long hot red pepper, cut in thirds

4 heads fresh dill, the fresher the better. Be sure heads are full of seeds. Do not use leaves or stems.

Put part of above ingredients on the bottom of the jar, fit cucumbers on end into the jar, being careful not to bruise them. Add more of the dill, pepper and garlic, another row of pickles, standing on end, and so on, until all ingredients are used. Pour into jars the following:

### The Brine
### (Enough for 1 peck of cucumbers)

4 qts. water
1½ C cider vinegar

⅔ C salt

Boil water, vinegar and salt. Pour this over the cucumbers in the jars for three successive days; sometimes it will be necessary to make up an extra amount of brine, for the cucumbers must be completely covered each time. Spread a clean kitchen towel over the tops of the jars until ready to seal. On the second and third mornings the brine must be poured off the cucumbers, reboiled, and poured back again while still piping hot. The three boilings are necessary to kill the spores that form, for it is the spores which cause the pickles to spoil. If there should not be enough brine to completely cover the pickles in the jars make up half the above recipe, heat and use.

On the third day the jars are sealed and the lids screwed down tightly. Store in a cool dark place for at least six weeks before using. If properly processed, these pickles keep indefinitely.

## MY PRIZE DILL PICKLES        *(Quickie!)*
### *(For summer use)*

We use a crock for quick pickles. They will not keep as long as the Prize Dill Pickles for Winter Use, but they are very good if eaten at once.

Wash a stone or pottery crock, preferably one that has a lid. Add the peppers, garlic and dill in the proportion given for the winter dills. Fill with the scrubbed cucumbers and pour the boiling brine over them. Cover and let stand 3 weeks or until pickles taste done. Remove scum. Chill pickles before serving.

## TOMATO DILLS

Hungarian dishes, such as Paprika Veal, Goulash, etc., scream for Tomato Dills. To make them, follow the recipe for My Prize Dill Pickles for Winter Use, substituting green tomatoes for cucumbers. The tomatoes should be firm and perfect, of a medium and uniform size. If pickled too early, they are apt to have a bitter taste, and if too ripe they will get soft. To test, cut one of the lot and see if it is green and firm throughout. Wash them, but do not peel. Pack into jars with the required herbs, etc. and pour the boiling brine over them just as for the cucumbers. They require the same length of time to age as the Winter Dill Pickles.

## GREEN TOMATO CATSUP
### *(8 quarts)*

½ peck green tomatoes  
1 head white cabbage  
6 large onions  
6 bell peppers  
1 hot red pepper  
1 oz. black mustard seed  
12 large cucumbers, seeds removed  

½ C prepared horseradish  
1 C salt  
1 oz. white mustard seed  
2 ozs. celery seed  
3 qts. cider vinegar  
2½ lbs. brown sugar  

Grind or chop all vegetables fine. Mix with salt and let stand overnight. Drain and squeeze out all water. Mix all ingredients together, heat well and bottle or pour into jars and seal. Do not use for a few days.

## MUSTARD CHOW CHOW

4 qts. green tomatoes  
6 sweet green peppers  
1 qt. button onions, peeled but left whole  

1 large or 2 small cauliflowers  
3 large cucumbers or 1 doz. small ones

Peel onions but do not slice. Slice peppers (discarding seeds) and tomatoes. Use tiny cucumbers whole without peeling; if large ones are used, cut in thin slices. Separate the cauliflower flowerets, cover with water, bring to a boil, then drain. Soak all vegetables overnight in a brine made according to the recipe given below. Next morning let come to a boil in the same brine. Drain and pat dry in a towel.

## Brine for Soaking Vegetables

4 qts. cold water                    1 C salt

After the vegetables have been soaked, boiled in the brine and drained, add them to the mixture given below. Let them come to a boil, stirring to prevent lumping, and pour at once into hot sterile jars and seal. Be sure the vegetables are hot throughout before putting in jars.

2 qts. vinegar (cider)          6 T powdered or dry mustard
1 C flour                              2½ C dark brown sugar

Put vinegar on to boil in a preserving kettle, reserving a cup or so to blend, cold, with the sifted flour and mustard to make a smooth paste. If the paste is lumpy, strain it, adding more vinegar if necessary. Stir paste into the hot vinegar with the sugar and when it makes a smooth sauce add the drained prepared vegetables. Lower the flame and stir until the mixture begins to boil once more and the vegetables are heated thoroughly throughout. Seal at once in sterile jars.

## ED WEST'S SLICED GREEN TOMATO PICKLE

Ed West is a smart engineer who was once in the pickle business. Here is an easy recipe to prepare, an excellent way to use green tomatoes and a good alternate for Nell Wolfe's Bread and Butter Pickle.

Slice large, firm green tomatoes in ¼-inch rings. Place in wide-mouthed sterile jars (use smaller tomatoes if no wide-mouthed jars are available). Pack firmly, filling the jars.

Pour the following ingredients into a preserving kettle:

1 qt. vinegar                     1 t cinnamon
1 lb. brown sugar             1 t allspice
2 T salt                             1 t nutmeg
1 t red pepper                  1 t cloves

Put on stove and let boil hard 5 minutes. Pour over the tomatoes and seal at once. Ready to use in about 3 weeks. You may put up as many tomatoes as you wish to at one time. Extra pickling syrup may be stored in a covered jar in the refrigerator.

## SPICED PICKLED CHERRIES
### *(3 pints)*

3 lbs. cherries, stoned (about 6    3 lbs. sugar
   C) (We use sour red cher-    6 sticks cinnamon bark
   ries)    9 cloves
2 C cider vinegar, or enough to    9 allspice berries
   barely cover fruit

Place cherries in a pottery or china bowl and add the cider vinegar. Cover and let stand 24 hours. Pour off the juice, add to it the sugar, let come to a boil with the spices. Pour this hot pickle juice over the cherries and let stand another 24 hours. Then pour off the liquid, boil it and pour over the fruit again. Repeat this process in another 24 hours, making 3 times altogether. On the third day, put the mixture into pint jars which have been sterilized, and seal. This relish is a delicious accompaniment for games or roasts.

## MINNIE BUECHEL'S TOMATO CATSUP
### *(Adapted from an old Louisville recipe)*

1 peck dead-ripe tomatoes    4 medium-sized onions
24 peach leaves tied in a bunch    2 bay leaves
   (optional)    2 long hot red peppers cut in
2 C cider vinegar        thirds, or 1 t cayenne pepper
3 T salt, or more to taste    1 T cinnamon
1 C sugar, or more to taste    2 t cloves
1 t mace    1 t nutmeg
1 t dry mustard

Wash tomatoes and remove spots; it is not necessary to peel. Put into a deep preserving kettle. Mash with a potato masher. Add peach leaves if you can conveniently get them—they do add a delicate flavor, but are not absolutely necessary. Add bay leaves, onions, garlic, salt and pepper. Put on the stove over a high flame and let come to a boil, then lower the heat to a simmer. Cover pot, and let cook 1 hour, stirring occasionally to prevent sticking. Remove peach leaves. Strain the tomato-onion mixture and press through a strainer to make a purée—I use a food mill. Mix spices to a paste with some of the hot tomato purée and add to the vinegar. Pour into the rest of the purée. Add the sugar and all other ingredients, putting in more salt and pepper if necessary. Cook 2 hours longer over a slow flame, stirring to prevent sticking. By that time the mixture should be thick; if not, allow to cook a little longer. It will thicken even more as it stands but will never be as thick as bought catsup. Pour while still hot into sterile jars or bottles, and seal. I dip the tops of my bottles in paraffin or sealing wax when catsup cools. It is, of course, safer to process these catsup-filled. containers in a pressure cooker if you want to keep them for a long time. Cook 5 minutes at 10 pounds pressure. If you desire a red-hot catsup for fish or cocktail sauce, add an extra ½ teaspoon of tabasco to each pint before processing or bottling it.

# Candies and Nuts

✠✠✠✠✠✠✠✠✠✠✠✠✠✠✠✠✠✠✠✠✠✠✠✠✠✠✠✠✠✠✠✠✠✠✠✠✠✠✠✠✠✠✠✠✠✠✠

## BITTER CHOCOLATE TRUFFLES

¼ lb. butter
1 egg, well beaten
1 T black coffee
F. G. salt (if sweet butter is used)

3 squares bitter chocolate (3 oz.)
½ C double cream
1 T vanilla
Powdered sugar to make a paste stiff enough to handle

Soften butter to room temperature but do not melt. Add egg and mix well. Dissolve chocolate in top of double boiler with coffee. Dump 2 cups of sifted powdered sugar in a bowl. Add butter mixture, melted chocolate, and cream, salt and vanilla. Stir well. Add more sugar to make a paste stiff enough to handle. Make into balls the size of butter balls— use a teaspoon measuring spoon to be sure the truffles will be of uniform size. While truffles are still soft, roll in chocolate shot or shredded semi-sweet chocolate. Put in icebox until firm. Wrap in waxed paper or foil and pack in tin boxes.

## BRANDY OR RUM TRUFFLES

Remove 1 tablespoon of cream from the cream used in the recipe for Bitter Chocolate Truffles and omit vanilla, substituting 2 tablespoons of brandy or rum. The rest of the recipe is the same.

## SOLGER'S CHOCOLATE TRUFFLES

*(Recipe from Solger's Candy Shop—a famous Louisville institution before World War I)*

1 lb. Whitman's powdered sweet chocolate, or any preferred brand of instant chocolate

1 t vanilla
1 pt. double cream measured after whipping

Mix, make into small balls the size of butter balls and roll in grated semi-sweet chocolate or chocolate shot.

## LELLIE ISHMAEL'S CREAM CANDY

This is a pulled sugar candy rich with cream, one of Kentucky's specialties. After the candy has been allowed to stand 3 to 4 hours in a warm room, it creams, but at first it is chewy, like molasses taffy. Mrs. Ishmael does not add any flavoring, claiming that the sugar and cream are flavor enough, and I am inclined to agree with her. There are many tricks in achieving success with this candy, but Mrs. Ishmael has kindly shared them all with us. Here is her foolproof recipe which I watched her make while I took down everything she did, step by step. Her ingredients were:

| | |
|---|---|
| 4 C sugar | ⅛ t soda |
| ½ t salt | 1 C cream (single) |
| 1 C water | |

A heavy metal saucepan is required for this candy. Mrs. Ishmael used a heavy aluminum chicken roaster, but a Dutch oven will do. Put the water, sugar, salt and soda in the pan. Do not stir these ingredients. Put on top of the stove over a high flame, or if you have an electric stove, over a high burner. When the mixture has cooked long enough so that it makes large clear bubbles, called "sheeps' eyes" by Mrs. Ishmael, and will spin a hair thread 3 to 6 inches long, add the cream. This is an important step in making this candy successfully, for the cream must be added almost drop by drop as if you were making mayonnaise. The candy must never stop boiling and this process of adding the cream cannot be rushed. After the last bit of cream has been added, lower the heat and simmer until the mixture gets "butterscotch-brown" and will once more spin a thread 3 to 6 inches long. The whole cooking process does not take more than 15 to 20 minutes.

Now pour the mixture on a greased marble slab or enamel table top. Use only butter to grease the slab, for the taste will be incorporated in the candy. The pouring-out process is important, too. Mrs. Ishmael pours the candy in a thin, narrow stream, making a "rivulet" about 6 to 8 inches long, then she leaves a space and pours another narrow stream of candy, and so on. She does not scrape the pan, as this, she says, causes the candy to sugar too soon. (You can scrape the pan and lick the spoon or turn the job over to your children. The candy at this stage tastes like delicious butterscotch taffy.)

Begin to pull the candy as soon as the last bit has been poured on the slab or table. Beginning with the first little stream, take that up and begin to pull, then add the next and incorporate that, and so on until you have used all the candy. Continue to pull until candy gets white or just the palest ivory color and is too stiff to continue pulling. The room should be warm while the candy is being pulled and Mrs. Ishmael leaves the door of the lighted oven open (she had the stove thermometer registering about 375°). When the candy begins to get stiff she pulls it while standing in front of the stove door. When the candy becomes too stiff to pull any longer, it is twisted into a rope about 1½ inches thick, cut in pieces 1 to 1½ inches wide with the kitchen scissors, then spread out on the greased table or slab. It is necessary to work quickly, as the candy gets hard very suddenly, and at this stage two hands are better than one. One person can cut from one end of the rope, another from the other end. In pulling the candy, too, it will be found that two people can handle the stiff candy better than one. Either leave the candy to cream on the table or pack it into tin boxes, putting a sheet of wax paper or foil between each layer. Put the lids on the boxes and leave candy in a warm room until it becomes creamy and melts when touched with the tongue.

Mrs. Ishmael says she sometimes dips the candy in melted semi-sweet chocolate after a few days, to keep it fresh—or it can be dipped as soon as it creams, if desired. I find it keeps indefinitely if each piece is wrapped separately in wax paper or foil before being put in the tin boxes.

## ORANGE CARAMEL FUDGE
### (A Kentucky specialty)

| | |
|---|---|
| 2 C dark brown sugar | 1 saltspoon soda |
| ½ C cream | 1 C chopped nuts |
| Grated rind 1 orange | 1 t butter |

Boil sugar, cream and soda until it makes a thick syrup or forms a medium-soft ball in cold water. Take off stove and add butter, orange rind, nuts and pinch of salt. Beat well until mixture becomes quite thick. Pour on buttered plate and cut in inch squares, or drop by teaspoons onto a greased platter.

## ALICE'S PECAN PÂTÉS

When I was a child in Montgomery, Alabama, one of the delights of my life was to stand on the corner with the neighborhood gang and wait for Alice's candy wagon. It was a small covered wagon drawn by a small horse and driven by an intrepid little boy.

There was a varied assortment of cocoanut mounds, which did not especially appeal to me; fudge, which was more or less a commonplace article; and, best of all, a creamy praline, known throughout the city as "Alice's pecan candy." Alice, in an unguarded moment, gave the recipe to my mother, and I pass it on to you. I find it one of the few recipes as good now as I remember it so many years ago.

| | |
|---|---|
| 1 C pecans (coarsely chopped) | ¼ t cream of tartar |
| 1 C cream (single cream) | 1 C granulated sugar |
| 1 T butter | 2 C dark brown sugar |
| 2 t vanilla | ⅛ t salt |

Put sugar, butter, salt and cream in a saucepan. Stir to dissolve. Set over a flame on top of stove and stir occasionally until it makes a medium ball when dropped in ice water. Have greased platter ready. Add vanilla, broken pecans and cream of tartar, and beat hard until mixture becomes stiff and creamy. Drop from a tablespoon into cakes on greased platter or greased marble slab. Should mixture harden too quickly, pour into the platter and cut in squares when cool. Wrap each piece separately in wax paper. They will keep for a long time in a tin box if tightly sealed. This recipe won first prize in a Louisville *Courier-Journal* candy recipe contest.

## SALTED ROASTED NUTS

To every cup of blanched almonds or large halves of jumbo pecans or walnuts, allow 1 tablespoon of butter or olive oil. Place butter or oil in biscuit pan and heat in a moderate oven (375°). Add pecans or almonds. Rub nuts with melted fat so that they are well coated. Keep in oven until thoroughly heated, shaking to prevent burning (15 to 20 minutes). Drain on absorbent paper. Sprinkle with fine salt while nuts are hot. Let stand until cold. Put in sieve or strainer and shake to remove excess salt. When cold, put in jars and seal tight.

## STUFFED PRUNES OR DATES WITH
## WINE OR WHISKEY

Steam large prunes or dates until soft. Remove seeds. (Do not cook until mushy.) Soak one hour or longer in sherry, Madeira, port or whiskey. Fill each prune or date with ½ marshmallow and a jumbo pecan, walnut or almond half. Roll in granulated sugar and leave on a wooden board several hours, or until dry enough to transfer to a plate or box. If wrapped separately in foil or wax paper before being put in boxes, they will keep indefinitely.

## SUGARED NUTS

1 lb. almonds,* Brazil nuts,    1 t vanilla or 1 T cinnamon or
   pecans or walnuts             1 T sherry
1 C water                       1 lb. sugar
⅛ t salt

Boil sugar and water to a very thick syrup. Add flavoring and salt. Stir in nuts and keep stirring until the syrup sugars. When cold, separate nuts and put in jar until ready to use.

* If almonds are used, blanch and dry before using in this recipe.

# Index

291

Breads and rolls (*continued*)
  Sauces for pancakes and waffles, 67
  Skillet corn pones, 66
  Southern potato rolls, 78
  Syrups for pancakes and waffles, 67
  Tea biscuits, 56
  Twin dinner rolls, 73
  Waffles, corn meal, 65
    gingerbread, 60
    perfection, 61
  Whole wheat honey bread, 57
Breakfast, Kentucky Derby, 18
Breast of veal, 136
Brittle brown sugar cookies, 262
Broiled porterhouse or sirloin steak, 114
  spring chicken, 98
Bronger, Charles: Louisville turtle soup, 50
Broomstick crunch wafers, 262
Brown crumb gravy for fried chicken, 105
Brown crumb sauce for noodles, 159
Brown Hotel sandwich specials, 31
Brown sandwich, 31
Brown sugar cookies, 262
  frosting for stack pies, 218
  sauce, 67
Browned butter and bourbon pie, 209
  and bourbon sauce, 198
Brownies, butterless, 243
Browning flour for cakes, etc., 231
Brussels sprouts with pecan sauce, 144
Buckner, Ben: sauce for roast lamb, 124
Buckner, Sarah: pot de crême, 189
Buechel, Minnie: tomato catsup, 284
Burger, Alene: avocados stuffed with deviled eggs, 167
  chicken chow mein with noodles, 100
Burgoo, 45
Burnt sugar sauce, 199
Butter, herbed, for shrimps de Jonghe, 89
  plum, 272
  and bourbon pie, 209
  and bourbon sauce, 198
  cookies, 263
  rolls, 70
*Butter Cakes*, 231-240
  Black walnut cake, 231
  Chocolate cake, 232
  Hickory nut cake, 231
  Hundred-Dollar chocolate cake, 232
  Isle of Spice cake, 234
  Maple loaf cake, 235
  Mary Todd's white cake, 237
  Raspberry jam cake, 236
  Union cake, 239
  Walnut, black, cake, 231
  White cake, 237
Butterless brownies, 243
*Butterless Cakes*, 240-244
  Angel food cake, chocolate, 241
    yellow, 244
  Carrie Byck's double fudge cake, 242
  Chocolate angel food cake, 241
  Cold water sponge cake, 244
  Double fudge cake, 242
  Mary Clegg's yellow angel food cake, 244
  Pauline Park Wilson's chocolate angel food cake, 241
  Sponge cake, cold water, 244
  Yellow angel food cake, 244
Buttermilk bourbon pie, 210
  coffee cake, 244
  pie, 210
  refrigerator dough, 69
  refrigerator rye rolls, 70
  refrigerator rye salt sticks, 71
  refrigerator whole wheat rolls, 71
  roll dough, 71
Butterscotch icing, 236
Byck, Carrie: double fudge cake, 242-3

Tomato (continued)
  soy, 278
Tomatoes, fried, 150-1
Tomatoes au caramel, 150
Tomato juice dressing for crab-meat
  slaw, 169
Tomato, okra, and corn melange,
  146
Tongue, 121
Toppings for vegetables, 161
Torte, almond rum, 250
  chocolate, 243
Tossed salad, 163
Transparent pie, 219
  strawberry pie, 225
Trigg County fried country ham,
  131
Trout, 84
Truffles, bitter chocolate, 286
  brandy or rum, 286
Turkey, barbecued, 109
  dressing for, 111
  à la King, 110
Turnip salad greens, 151
Turnovers, 204
Turtle soup, 50
Twin dinner rolls, 73
Tye, Judge H. H.: Woodford pud-
  ding, 194
Tyler, President: puddin' pie, 216


Uncooked fruit cake, 259
Union cake, 239
Uri, Sonia: icebox cocktail pâté, 34


Vanilla glaze for rolls, 76
Veal, 134-138
  Aunt Mena's casserole of sweet-
    breads, 134
  Boiled sweetbreads, 134
  Braised veal chops in casserole,
    133
  Breast of veal with caraway dress-
    ing, 136
  Casserole of sweetbreads in wine
    sauce, 134

Veal (continued)
  Chops, braised, in casserole, 133
  Croquettes, 137
  Cutlet au vin en casserole, 136
  Nick Marlowe's braised veal
    chops, 133
  Roast veal with anchovies, 137
  Sautéed sweetbreads, 134
VEGETABLES, 141-162
  Arnold Griswold's Italian spa-
    ghetti, 160
  Artichokes, boiled, 141
  Asparagus in tarragon butter, 142
  Asparagus sauce, 161
  Barley for roast goose or duck,
    154
  Black-eye peas, 154
  Brussels sprouts with pecan
    sauce, 144
  Cabbage, fried, 144
  Celery leaf soufflé, 145
  Chestnuts, 152
    and prunes, 152
    and raisins in wine sauce, 152
  Corn, fried, 156
  Corn pudding, 155
  Cornfield peas, 154
  Cowpeas, 154
  Cucumbers with mock hollan-
    daise sauce, 145
    stuffed, 145
  Eggplant, stuffed, 146
  Elizabeth Pleus's baked stuffed
    yellow squash, 148
  Fried cabbage, 144
  Fried corn, 156
  Grandmother Flexner's asparagus
    sauce, 161
    green beans, 142
  Green beans with brown roux,
    142
    with corn, 143
    with ham hock, 143
    with jowl or bacon, 143
  Green peas, 148
  Green rice, 157
  Hashed brown potatoes, 156